The New Life

Six Studies on the New Life in Christ

Allan R. Knight
Gordon H. Schroeder

Judson Press ® Valley Forge

THE NEW LIFE
Second Revised Edition
Copyright 1971 by Allan R. Knight and Gordon H. Schroeder
© 1993 by Allan R. Knight and Pearl P. Knight, Trustees Allan and Pearl Knight Trust
UAD 6/15/88

Judson Press, P.O. Box 851, Valley Forge, PA 19482-0851

ISBN 0-8170-0120-4   Printed in the U.S.A.

   98 99 00 01 02 03 04 05   42 41 40 39 38 37 36 35 34

CONTENTS

A WORD AT THE BEGINNING

The new life in Christ! To live that life is the most wonderful goal any person can possibly have. This booklet is written to help you reach that goal. It attempts to cover as completely as possible in one brief manual the teachings essential for the new Christian. This booklet may be used by youth and adults alike. Although this booklet was written primarily for use in a pastor's class, it may be used with great effectiveness in other classes, study groups, or conferences.

A study of this book will aid you in learning the basic truths about the Christian life. It should be one of the most helpful courses you will ever take. Study each lesson assignment well before the class period. Bring your own Bible to the class.

If you have difficulty with any of your lesson assignments or if you have problems and questions about the Christian life, ask your Sunday church school teacher or your pastor for help. During the months ahead they will be eager to talk with you about these matters and about your service to Christ through his church.

Since you are committed to follow Christ and to be a part of his church, you will also be expected to attend the church school and the worship services each Sunday.

ACCEPT
the New Life

WHO IS A CHRISTIAN?

Christians are those who love Jesus Christ, trust in him as Savior, and are obedient to him as Lord. Christians believe what the Bible says about Christ and have opened the door of their lives for Christ to enter. They say, "I know whom I have believed" (2 Timothy 1:12, KJV). Whether it was through a sudden or a gradual experience, they have become certain of one thing: The living Christ is with them as Guide, Helper, and Savior.

Christians, then, become more and more like their Friend and Master. They obey him and seek to model their lives after him. It is said that a Christian is one who reminds other people of Jesus.

WHY BE A CHRISTIAN?

BECAUSE GOD LOVES YOU. God has given you far more than you have received from your parents or others. Such gifts as life, health, talents, and natural resources come from him. The Bible says that God "furnishes us with everything to enjoy" (1 Timothy 6:17). In John 3:16 we are told of God's greatest gift, Jesus Christ. God sent his Son to the world because of his great love for us. In response to this love, we should love and serve God willingly all our lives.

BECAUSE CHRIST WILL HELP YOU FACE LIFE. Your experiences

in life will include all you are or ever will be, all you ever will do, all your hopes and ambitions, all your accomplishments. Your job or profession is a part of life. So are those whom you love or will love. Your decisions, desires, likes and dislikes, thoughts and words are included in life. All who do much serious thinking about life realize that to be a success one needs the help and advice of others. Your greatest friend is Jesus Christ. He gave the rules for happy and purposeful living. Jesus quoted from the Old Testament when he said, " 'You shall love the Lord your God with all your heart, and with all your soul, and with all your mind, and with all your strength' . . . and 'You shall love your neighbor as yourself' " (Mark 12:29-31, quoting from Deuteronomy 6:4 and Leviticus 19:18). He taught, "Strive first for the kingdom of God and his righteousness" (Matthew 6:33); "Love your enemies and pray for those who persecute you" (Matthew 5:44); "Do not judge, so that you may not be judged" (Matthew 7:1); "If you forgive others . . . , your heavenly Father will also forgive you" (Matthew 6:15). Christ teaches you how to face life. He not only gives you lofty goals for life, but he also offers help to attain those goals. He will help to make your life useful and worthwhile. That which is harmful, impure, or second-rate cannot remain in one who lives life with Christ.

BECAUSE CHRIST WILL GIVE YOU ETERNAL LIFE. Being a Christian is the only way to experience a meaningful and complete life. Jesus said, "I came that they may have life, and have it abundantly" (John 10:10). He was talking not only about physical existence but also about the spiritual life that he imparts to those who trust in him. The Bible calls it "eternal" or "everlasting" life. "Whoever believes in the Son has eternal life; whoever disobeys the Son will not see life, but must endure God's wrath" (John 3:36).

For close to two thousand years, those who have placed their trust in Christ have found true joy and purpose. Becoming Christ's follower does not mean the end of fun and laughter. Rather, it is the beginning of a rich, full, radiant, and satisfying life with Christ. Furthermore, this abundant life does not end when this earthly life is over. Christ gives assurance that the life which he imparts is never ending.

BECAUSE CHRIST WILL RECLAIM YOU FROM SELFISHNESS AND SIN.

What sin is. Sin is a broken relationship between human beings and God. Any thought, word, or act contrary to God's law is sin. "Sin is lawlessness" (1 John 3:4). Moreover, when we fail to do what we know is right, when we do not measure up to our best, when we fail to achieve God's will for our lives, we sin. "Anyone, then, who knows the right thing to do and fails

to do it, commits sin" (James 4:17). The supreme sin is to refuse to believe in Jesus Christ. Our Lord said that when the Holy Spirit came, he would convict the world of sin "because they do not believe in me" (John 16:9).

What sin does. The Bible gives God's verdict against sin. "The person who sins . . . shall die" (Ezekiel 18:4). "The wages of sin is death" (Romans 6:23). The Scriptures are speaking here not only of physical death but also of the fact that disobedience separates us from God, both here and in the future life. Do you remember the story of the prodigal son (Luke 15:11-32)? When he decided to live in his own willful, selfish way, he turned his back on both his father and his father's desires for him and went to a "far country." His father had to say that the son "was dead."

When you disobey God, you go away from God, just as the prodigal son went away from his father. You choose to walk your own way rather than God's way, showing by your attitude that you do not want God's life, love, or fellowship. In a real sense, when you sin, you are "dead" to God, even though your body is very much alive. You do not have the abundant life which only Christ can give.

Who has sinned. We must all plead guilty. No one can say truthfully that he or she has done no wrong. What does the Bible say? "If we say that we have no sin, we deceive ourselves, and the truth is not in us" (1 John 1:8). "All have sinned and fall short of the glory of God" (Romans 3:23).

Two workers wanted to reach the roof of a building thirty feet high. One had an eight-foot stepladder, while the other had a ladder twenty feet long. Although both climbed as high as possible and stretched as far as possible, neither could reach the roof. So it is with all of us. Some, like the worker on the stepladder, fall far short of God's noble purpose for them. Others, like the worker with the twenty-foot ladder, though living outwardly moral lives, still fall short of the life that completely pleases God. No one lives as fully as Jesus Christ did. All have sinned before God. Therefore all need to be saved from sin and given the power to obey God.

Jesus came to save each of us from sin. He can reclaim us from the selfishness in our lives, which is at the center of most sin. When Christ died on the cross at Calvary, he gave his life in payment for the sins of all of us. Because God loved us enough to sacrifice his only Son, who had never sinned, we know that God will forgive any wrong we have done. As we repent of our sin and ask for forgiveness, we shall receive it.

HOW TO BECOME A CHRISTIAN

A person does not unconsciously develop a Christian life. One makes a decision to become a Christian; one chooses to trust and follow Jesus

Christ. Christian faith is not inherited; no one can make this all-important decision for another. Nor can one become a Christian merely by enrolling in a pastor's class or by becoming a member of a church. God does not force anyone to follow him. God prepares a table for us, but we shall starve to death unless we decide to come and eat.

The requirements for becoming a Christian are clearly revealed:

1. REPENT OF YOUR SINFUL AND SELFISH WAYS. The only way you can enjoy God's eternal companionship is to repent or turn away from selfishness and sin. "He commands all people everywhere to repent" (Acts 17:30). Jesus said, "The time is fulfilled, and the kingdom of God is at hand; repent, and believe in the gospel" (Mark 1:15, RSV). You must make an "about-face" in the direction your life is taking. You must turn *from* your own selfish way and turn to Christ.

2. BELIEVE IN JESUS CHRIST. You must receive Christ as your Lord and Savior, believing that Christ forgives your sins and gives you eternal life. The Bible says, "Believe on the Lord Jesus, and you will be saved" (Acts 16:31). "To all who received him, who believed in his name, he gave power to become children of God" (John 1:12).

3. OBEY THE COMMANDS OF CHRIST. Jesus said, "If you love me, you will keep my commandments" (John 14:15). This means that you will constantly seek Christ's help in order that you may be a loyal, stalwart follower, obedient to his commands, living a joyful, radiant, dedicated Christian life.

DECIDE NOW TO BECOME A CHRISTIAN

If you have not made your decision to become a Christian, decide to do so now. In John 3:16 we read:

"For God so loved the world—	[that includes everyone]
"that he gave his only Son—	[Jesus Christ]
"so that everyone—	[which means anyone who will]
"who believes in him—	[you are saved by believing that Jesus died for you and by receiving him as your Savior]
"may not perish—	[the wages of sin is death]
"but may have eternal life—	[this is God's promise, believe it]."

Do you want Jesus Christ to help you be the kind of person you wish to be? Are you truly sorry for neglecting God and failing to do God's will? Will you turn from your selfishness and sin and put your trust in Jesus Christ now as your Savior? If so, or if you have previously done so, write your name below.

Name _____ Date _____

PRAYER MOMENT

> Thank God for his gift of Jesus Christ, who died for you.
> Ask God to forgive your wrongdoings.
> Tell God that you have put your trust in Jesus.
> Ask God to save you now for Jesus' sake.
> Promise God that with his help you will live for Christ all your life.

QUESTIONS

1. Is it sufficient merely to pattern your life after Christ? Give reasons for your answer.
2. Why should a person become a Christian?
3. How does one become a Christian?
4. Will life be easier or more difficult after receiving Christ as your Lord and Savior? Why?

DECLARE
the New Life

CHRISTIANS SHOULD BE BAPTIZED

Baptism is taught in the Bible as the next step following conversion in the Christian life. "Repent, and be baptized every one of you in the name of Jesus Christ so that your sins may be forgiven; and you will receive the gift of the Holy Spirit" (Acts 2:38). Baptists practice baptism by immersion, in which a person, after confessing faith in Christ, is lowered fully under water and then immediately brought forth. A baptismal service, whether in the church baptistry or in a stream or lake, is a beautiful and impressive service. There are four reasons why a new Christian should be baptized:

1. A CHRISTIAN SHOULD FOLLOW CHRIST'S EXAMPLE. Jesus was baptized by John the Baptist in the Jordan River (Matthew 3:13-17). Baptists practice baptism in the same form that Christ and the early Christians did—that is, by immersion.

2. A CHRISTIAN SHOULD OBEY CHRIST'S COMMAND. Not only should you follow Christ's example in baptism, but you should obey his direct commandment to be baptized. He taught his disciples to baptize all those in every nation who decided to become his followers (Matthew 28:19).

We discover that the apostles obeyed this teaching of Jesus. Peter preached baptism (Acts 2:38). Men and women were baptized by Philip

after they were converted (Acts 8:12-13). The Ethiopian government official, after expressing his belief in Christ when Philip had presented the
good news of Jesus, was baptized in water near the road (Acts 8:35-39).
Read also Acts 10:44-48; 16:29-33; 18:8.

The reason for differing beliefs concerning baptism goes back to the mis-
taken idea that baptism is necessary for salvation. This resulted in parents
desiring to baptize their babies so that they would go to heaven if they died
in infancy. We believe, however, that babies are safe in God's love until they
are old enough to receive or reject Christ for themselves. Jesus said, "Let
the little children come to me, and do not stop them; for it is to such as
these that the kingdom of heaven belongs" (Matthew 19:14). Baptist parents often dedicate their babies to the Lord, not in baptism but in a public
service of dedication, in much the same spirit that Joseph and Mary presented the baby Jesus to God in the temple. (This story is found in Luke
2:22-38.)

The unscriptural belief that baptism is necessary for salvation also resulted in the substitution of sprinkling for immersion, sprinkling being
adopted because of its convenience. The Greek word for baptize, *baptizo,*
means "to dip," "to submerge," "to cleanse by dipping or submerging"
(Joseph Henry Thayer, *The New Thayer's Greek-English Lexicon of the
New Testament,* Peabody: Hendrickson Publishers, 1981). The meaning of
baptism is therefore evident. Most leading biblical scholars today believe
that Jesus was immersed. Many of the early churches of Europe still standing contain large baptismal pools, proving that in the early centuries people
were baptized by immersion. The baptistry in the Cathedral of Pisa (Italy)
is one hundred feet in diameter. Immersion was common in the medieval
Roman Catholic churches; however, sprinkling or pouring had become
customary by the time of the Reformation.

A group of Christians in the sixteenth century became convinced that
baptism was for believers only, that is, for those who had actually put their
trust in Christ. For this reason they were called Anabaptists or "those who
baptize again." Some of the spiritual descendants of these stalwart Christians became known as Baptists because they shared the same emphasis
upon believer's baptism.

Few people realize the persecution early Baptists endured for their scriptural observance of baptism. For administering believer's baptism to adults,
Balthasar Hubmaier of Germany was tortured with hot pincers and then
beheaded and his body burned. In the Netherlands in 1535 Charles V or-
dered the death penalty for all Anabaptists. Within two years thirty thou-

sand were killed. Even in America approximately three hundred years ago, Obadiah Holmes was declared worthy of death because he did not believe in infant baptism and was not afraid to say so. He finally received as his punishment a whipping of thirty stripes.

3. BAPTISM IS A PUBLIC CONFESSION OF CHRIST. A person becomes a soldier upon taking the soldier's oath. The public, however, may not realize this until that person is seen in a military uniform. The uniform does not make a soldier; it simply proclaims that person to be a soldier. In a similar way one becomes a Christian through trusting in Christ and proclaims this faith publicly through the act of being baptized. Baptism is an outward act portraying an inward change. A baptismal service is usually open to the public. One of the first opportunities a new Christian has to witness for Christ is the moment when he or she stands in the baptistry. The early Christians, after gladly receiving the gospel, were baptized to show others that they were to be counted among the followers of Christ (Acts 2:41).

4. BAPTISM SHOWS A BELIEVER'S DEATH TO SIN AND DETERMINATION TO LIVE A CHRISTIAN LIFE. The apostle Paul explains baptism as an outward act that pictures an inward change. Read Romans 6:4 several times. Here Paul compares baptism to the burial and resurrection of Christ. When a person is being lowered into the water, it is as though he or she were saying, "I am burying my sinful life, everything about me that is not pleasing to Christ." When a person is being raised from the water, just as Jesus arose from the grave, he or she is saying by this act, "From now on I will live the new life in Christ." Baptism by itself does not produce any of these changes. It is an act by which you tell others that you have received Christ as your Lord and Savior and that from now on you are going to be his follower. Baptism also pictures the resurrection of Christ and reminds those who believe and follow Christ that they too shall live after death. You can now understand why Baptists practice immersion. Only immersion can picture Jesus' death, burial, and resurrection as Paul explains in Romans. Only immersion can picture your death to sinful living and your being raised to the new life in Christ.

CHRISTIANS SHOULD UNITE WITH THE CHURCH

Christ established the church. He expects every follower to unite with a local church and to support it. In Acts 2:41 we read that the early Christians followed three steps in uniting with the church: (1) They "welcomed his message," that is, they believed in Jesus Christ. (2) They "were baptized" in obedience to the command of Jesus as proclaimed by Peter. (3) They immediately joined the church and "that day about three thousand persons were added."

The account of what the first-century Christians did after they were baptized and received into the fellowship of the church in Jerusalem gives excellent reasons for uniting with and serving in the church today.

IN THE CHURCH . . .

YOU LEARN ABOUT THE BIBLE. "They devoted themselves to the apostles' teaching . . ." (Acts 2:42). Sincere Christians should learn the teachings of Christ and the apostles. Today Christians study the Bible and hear it explained in worship services and Sunday church school. This knowledge helps them to live the Christian life and to deal with perplexing problems.

YOU FIND FELLOWSHIP WITH OTHER CHRISTIANS. They "devoted themselves to . . . fellowship" (Acts 2:42). The church provides Christian fellowship. Through this means, Christians can help one another in their efforts to be like Christ. Outside the church, and alone, we easily develop unbalanced conceptions of Christianity; but in the church, in contact with Christian people of varying experiences and outlooks, our views become more stable and meaningful.

YOU PARTAKE OF THE LORD'S SUPPER. They "devoted themselves to . . . the breaking of bread" (Acts 2:42). This refers to the Lord's Supper, an ordinance of the church established by Christ. The bread of the Lord's Supper represents the body of Christ, which was given (broken) on the cross for us. The eating of the bread symbolizes our dependence on Christ for spiritual nourishment. The cup of grape juice is a symbol of his blood, which was shed for us on the cross. The partaking of these elements is a reminder of Christ's death for us and a renewal of our commitment to our Lord (1 Corinthians 11:23-29).

YOU PRAY WITH OTHER CHRISTIANS. The early Christians "devoted themselves to . . . the prayers" (Acts 2:42). Group prayer has a place in the life of every Christian. You can make the prayer of the minister your own, for usually these prayers will express the needs of every Christian believer. Moreover, you can take part in public prayer yourself, whether in the worship service, study hour, or prayer groups.

YOU WORSHIP GOD. Acts 2:47 tells of the Christians "praising God." The entire service of singing, praying, preaching, and giving offerings is really the worship of God. In the worship service you need to realize that, although unseen, God is present. When you are in an attitude of worship,

you will hear God speak to you and understand with greater clarity God's will for your life.

YOU SERVE GOD. "You will be my witnesses in Jerusalem, in all Judea and Samaria, and to the ends of the earth" (Acts 1:8). The church provides the most effective means for carrying on Christ's work. As individual Christians, we find difficulty in overcoming the organized efforts of evil, but by working together with other Christians we can counteract evil forces. Join the church not only for what you can get out of it, but also for what you can give to it. There is no greater opportunity for service anywhere than through the church of Christ.

YOU GIVE TO GOD'S WORK. We are instructed to give each week to the church for God's work (1 Corinthians 16:1-2). This offering is to be in proportion to the blessings we have received from God. What a thrilling thought that the money you give not only supports your local church but also helps people around the world to know Jesus Christ! The great task of evangelizing the world can be accomplished only by the united efforts of all Christians.

YOU DO CHRIST'S WILL. Jesus said, "On this rock I will build my church, and the gates of Hades will not prevail against it" (Matthew 16:18). Our faith and loyalty to Jesus Christ are the foundation upon which he builds his church. If you are not a part of Christ's church, then its foundation is weakened. Someone may say, "Can a person be a Christian without being a church member?" In answer we may ask, "Can a person be educated without going to school?" The answer is: "Yes, after a fashion, but how well educated would that person be? The routine of regular class sessions, the discipline of assignments, the help of teachers—all these are needed." In like manner we need the routine of regular worship, study, service, and giving; the discipline of the church covenant; and the help of those trained to interpret the Scriptures. We can be Christians without the church about as well as we can be educated without a school system. Those who say they can be as good Christians outside the church as in it are deceiving themselves. They cannot be as good, for they are disobedient to the will of Christ. They are failing to be a "rock" upon which Christ can build his church.

You should be a Christian before you join any church. Those who are not Christians do not belong in the membership of the church, and those who are Christians do not belong outside. When you join the church, you identify yourself with other Christians. You are stronger against temptations, the church is stronger, and your influence and testimony are stronger. You cannot believe in Christ for yourself without believing in sharing him with others.

CHRISTIANS SHOULD KEEP THEIR COVENANT WITH CHRIST AND THE CHURCH

In uniting with a Baptist church, a Christian believer voluntarily attempts to obey the teachings of Christ and live according to the church covenant. There have been traditional church covenants used in thousands of our Baptist churches. However, in recent years an increasing number of churches are revising their covenants to meet more adequately the needs of the Christians of today. Become familiar with the covenant of your church and live up to it.

STEPS IN UNITING WITH A BAPTIST CHURCH

The following steps are practiced in uniting with a Baptist church, with perhaps some local variations:

1. Tell your pastor that you have received Christ and want to live for him, and that you desire to be baptized and unite with the church.
2. Sometimes a pastor, at the close of a worship service, invites those who have received Christ and wish to unite with the church to come forward. This is a public way to show your faith in the Lord. If such an invitation is given, be proud to step forward.

3. You will regularly attend the church worship services and the pastor's instruction class.
4. You will be asked to live your life according to the teachings of Christ and the church covenant.
5. You may be asked to meet with an appropriate church committee to relate in simple words your Christian faith. You will then be voted on as a candidate for baptism and church membership.
6. The pastor will arrange with you for the baptismal service and tell you what preparations are necessary.
7. You will be baptized during a regular worship service of your church.
8. You will receive the hand of fellowship as a welcome into the church. At this time you will receive a baptismal certificate or a new member's kit.

QUESTIONS
1. Why should a Christian be baptized? How? When?
2. What does the act of being immersed in water picture to you?
3. Is it necessary to unite with a church? If so, why?
4. What are some ways in which a church member can serve others through the church?

GROW
in the New Life

The first time a baby uses a spoon it may get more food outside its mouth than inside. Why? Because it has not had practice in using a spoon. But "practice makes perfect," and it will not be very long before the child can use the spoon well. In fact, the skillful use of a spoon will become a habit.

This is what practice does. Constant practice makes an act become a habit or an integral part of your life. When you receive Christ, you are as a baby born into God's family. Some Christian habits must be acquired. You must practice these suggested duties faithfully so that they become a part of your Christian life.

PRAY EVERY DAY

What would a father think if his son should go all day long without saying a word to him, either in the morning, at meals, in the evening, or when he went to bed? What does our heavenly Father think of us if we go through the day without talking with him in prayer? Prayer is simply conversation with God. When we pray, we talk to God and we listen quietly to hear what God says to us. We must pray if we are to grow as Christians. We "need to pray always" (Luke 18:1).

Some time each day should be set apart for the purpose of praying. It is wise to spend a few minutes in prayer in the morning, just after you awake.

Begin the day with God, asking God's blessing and guidance. Take time at night before you retire to thank God for his help. Confess your sins to God and receive forgiveness. Give yourself to God anew. Pray for others. Thus you begin and end the day with God. Of course, anywhere and at any time during the day you can thank God for his love and for the helpfulness of his presence. No one is too busy to be aware of God's nearness and to have fellowship each day with our heavenly Father. Will you make this a daily habit?

READ THE BIBLE EVERY DAY

We desire not only to talk to God but that God talk to us, telling us which way to go and what to do. God can speak to us through the Bible. It is our road map through life. Travelers who decide they will not be bothered by a road map can blame no one but themselves if they get lost. Many Christians lose their way in the Christian life because they do not read the Bible.

The best way to be faithful in Bible reading is to have your Bible in the room where you pray. Read it before or after prayer. Thus you hold two-way conversation with God. You talk to God in prayer, and God talks to you as you read the Bible and think quietly about him and his Word.

The Bible is the most valuable book ever written and can become the most interesting to you. But do not start with Genesis. As a suggestion, begin with the story of the Savior as found in the **Gospel of Mark.** Then read the wonderful **Gospel of John.** Follow this with the **Acts of the Apostles** in order to see how the first Christians lived. The **Psalms** will deepen your spiritual life. **Philippians** will make you thankful. **Romans** will instruct you in the great teachings of the Christian faith. **First John** describes the marks of a true Christian. The **Gospel of Luke** has been called the "most beautiful book ever written." **Hebrews** shows how the Old Testament is fulfilled in the Christian message. The **Gospel of Matthew** particularly tells how Jesus' life fulfilled the Old Testament prophecies. After reading the New Testament, you will find the Old Testament stories of great help.

Sometimes you may want to read two or three chapters at a time. Other times you may spend all your moments and thought on just a verse or a section. Read until God gives you a message for the day. Remember the statement of the psalmist, "I treasure your word in my heart, so that I may not sin against you" (Psalm 119:11). Will you make this one of your daily habits?

GO TO CHURCH REGULARLY

The reasons you studied previously for joining a Christian church are also reasons for attending the services of the church. You receive little help and encouragement in the Christian life if you do not go to church. Christian fellowship, group worship, prayer, and study are not often experienced by those absent from the church services. Just as an ember that is separated from the fire soon dies, so will a Christian lose a certain spiritual glow and joy by failing to attend church regularly. The growing, active Christian is one who attends the services of the church and who shares unselfishly in its work. The Bible warns us about "neglecting to meet together, as is the habit of some" (Hebrews 10:25).

Attend the church services for the purpose of worshiping God. Enter the sanctuary remembering that you are in God's house. When you have been seated, pray for your pastor, for others who are worshiping with you, and for yourself. Your prayerful attitude will enable you to be aware of the presence of God.

Your church probably provides several different types of services each week. Try to be present at all of them. One opportunity for worship a week is not enough, just as one meal a day is not sufficient.

1. The Sunday morning worship service is a time to worship God and to receive food for Christian living.

2. In Sunday church school the Bible is studied and its teachings are applied to everyday life. You will make new friends here.

3. The young people's meetings are conducted by and for youth. Here young people study Christian truths and receive training for Christian service.

4. The Sunday evening services, in churches that have them, are more informal and provide opportunity for a varied program of worship, study, discussion, and Christian fellowship.

5. The midweek program is like a foundation base in the middle of a long bridge spanning a river. Meetings for Christian dialogue, prayer, and Bible study strengthen Christians in the midst of the week. Some churches sponsor small group meetings in homes for the same purpose.

As a Christian you need encouragement in worship, study, and service, and you should plan to take advantage of the opportunities for Christian growth provided by your church. Will you do this?

GIVE REGULARLY TO THE LORD

It is very easy to forget that the world and everything in it belongs not to people but to God, who created all things. "The earth is the Lord's and all that is in it, the world, and those who live in it" (Psalm 24:1). God is the owner of all you possess. Even the money you earn does not belong to you. It is a trust from God. You earn money by the abilities God has given you, by making use of the natural resources of the earth—land, minerals, water, vegetation, electricity—all products of God's creation.

Stewardship means that a Christian is accountable to God for the way in which his or her life, health, body, talents, time, and money are used. The first step to be taken is to give oneself to God. Christians who do not support the Lord's work financially as they should must face this truth: They have not yet given themselves to God. When we have surrendered our lives to God, then we shall give our money joyously to God's work. That is the test. Do you really enjoy giving generously to God's work?

God knows our needs. God also knows that multitudes of people worry too much about what they have and what they do not have. Some people never give to God's work because of selfish or unsatisfied desires. Jesus urged his followers not to be too concerned about food and clothing but rather to be concerned about doing God's will (Matthew 6:31-33).

Every committed disciple desires to give to the Lord's work. But the amount to give is the difficult question. The Bible suggests an amount—a tenth. In the Old Testament the giving of a tithe (a tenth) of one's income to God's work was a part of the law (Malachi 3:10). In the New Testament believers are urged to give regularly and proportionately (1 Corinthians 16:2). If the Old Testament believers gave a tenth, surely we, who live not under law but under the grace of our Lord Jesus Christ, cannot do less. Persons who give at least a tenth of their income to God's work are being faithful to God's Word.

Tithing means keeping a record of your income and then regularly giving a tenth of it to the Lord. A person earning five hundred dollars a week will give at least fifty dollars each week to God's work. A young person earning fifty dollars a week should plan to give at least five dollars a week to God. We must remember that "each of us will be accountable to God" (Romans 14:12).

When you join the church, you will probably receive offering envelopes. Use them regularly so that the local ministry of your church and the wider mission work which your church supports will grow in scope and effectiveness. "For we are God's servants, working together" (1 Corinthians 3:9). Will you begin tithing?

WITNESS FOR CHRIST FAITHFULLY

Jesus said to all Christians, "You will be my witnesses" (Acts 1:8). You have been led to Christ because someone told you about him and his love. Now it is your turn. Will you tell others, that they also may experience the joy of being followers of Christ?

In John 1:35-49 we read that John the Baptist directed two of his disciples to Jesus. Both of them became his followers. One of these, Andrew, went immediately to find his brother so he could tell him about the Savior. Similarly, Philip, when he became a Christian, told Nathanael, who also became a follower of Christ.

Do not make the matter of witnessing a difficult one. Tell others, by your deeds and by your words, what Jesus has done for you and what he means to you. Tell others how they can learn about Christ and experience his love. Invite them to church or to talk with your pastor.

Witnessing includes more than speaking to others about Christ. By the acts of service that you do at home, in the church, and in the community, you can be a witness for Christ. Your attitude of love toward all people regardless of their race, cultural background, or religious beliefs; your honesty and faithfulness in your tasks; your concern for the less fortunate and efforts to alleviate their needs—all speak of your inner faith. Ask your pastor if there is a definite task that you can do, and then perform it faithfully. A deed of kindness; a word of cheer; a quiet, helpful act—in all these ways you can be Christ's witness. You must constantly live as a loyal follower of Jesus Christ, remembering also to speak to your friends about Christ and the church whenever you have an opportunity to do so.

DECISION MOMENT

If you will faithfully endeavor with God's help to acquire these five habits in your Christian life, you will never lose your love for your Lord. Instead, you will grow in your Christian faith, and you will be a happy, useful

Christian. Check below the responsibilities which you will earnestly seek to fulfill in your life.

God being my helper,

I will pray every day . . . . □
I will read the Bible every day . . . . □
I will go to church regularly . . . . □
I will give at least a tenth of my earnings to the Lord . . . . □
I will witness for Christ faithfully . . . . □

At the back of this booklet is a check-up chart where for eight weeks you can keep a record of your weekly progress in acquiring the habits that will enable you to grow in the Christian life.

Bow in prayer now, asking for God's strength and guidance.

"Eternal God, help me to live each day in the spirit of Jesus Christ. Support me in my efforts to grow in Christian love and service. Keep me strong in my faith and true to him who surrendered his life for me, in Jesus' name. Amen."

QUESTIONS

1. Why is prayer of great importance to a Christian? How can we make it meaningful in our lives?
2. Why is church attendance important?
3. What Christian truths should be a guide for spending money? How does Christian stewardship enhance our lives?
4. How can Christians effectively share their faith in Christ?
5. Who is helped more when you share your faith—you or the one to whom you witness? Why?

ENJOY
the New Life

Christ puts a song in one's heart and gives a joyous lift to every day. Christians should be the most joyful of all people, for they have the greatest reason for being genuinely happy. They find the real meaning of life in being workers for God in the world, in being concerned for their fellow human beings, in standing for justice and love, in overcoming their own inner weaknesses, and in finding a sense of security and inner peace. Are you enjoying the Christian life as you should? Here are suggestions that will help you.

ASSURANCE

You have daily assurance that you are a Christian when you keep three things clearly in mind:

1. GOD'S SON IS YOUR SAVIOR. You believe in Jesus, and he is the one who has saved you from spiritual death and given you eternal life. Since you have become a Christian, you are aware of God's presence with you and of the strength and care God gives you for day-by-day living. Read John 10:27-30 to see how Jesus Christ and the Father care for you.

2. GOD'S WORD IS TRUE. Your faith rests on God's own Word, not on the unreliable promise of a human being. First John 5:13 states, "I write these things to you who believe in the name of the Son of God, so that you

may know that you have eternal life." When he was tempted, Jesus trusted God's Word, replying three times, "It is written . . ." (Matthew 4:4,7,10). Jesus has said, "Listen! I am standing at the door, knocking; if you hear my voice and open the door, I will come in to you and eat with you, and you with me" (Revelation 3:20). If you honestly open the door of your life to Christ, you know that he comes in because he said he would. If you do your part and believe, Jesus is certain to do his. Rely on him. Jesus Christ is worthy of belief and will not fail in his promises.

3. GOD'S SPIRIT ASSURES YOU. You need not depend on your feelings, for the Holy Spirit of God adds certainty to your own assurance that you are God's child. "It is that very Spirit bearing witness with our spirit that we are children of God" (Romans 8:16).

FORGIVENESS

Undoubtedly you have found that even after becoming a Christian, you have displeased God with wrong words, thoughts, and deeds. Certainly you have displeased yourself by so doing. Where do you stand now? It is wrong for a Christian to sin. The teachings of the Bible and your own conscience tell you that sinning is wrong. Your Christian friends will be disappointed in you, and those not yet Christians will wonder or scoff. Worst of all, sin on your part grieves your heavenly Father.

Fortunately God will forgive your sin. A Christian strives to do God's will. However, since no one is perfect, all make mistakes and fail God, even those who are Christians. Can a Christian ask God for forgiveness? Certainly, provided that person is truly sorry for the sin and determines, with God's help, not to repeat it. To do otherwise is to mock God's forgiveness. A wonderful verse for you to learn is 1 John 1:9: "If we confess our sins, he who is faithful and just will forgive us our sins and cleanse us from all unrighteousness."

VICTORY

"Can I live a victorious Christian life? Will I be able to overcome the temptations that come my way? Or will I be continually defeated?" You can live a successful Christian life. It is God's will that you have victory over temptation (1 Corinthians 10:13).

You will experience temptations. Accept that as a reality. But here is a glorious secret: You do not have to fight the battle alone. Jesus Christ is your helper. Whenever or wherever you are tempted, breathe a prayer to him asking for help to overcome the temptation. Memorize now, for use when you need it, Philippians 4:13: "I can do all things through him who strengthens me." Say it over every day. Believe it and act on it.

GUIDANCE

Many times in your Christian life you will have to make decisions. As a disciple of Jesus you will want to do God's will. How can you be sure what God's will is? God shows you the way by at least four guideposts.

1. THE TEACHINGS OF THE BIBLE. The psalmist said, "Your word is a lamp to my feet and a light to my path" (Psalm 119:105). The Word of God lays down principles to guide you in your choices. Read the Bible prayerfully to obtain God's guidance. Then apply its principles to your particular problem.

2. THE GUIDANCE OF THE HOLY SPIRIT. As you wait before God in earnest prayer and thought, the Spirit of God who dwells within you will make clear the right way for you to go. "For all who are led by the Spirit of God are children of God" (Romans 8:14). The Holy Spirit will help to form a conviction as to what is right—if you are willing to follow the Spirit's leading.

3. THE ADVICE OF CHRISTIAN FRIENDS. God tells you, not someone else, what his will is for you. Nonetheless, the experience and advice of earnest Christian friends who have good common sense will be of great help. To seek your pastor's advice is wise. He or she has been trained to help people with their problems and will pray with you for divine guidance.

4. THE INDICATION OF OUTWARD CIRCUMSTANCES. For a committed Christian, God shapes circumstances generally in the direction of his divine will. This is not an infallible test, for sometimes God leads against apparent circumstances. Decisions must always be considered in the light of Bible teachings, the guidance of the Holy Spirit, and the advice of Christian friends. For example, God does not normally call one with failing health to be a foreign missionary, or an uneducated person to be a Bible translator, or one with very weak eyes to be a surgeon. The God who controls all things guides events in the lives of his children into the direction of his will. "Our steps are made firm by the Lord" (Psalm 37:23).

God will show you his will by means of these four guideposts, provided you are open and honestly prepared to obey God's will when it is revealed, even though it may be contrary to your natural desires. You cannot expect God to lead you if you are determined to have your own way.

JESUS IS YOUR EXAMPLE

Before a building is erected, an architect draws plans showing just what the building should be like. The carpenters and masons follow that plan. You are building a Christian life. Jesus has drawn the plans. If you are a Christian, then Christ must be the example for your life.

Many times you will wonder what is right or wrong for a Christian to do. Study the Gospels and see what Jesus taught or did in similar cases. Pray for guidance. Ask yourself this question: "What would Jesus do now?" Answer it honestly in the light of Bible teaching and your Christian conscience. Then act accordingly. If what you are about to do

1. can be done in Jesus' name,
2. will help other Christians by your example,
3. can be done to the glory of God,

then you are doing right. If you are in doubt, give God the benefit of your doubt. In John 13:15 Jesus said, "For I have set you an example, that you also should do as I have done to you."

SERVICE FOR CHRIST AND HIS CHURCH

Jesus always lived for others, not for himself. He said he came "not to be served but to serve" (Matthew 20:28). He enjoyed doing the will of God. The selfish life is always the unhappy life. The unselfish way is the way of joy and peace.

Since Christ has done so much for you and you wish to follow his example, you will be glad to work for him. According to Matthew 5:16, people will glorify God when they see your good works as a Christian. Ask your pastor how you can be of service. Do loving acts of service regularly for Christ and for others. Try to become more sensitive to the needs of others so that you may respond to them as Jesus did. Be a true disciple for Christ in the world today.

COMPLETE DEDICATION TO GOD

There was no halfway business with Jesus. He did his Father's will completely, even though he knew it meant dying on the cross of Calvary in the end.

How sad, then, when a Christian says to the Lord of life, "I will go part way with you, and serve you only when it is convenient; you can save my soul, but I want my life to live as I please." Since the Christian really belongs to Christ (1 Corinthians 7:23), that person should be willing to say with Paul, "For to me, living is Christ" (Philippians 1:21). The very name "Lord" means "Master." In using this great word, the believer is becoming the servant to Jesus the "owner." Either self controls life or Jesus does; either self is on the throne or Christ is there. When Christ is on the throne, he is the true Master of life, and self takes the last place.

Are you willing to let your life—all your plans, ambitions, service, ability, everything—belong to Jesus and be under his control? Will you live for him completely where you are? Are you willing to say yes if he calls you as a minister, a missionary, or other full-time Christian worker? If he wants you to be a Christian servant in a business or profession, in a factory, in school, or at home, will you take this as your Christian calling?

FRIENDSHIPS

One result of your discipleship and dedication will be a growing friendship with Jesus Christ. You will want to recognize him as your daily companion. He said, "You are my friends" (John 15:14). This companionship with Christ will have certain effects in your life. Because he is the Master Friend, all other friendships will be judged in this light.

One is influenced for good or evil by the company one keeps. Before you became a disciple for Christ, you had many interests and attitudes in common with non-Christian friends. Now your interests, desires, and attitudes are increasingly different from theirs. You must influence them for Christ and not allow them to influence you away from Christ. You will desire, also, to form lasting acquaintances with other earnest Christians. Such fellowship will bring great joy and meaning to your life.

Another important consideration to keep in mind is that friendships formed with non-Christians of the opposite sex may end up leading to the consideration of marriage. A Bible teaching regarding this is found in 2 Corinthians 6:14-15: "Do not be mismatched with unbelievers. . . . What fellowship is there between light and darkness? . . . Or what does a believer share with an unbeliever?" In 1 Corinthians 7:39 we read that Christians should marry "only in the Lord." A wise young Christian who is looking forward to a happy, united, congenial home with Christ as the head should seek one who shares the same Christian beliefs. Otherwise, misunderstanding and a lack of unity in spiritual things may result. Many Christians have unfortunately discovered this problem all too late. A wise Christian will not allow such a friendship to develop deeply for fear that, when it begins to deepen, love will blind the eyes to religious conviction and loyalty to Christ. Pray earnestly for God's guidance in the choice of a mate so that you may be united with an earnest, active Christian as your life companion.

SOCIAL RESPONSIBILITY

Another result of your discipleship will be a concern that Jesus Christ may have a growing influence in all the relationships of society. You should use your influence to remedy evil and unhealthful conditions in your community and nation. Where needs go unattended and problems need solutions, you can make your influence felt. Such conditions challenge red-blooded Christians who have plenty of common sense and a dedicated spirit. These areas of great need surely call forth your best efforts for Christ:

1. The spirit of militarism that leads to conflicts and wars
2. The injustice of inadequate education, jobs, housing, and food for so many people
3. The discrimination against people because of race, gender, religion, or national background
4. The growing amount of organized crime, violence, and disrespect for law
5. The dangers to the mind and body in drugs, smoking, and alcoholic beverages
6. The pollution of the environment and the overuse of natural resources
7. The disregard for basic moral standards
8. The breakdown of the home and family life
9. The growing disregard of Sunday as a day of rest, worship, and witnessing for Christ.

QUESTIONS

1. How can we be certain that we are Christians?
2. Why are some Christians not happy Christians?
3. How may Christians be guided in making decisions?
4. How may Christians determine which habits, amusements, and work are Christian and which are not Christian?

STUDY
the New Life

As a new believer, you have much to learn about the life into which you have entered. The truths presented in this chapter will become more meaningful as you grow in Christ. You will want to refer to this chapter often.

THE BIBLE

IT IS A BOOK. The Bible contains sixty-six books, written by at least forty different authors over a period of about fifteen hundred years. There are two main parts: The Old Testament of thirty-nine books tells of God's dealing with the human race before his Son, Jesus Christ, came to earth; the New Testament of twenty-seven books relates the story of Jesus' birth, life, death, and resurrection, as well as the beginnings of the church.

IT IS GOD'S MESSAGE. Though forty different human authors recorded the words, the one author behind them all was the Holy Spirit. For example, David, Luke, Peter, or Paul each expressed himself in his own way, yet all the while each was directed by the Holy Spirit. "All scripture is inspired by God" (2 Timothy 3:16). "No prophecy ever came by human will, but men and women moved by the Holy Spirit spoke from God" (2 Peter 1:21). While many other books contain much that is true, the Bible is different, for it does more than record people's thoughts about God. It is the truth of God.

IT IS OUR GUIDE. When God speaks, we must listen, believe, and obey. The Bible will direct our lives into God's path. "Your word is a lamp to my feet and a light to my path" (Psalm 119:105).

GOD

GOD IS. "In the beginning God . . ." (Genesis 1:1, RSV). The Bible does not seek to prove that there is a God but simply takes God's existence for granted. So should we, as we see so many evidences of God in nature, in life, and in God's dealings with us.

WHO GOD IS

God is a personal being. As an individual person, you think, feel, decide, and act for yourself. Likewise God is a personal being who does all these things to a supreme degree. As you can say, "I live," and "I am," God described himself once as the almighty "I AM" (Exodus 3:14).

God is spirit. "God is spirit," said Jesus (John 4:24). God does not have a male or female body. God is not limited to any one place but is present everywhere (Psalm 139:7-10). Neither is God limited by time as we are. God is beyond time, for God is eternal (Psalm 90:2).

God is all powerful. Jesus said, "With God all things are possible" (Matthew 19:26, RSV). No person or force in this universe is as great as God is. Indeed through his power God created this universe of which we are a part. "In the beginning God created the heavens and the earth" (Genesis 1:1, RSV). God is the ruler of the universe and of the ultimate destiny of humankind.

God is the God of truth. All truth, if followed far enough, will lead to God. All that is true in chemistry, geology, space technology, philosophy, sociology, or other sciences is true because it is in harmony with God. God is the standard of truth. "Your word is truth" (John 17:17).

God is the God of holiness. Holiness is that which is morally right. Again in this realm, God is the standard. We judge whether a thing is right or wrong by whether or not it conforms to God's holy nature. "Shall not the Judge of all the earth do what is just?" (Genesis 18:25). God is holy. Because human beings became sinful and selfish, they could not dwell in God's presence. Their sin had to be removed before God could receive them. Jesus died to remove that sin.

God is the God of love. That which appeals the most about God is his love. "God is love" (1 John 4:8). Love gives itself to others. "For God so loved the world that he gave his only Son" (John 3:16). God is always yearning for human beings and seeking to give himself to those who will receive him. His love has made possible our salvation through Christ.

GOD'S ONENESS

God is one. There is only one God. Every Jewish child was taught to repeat that which Christians also believe, "Hear, O Israel: The Lord our God, the Lord is one" (Mark 12:29, see also Deuteronomy 6:4). For this reason the Lord deserves complete love and loyalty. No one should set up other gods in place of or in addition to God.

God is three-in-one. Though God is one, yet God has been revealed to us in three forms: God, Jesus the Christ (Messiah), and the Holy Spirit. Each is distinct, yet each is of the one God. The Son reveals the Father; the Holy Spirit helps us to understand this revelation. Illustrations from nature, though inadequate, help to picture this triune relationship. Ice, water, and steam are all forms of H_2O. Each presents a different appearance, yet each is the same chemical substance. The rain falling from heaven, the river which it feeds, and the ocean into which the river flows are all one water system, yet each is distinct. At the baptism of Christ the three members of the Trinity were present. Identify them in Matthew 3:16-17.

THE HUMAN RACE

WHAT WE ARE. We are the highest of God's creatures. Only to human beings did God give his own image (Genesis 1:26). We know the difference between right and wrong and can choose freely between the two.

HOW WE FAILED. We human beings were made to live in the full likeness of God through perfect obedience to God. But the Bible tells of humankind's early disobedience (Genesis 3:1-7), which marred God's image, just as dropping a clay figure would ruin the likeness it portrayed. In sinning, human beings departed from God, felt the guilt of breaking God's law, and created a sinful tendency that has been passed on to every member of the human race. Disbelief in God caused sin. Unbelief and separation from God still lead to all forms of evil.

JESUS CHRIST

SON OF GOD. In a way which no one else can claim, Jesus Christ is the Son of God. He said, "I and the Father are one" (John 10:30). Christ has always existed as God the Son. While he was on this earth, he forgave sins; he taught with divine authority; he performed miracles; he made claims which could be made only by one who was truly God.

SON OF MAN. No one must doubt the fact, however, that Jesus was a real human being. He came as a male baby, grew into manhood, worked, prayed, ate, talked, and became as weary as we can become. He shared the problems and temptations of us all. As God's Son, however, he was without sin, and therefore could take our place in death. He was "one who in every respect has been tested as we are, yet without sin" (Hebrews 4:15).

SAVIOR. Jesus came to earth to be our Savior. "You shall call his name Jesus, for he will save his people from their sins" (Matthew 1:21). Though sinless himself, he identified himself with us in our sin. He suffered the end result of our sin, which was death (that is, being spiritually separated from God), in order that we need not die but rather might receive life and forgiveness as a free gift of God. God can look with favor upon us because Christ's death took away the sin that was an obstacle between God and us. Christ broke the power of sin and death when he rose from the grave. We can become children of God by placing our faith in him.

THE HOLY SPIRIT

WHO THE HOLY SPIRIT IS

A personal being. Wherever the Bible refers to the Holy Spirit, it pictures that Spirit as a personal being. The Holy Spirit knows, loves, wills, leads, can be grieved, convicts us of sin, inspires. All of these only a personal being can do.

God. Moreover, the Holy Spirit is divine in the same sense that the Father and the Son are divine. The Holy Spirit is called "God's Spirit" (1 Corinthians 3:16). The Spirit is named on an equal basis with the Father and Son (Matthew 28:19).

WHAT THE HOLY SPIRIT DOES

The Spirit reveals truth. As was stated in the section on the Bible, the Holy Spirit inspired certain authors to write God's message. But the Spirit did not stop there. Each time we open the Bible to read it, the Spirit is our teacher, helping us to understand and apply its meaning.

The Spirit leads us to Christ. The Spirit of God wants all men and women to come to Christ. Jesus said, "When he comes, he will convince the world

concerning sin and righteousness and judgment" (John 16:8, RSV). The Spirit holds up the living Christ as the One who is ready to receive all who trust him. The Spirit shows the disbelieving person just how far he or she is from the life that pleases God. The Spirit warns that person of the great danger of continuing on that course. When we are willing to be led, the Spirit brings us to a childlike trust in the Savior and puts the very life of God within our soul. Jesus called this change the "new birth" or the "birth from above" (John 3:3).

The Spirit helps Christians grow. A true believer has a new power, that of the Holy Spirit. The Spirit makes the Christian increasingly sensitive to what is displeasing to God and gives instruction regarding the will of God. The Spirit teaches the practice of prayer and produces the fruit of the Spirit (Galatians 5: 22-23). The Holy Spirit gives strength to perform Christian service.

THE CHURCH

ITS MEANINGS

A worldwide family. The word *church* is used with two meanings in the New Testament. In one sense it means the church of Christ as a worldwide family, that is, the whole body of believers throughout the world rather than a particular group of Christians in a certain place. Jesus had this meaning in mind when he said he was the founder of his church and that no stronghold, not even the gates of Hades, could withstand the church's influence (Matthew 16:18). All who have truly trusted in Jesus Christ for their salvation are members of the church of Christ.

A local organization. The word *church* is also used to refer to a local organized group of believers in Christ, such as the Philippian church or the Ephesian church. This is the more familiar meaning. The church gathers at its base of operations for worship, inspiration, and instruction on the Lord's Day. It disperses into the world during the week for the ministry of witness and service in all areas of life. In accordance with the New Testament pattern, each Baptist church is self-governing, with each member having an equal right to vote. Each church is expected to cooperate with other churches.

ITS OFFICERS

Pastor. Read Ephesians 4:11. The New Testament refers to pastors, elders, and bishops, all of whom seem to have had similar duties. The pastor is to serve, to teach, to lead, to oversee the local group of believers. The pastor is like a shepherd.

Deacons. Read 1 Timothy 3:8-13. This office probably originated as de-

scribed in Acts 6:1-7. Deacons are to serve in the spiritual and temporal affairs of the church.

Other officers. Other officers, such as treasurers and clerks, may have served in the New Testament churches. Still others have been added since then, as needs have arisen.

ITS ORDINANCES. An ordinance is an acted-out symbol portraying a spiritual truth. The two ordinances that Christ commanded the church to observe are baptism and the Lord's Supper. They are discussed in "Study 2."

THE THINGS OF THE FUTURE

DEATH. For a Christian, death has lost its sting. Believers still die, but for us it is "away from the body and at home with the Lord" (2 Corinthians 5:8). Jesus has gone on ahead to prepare a place for us (John 14:2).

THE RETURN OF CHRIST. Jesus promised, "The Son of Man is to come with his angels in the glory of his Father, and then he will repay everyone for what has been done" (Matthew 16:27). When Jesus left the earth, two divine messengers assured his watching disciples, "This Jesus, who has been taken up from you into heaven, will come in the same way as you saw him go into heaven" (Acts 1:11). This event is yet in the future. No one knows when it will come to pass (Mark 13:32). But the Bible declares that this event will be a personal return of Christ to earth in great glory and power.

THE RESURRECTION. Just as Jesus Christ could not be held in the grave by death but rose in new life from it, so those who have died believing in Christ will experience the same victory over death. The Christian believer will be given a new and glorified body. Read John 11:25-26 and 1 Corinthians 15:51-53. Those who do not believe in Christ will experience the "resurrection of judgment" (John 5:29, RSV).

JUDGMENT. The Bible very clearly states the fact of judgment. Jesus spoke of it and said that he himself would be the judge (Matthew 25:31). He will judge with absolute correctness. Those who have refused to believe in him as Savior in this life will be condemned by that fact and by their evil deeds (John 3:18-19). Hell is the eternal state of those who have continued in rebellion against God. Believers in Christ will not come into this judgment, since their sins have already been judged in the death of Christ on the cross at Calvary. But they will come before the judgment seat of Christ to receive the full reward for their faithful service for Christ in this life (2 Corinthians 5:10). Heaven is prepared for those who are true believers and followers of Christ. The supreme delight of heaven is the perfect fellowship that believers will share throughout eternity with God and with all others who love God.

QUESTIONS
1. How is the Bible helpful to the Christian?
2. Who is Jesus Christ? What does he mean to you?
3. What is the work of the Holy Spirit today?
4. What do we mean by the word *church?*

SHARE
the New Life

OUR BAPTIST HISTORY

The churches mentioned in the New Testament were groups of believers in Christ who met in homes to worship and study. When their numbers grew larger, buildings set apart especially for worship were secured.

The early Christians were cruelly persecuted by some of the Roman emperors. Even before the death of the apostles, the common danger of persecution drew the Christians together. In the year 313 A.D. the emperor Constantine stopped all persecutions of Christians and brought about an alliance between the church and the state. This appeared to be a great blessing to the churches. Unfortunately, it led ultimately to many evils, including the receiving of unconverted people into church membership, the tendency to inject pagan ideas into the church's worship, the use of the church by the government for its own ends, and the tendency of the church to depend on the power and authority of the government rather than on God for its growth and influence.

The first-century believers organized into many independent local churches, united only by a common faith, love, and a mutual responsibility to win the world for Christ. They had no overall organization, no priest or pope, no creedal statement, mass, or highly formal ritual, all of which developed later. Theirs was a free, spiritual, Christ-centered faith that gave rise to the New Testament Scriptures and led to a vital unity in the Spirit. After the destruction of Jerusalem in 70 A.D., a new location for church leadership became necessary. Antioch served for some years. Later Rome became increasingly important as a church center. Not until about the fifth century was there any serious effort by the bishop of Rome to claim or exercise wider authority. The group of Western churches that later accepted papal authority was known as the Roman Catholic Church.

As centuries passed, various unbiblical practices developed, such as the rise of a sacred priesthood, the practice of confessing sins to priests, infant baptism, sprinkling, the withholding of the Bible from the people, authoritarian rule of the church by a priestly group headed by the pope, the loss of personal religious freedom, the raising of human rules and decisions to a place equal in authority to the Bible, prayers to saints, the adoration of the virgin Mary, buying from priests permission slips to sin, and depending for salvation on good works rather than on faith in Jesus Christ.

As early as the twelfth century, voices were raised to protest the various unscriptural practices of the prevailing church. Pierre de Bruys, Arnold of Brescia, and Peter Waldo in that century were followed later by John Wycliffe of England, John Huss of Bohemia, and Balthasar Hubmaier of Germany. Their protests and teachings sound strikingly similar to our cherished Baptist principles today. They urged obedience to the Scriptures rather than to the pope. They taught that a true church is composed of those who have been born anew by faith in Jesus Christ and have publicly made a commitment to obey Christ and symbolized their commitment by immersion. They insisted that all believers are equal before God and that each local church is self-governing, subject only to Jesus Christ. They denied that the churches should rule the state or the state the churches, and they insisted on the right of every person to obey God according to his or her conscience. Indeed, while not bearing the name "Baptist," they can truly be said to be our spiritual forebears.

On October 31, 1517, Martin Luther, a German priest, openly opposed the corrupt practices of the Roman Catholic Church that were in contradiction to the Scriptures. His stand brought the smoldering fires of dissent into the open. The movement in Europe to restore New Testament Christianity became known as the Protestant Reformation.

Among the reformers were Christians who insisted on baptizing only those who personally committed themselves to Christ. These were called by their critics Anabaptists or "re-baptizers" because most European Christians had been baptized as infants. There were vigorous groups of Anabaptists in Moravia, Holland, Switzerland, and England. Baptists number these Anabaptists among their spiritual forebears.

Baptists emerged out of English Puritanism. A handful of Congregational Separatist refugees from England became convinced of the importance of believer's baptism and formed the first English Baptist church in 1609 in Amsterdam, the Netherlands. Part of this congregation later returned to England to give that land a Baptist witness. These Baptists shared many of the beliefs of the Anabaptists.

In America the story of Baptists begins with Roger Williams, a minister of the Church of England who fled to America. He was responsible for the founding of the colony of Rhode Island, where people were granted absolute religious liberty. The first Baptist church in America was founded in Providence in 1638 by Roger Williams. Although he is not so well known, John Clarke founded the Baptist church in Newport, Rhode Island, in 1644 and became one of the most important Baptists in the seventeenth century.

The Baptist conviction that every person is responsible only to God for his or her religious beliefs and practices is in a large measure responsible for religious freedom as we know it in America today. The American Bill of Rights was the result of the efforts of many liberty-loving people and evangelical Christians like the Baptists of Virginia and New England. Baptists, with their evangelistic zeal based on positive scriptural beliefs, gained many converts in America. They grew from an insignificant ten thousand in 1775 to one hundred thousand in 1800. In 1900 they numbered over 5 million. The Baptists compose the largest Protestant group in North America today, with a total of approximately 31 million members in the Baptist denominations. The world family of Baptists has approximately 38 million baptized believers representing a community of 80 million Baptists ministering in more than two hundred countries.

Baptists have made an outstanding contribution to the spiritual progress of the world. The first modern foreign missionary was William Carey, a Baptist from England. The first American foreign missionaries were Adoniram and Ann Judson, who were supported by Baptists. The author of *Pilgrim's Progress,* John Bunyan, was a Baptist pastor. John Hughes founded the British and Foreign Bible Society. The prince of preachers, Charles Haddon Spurgeon, and the renowned pulpiteer, Alexander Maclaren, were Baptists. The hymn "America" was written by Samuel F. Smith, a Baptist. The first Sunday school in America was founded in the First Baptist Church of Philadelphia in 1815. The first reservation day school for Indians in America was organized in Lodge Grass, Montana, by

Baptists. This denomination also has the honor of having instituted the first Christian center in America in Seattle, Washington. Other Baptists who have distinguished themselves include Walter Rauschenbusch, a great exponent of the social implications of the gospel; Charles Evans Hughes, former chief justice of the United States Supreme Court; Kenneth Scott Latourette, foremost church historian of the modern era; and Billy Graham, world famous evangelist. As of 1993, the historic roster of U.S. presidents contains the names of four Baptists.

OUR BAPTIST CHURCHES

THE LOCAL CHURCH. A local Baptist church is an organized group of baptized believers who have confessed Christ as their Lord and Savior and who desire to work together for the advancement of his kingdom. Each local Baptist church chooses its own pastor and officers, whose duties are usually outlined in the church constitution.

THE AREA OR ASSOCIATION. Each Baptist church controls its own business and ministry as the members decide. Baptists believe, however, that they can make a greater contribution to the cause of Christ by cooperating with churches of like faith in the great task of reaching the world for Christ. This helps them to relate to the whole body of Christ. Therefore they voluntarily join themselves into an association for fellowship, inspiration, and cooperative missionary endeavors. From ten to about fifty churches make up the average area or association. The term *area* is supplanting *association* in some locations today.

THE REGION, OR STATE, OR METROPOLITAN CONVENTION. Just as churches of a smaller location voluntarily band together into an area or an association, so Baptist churches in one or more states or in a metropolitan context unite. This larger organization assists churches and pastors; starts new churches; provides Christian camping opportunities; aids in Christian education, evangelism, and leadership training; and raises funds for carrying on the work of Christ in the region, nation, and world. Churches send delegates and visitors to the annual meeting for business and fellowship. To oversee all these tasks of the region, an executive is employed. Often area ministers, directors of evangelism, and specialists in Christian education, missionary promotion, community ministry, and other areas of service are employed as well.

NATIONAL BAPTIST BODIES (often called conventions, federations, unions, or conferences). Baptists must work together in units of cooperative organization larger than state or provincial conventions if they are to carry out their national and worldwide responsibilities. So they have various national bodies. These groups are formed (especially in the United States) on the basis of geographic proximity; common racial, national, or language background; or some particular doctrinal, social, or organizational interest that they share with one another. These national bodies work to evangelize their own nations and the world through home and foreign missionaries; establish and support colleges, seminaries, hospitals, and homes for children and the aged; organize and strengthen churches; publish literature; make their testimony felt in social, religious, public, and moral issues; and provide arrangements for pensions and grants for their ministers, missionaries, and official workers.

The Baptist bodies in the United States with the largest membership are given in order of their present size:

Southern Baptist Convention
National Baptist Convention, U.S.A., Inc. (African American origin)
National Baptist Convention of America (African American origin)
American Baptist Churches in the U.S.A.
American Baptist Association (Landmark Baptists)
Progressive National Baptist Convention, Inc. (African American origin)
Conservative Baptist Association of America
National Primitive Baptist Convention
North American Baptist Association
General Association of Regular Baptist Churches
United Free Will Baptist Church
Baptist General Conference of America (Swedish origin)
North American Baptist General Conference (German origin)

Baptists in some two hundred other countries of the world have their own organizations.

THE BAPTIST WORLD ALLIANCE. This is the official worldwide fellowship of Baptists. Organized in 1905 in London, it has its present headquarters in McLean, Virginia, with BWA regional secretaries in the Caribbean, Asia, Africa, Europe, and Latin America. Its stated purposes are to unite Baptists worldwide, lead in world evangelization, defend human rights, and respond to people in need.

The Baptist World Alliance has become a strong voice in many countries for religious liberty and Baptist principles. It gathers facts, aids refugees, provides relief, and proves an arm of strength for Baptist minorities.

In America the North American Baptist Fellowship was formed in 1965 to draw together the Baptists of the continent on the basis of their common interest and to inspire them to work together in fulfilling the directives of

Christ. The major Baptist groups of the continent cooperate in this fellowship, which is a part of the Baptist World Alliance.

OUR BAPTIST BELIEFS

Baptists share with other evangelical denominations belief in the great doctrines of the church, such as the Bible as God's holy Word; belief in the triune God—Father, Son, and Holy Spirit; the redemptive ministry of Jesus Christ; the believer's resurrection made possible by the resurrection of Jesus Christ; and the ultimate triumph of our Lord over sin and death. In addition to these great truths, Baptists stress the following beliefs:

THE LORDSHIP OF JESUS CHRIST. Christ is the only mediator between God and human beings. He is the living Lord of the Bible and the living Lord of today. He is the head of the church.

THE SUPREMACY OF THE SCRIPTURES. The Bible is our guide. Each believer, with the help of the Holy Spirit, can read and understand the Scriptures. Unlike many denominations, Baptists do not have a formal creed. Individual churches and certain groups of churches have formulated covenants and articles of faith that summarize their understanding of scriptural teachings, but as Baptists we have not officially adopted a creed to which all must conform. The Bible is our final authority in faith and conduct.

THE PRIESTHOOD OF BELIEVERS. Every person can approach God directly through Christ, without the aid of human priests, ritual, or baptism. Personal faith in Jesus Christ is the only way to God. "For by grace you have been saved through faith; and this is not your own doing, it is the gift of God" (Ephesians 2:8). However, one cannot be a priest all alone; one needs to be a part of the church and a witness to others.

BELIEVER'S BAPTISM. Baptism should be administered only to those who believe and follow Christ. The ordinance of baptism has no meaning apart from the spiritual change that has already taken place within the individual by accepting Christ. Baptism by immersion in water was taught in the Bible and used in the early church, for it pictured a person's death to sinful living and rising into a new life in Christ. For this reason Baptists have historically practiced immersion as the scriptural form of baptism.

REGENERATE CHURCH MEMBERSHIP. Church membership is only for baptized believers. The membership of the church should be composed only of those who have personally received Christ as their Lord and Savior and bear witness to the new life in Christ. This is referred to as a "regenerate church membership." Baptists oppose the inclusion of infants and unsaved people as members of the church. Anyone desiring to unite with a Baptist church should give evidence of a personal experience of faith in Christ.

SEPARATION OF CHURCH AND STATE. Baptists have always stressed the separation of church and state. The church must not dictate to the state nor the state to the church. The state should protect all religious groups but favor none.

RELIGIOUS FREEDOM. All persons are responsible to God for their religious beliefs and practices; they therefore should have the right to worship God as their own convictions and consciences dictate. Neither the state nor the organized church has the right to dictate what they shall believe.

THE INDEPENDENCE OF THE LOCAL CHURCH. Each local congregation is self-governing, choosing its own pastor, managing its inner life, and determining its relationship to other churches. Our churches realize we must work together to spread the gospel of Christ and bear our witness more effectively.

THE EVANGELIZATION OF THE WORLD. Baptists take seriously the Great Commission of Christ. Our remarkable growth is the result of constant endeavors to win both adults and youth to Christ. Baptists believe in taking the gospel to their local communities, to all sections of their state and nation, and to the uttermost parts of the world.

OUR FUTURE

Our Baptist history is a record of earnest commitment to Christ and to the sharing of his message with others. In humble gratitude we point to the growth and influence of Baptists in the past. The future demands that under the guidance of Almighty God the millions of Baptists of the world take their share of the responsibility for bringing the world to the feet of Jesus Christ in humble confession of him as Lord and Savior.

QUESTIONS

1. How and when did the church begin?
2. What was the origin of Protestantism?
3. What was the origin of the Baptists?
4. How do Baptists differ from other Protestant denominations?
5. What do you like about your church?
6. In what ways can the ministry of your church be more effective?

A New Member's Check-up Chart

I have for the week ending Saturday:	(Insert Saturday Dates Here)									
Prayed daily										
Read the Bible daily										
Attended the following church services: Morning Worship										
Church School										
Youth Activities										
Evening Service or Program										
Midweek Service										
Given at least a tenth of my earnings to the Lord										
Number of times witnessed for Christ										

$\mathcal{M}ary$
and the
FUNDAMENTALIST CHALLENGE

THE
REVEREND
PETER M. J. STRAVINSKAS,
PH.D., S.T.D.

PREFACE BY
THE MOST REVEREND
ROBERTO O. GONZALEZ, O.F.M.

Our Sunday Visitor Publishing Division
Our Sunday Visitor, Inc.
Huntington, Indiana 46750

The author and publisher are indebted to those individuals (including authors and publishers) who have kindly made their materials available for use in preparing this work. Most of the materials used in this book are cited in the Endnotes and Bibliography. If any copyrighted materials have been inadvertently used in this book without proper credit being given, please notify Our Sunday Visitor in writing so that future printings of this work may be corrected accordingly.

Contents

Preface

I am happy to recommend Father Peter Stravinskas's latest work, *Mary and the Fundamentalist Challenge.*

The place of Mary in the hearts and minds of the followers of Christ has been secure from the time of her intercession for the bride and groom at the wedding feast of Cana: " 'They have no wine.' . . . His mother said to the attendants, 'Do whatever he tells you' " (John 2:3, 5).

The ancient Fathers and Doctors of the Church, both East and West, glorified Mary because of her role as Mother of the Savior. The holy title *Theotokos* ("God-bearer"), given by the Council of Ephesus in 431, has been revered in the churches and homes of the faithful throughout the world. The theological authors may not necessarily be read in the ordinary home, but the picture of the Blessed Virgin Mary holding the Christ Child proclaims the Gospel of salvation through Christ Jesus.

Dr. Stravinskas shows with great scholarship the relevance of Mary to those who seek salvation through Christ. He addresses in particular the criticisms made of Catholic doctrine by Fundamentalists who carry a bias against Catholic belief and practice. It should be noted here that not every Christian who ascribes to a Fundamentalist interpretation of Christian Scripture and doctrine falls into the category of those addressed by Dr. Stravinskas. In a certain sense Catholicism can be classified as a Fundamentalist form of Christianity because of its strict adherence to Scripture and Tradition. However, this refers to the fundamental matters of belief for Catholics, not as a Fundamentalist interpretation of the Bible and Catholic teaching but as a fidelity to the Bible and the apostolic tradition from the beginning.

Dr. Stravinskas, while using sound biblical and theological arguments, addresses those more public evangelists who label Marian doctrine and devotion as idolatry and ignorance of the worst kind. Some of these critics use arguments that any mature person would recognize as specious. However, confrontation with their half truths and twisted history embarrasses Catholic laypersons. A thoughtful

reading of Dr. Stravinskas's book by clergy, religious, and laity —
especially religious educators and evangelists, RCIA leaders, pastoral planners, liturgists, theologians, and those in the ethnic and
multicultural ministries — will give rich source material to help the
faithful answer those whose main evangelical drive seems to be "to
convert a Catholic." Dr. Stravinskas will help Catholics, especially in
the Hispanic ministry, to respond more effectively to those non-Catholic proselytizers who utilize Catholic symbols to draw Catholics to
their churches. In a word, Dr. Stravinskas's book is most enlighten-
ing.

For myself, as for Father Stravinskas and for many others I am
sure, I ask: "Why is all this polemic necessary when the question of
devotion to Mary is simple, even fundamental?" The Gospel according to St. Luke puts the words of God into Gabriel's mouth: "Hail,
beloved daughter of God" or "highly favored of God," which the
Vulgate renders "full of grace." The answer is plain: if God so honored Mary, who are we to do any less? (See Luke 1:28.)

I thank Father Stravinskas for combining in his book an excellent presentation of the Church's teaching on Mary and its nexus with
the Church's pastoral mission of worship, evangelization, and service. I commend Father Stravinskas for enabling our devotion to the
Blessed Virgin Mary to be enriched by his scholarship.

May the Lord bless and keep you.

✠ *ROBERTO O. GONZALEZ, O.F.M.*
BISHOP OF CORPUS CHRISTI
Feast of Our Lady of the Rosary
October 7, 1997

Introduction

Most books have a history; that is particularly true in the present case. My work in apologetics quite naturally has made me interested in proselytism that, in many ways, makes apologetics necessary. Ten years ago, while wearing yet another hat, that of representative of the Most Reverend Paul Baltakis (Lithuanian Bishop for the Diaspora) to the National Conference of Catholic Bishops' Committee on the Pastoral Care of Migrants, I was approached by its director at the time, the Reverend Silvano Tomasi and the Committee's episcopal chairman, the Most Reverend Anthony Bevilacqua (auxiliary bishop of Brooklyn), to conduct a pilot study on the phenomenon of proselytism, with special attention given to its effects on traditionally Catholic immigrant groups. Also then serving on that Committee were the Most Reverend Sean O'Malley of St. Thomas in the Virgin Islands and the Most Reverend Roberto Gonzalez, auxiliary of the Archdiocese of Boston. Bishop Bevilacqua was succeeded by the Most Reverend Theodore E. McCarrick, founding bishop of Metuchen; he, too, saw the need for such a study and was most supportive.

The results of that preliminary effort bore fruit, so that the episcopal committee commissioned a full-blown analysis to be done by the Center for Applied Research in the Apostolate, under Sister Eleace King, IHM. This, in turn, spawned yet another project. In all three analyses, we found that Our Lady figured in the outreach of the proselytizers, and not too surprisingly. However, one detail kept surfacing, namely, that some proselytizers were using the Blessed Virgin not negatively (according to the usual *modus operandi*) but positively!

In the process of deciding upon a dissertation topic for my doctorate in Mariology at the University of Dayton and the Pontifical Institute Marianum in Rome, this fact suggested itself as both theologically significant and pastorally useful. What became obvious was that the concern could not be treated in isolation but had to be placed in a much larger context, so that we considered the roots of Fundamentalism in the Protestant Reformation, with a keen eye turned on the Reformers' attitudes toward the Blessed Mother. It was also deemed essential to reflect on the psychology and methods of proselytism.

Only then were we ready to look at the much smaller but fascinating element of how the Fundamentalist proselytizers use Mary as a "hook" — either positively or negatively — in their programs to attract Catholics to their communities. This venture also accorded me the marvelous privilege of observing numerous local situations in the United States, as well as the Church in Mexico, Guatemala, and Panama, where such activities are unfortunately all too common. I shall never forget the opportunity to address thousands of Panamanians in a week's worth of lectures, sermons, and discussions, organized by that great lay apologetics group of Panama City known as *Semper Gaudens*. What you are about to read is the pulling together of all that data.

One final step, however, was critical. Once the dissertation was written, approved, and defended, everyone agreed that the document had to be "translated" from "dissertationese" into standard English to make it more accessible. That task was admirably accomplished by a seminarian of the Diocese of Fall River, Thomas Kocik, himself a fine writer and budding theologian.

In this decade-long process, Father Tomasi has become Archbishop Tomasi and serves as the nuncio to Ethiopia and Eritrea; Bishop Bevilacqua is now the Cardinal-Archbishop of Philadelphia; Bishop McCarrick is the Archbishop of Newark; Bishop Gonzalez is the Ordinary of Corpus Christi; Bishop O'Malley serves the Church in Fall River; and Thomas Kocik is now a priest.

One thing has not changed, however, and that is the sad fact that proselytizers continue to assault the flock of Christ, especially the most vulnerable, who come among us as strangers and aliens. May Our Lady, Mother of Christ and Mother of the Church, give every reader the insight to appreciate the information contained in this volume and the determination to do all in one's power to preserve the unity of her Son's Church. May she also obtain from Our Lord the grace of being a maternal stimulus for proselytized and proselytizers alike.

Rev. Peter M. J. Stravinskas

CHAPTER 1

Disputes About Mary

Difficulties frequently arise because of misunderstanding and poor communication. The tension within Christianity between Catholics and Fundamentalists is a case in point. Nowhere is that strain more evident than in theological discussions regarding the place of the Blessed Virgin Mary in Christian theology and spirituality. The issue becomes particularly troublesome when Mary is made the centerpiece of Fundamentalist proselytizing aimed at Catholics.

The purpose of this book is to provide an overview of several related topics usually treated in isolation, if at all. These are: the theology and history of Christian Fundamentalism; the place of Mary in classical Fundamentalism; the methods and psychology of proselytism; the role of Mary in Fundamentalist proselytizing of Catholics. Each topic might well be the subject matter of exhaustive research in its own right. It is my opinion, however, that a balanced approach to understanding and combatting Fundamentalist incursions can come about only by treating these topics together.

This study of Fundamentalism was embarked upon in a spirit of ecumenism, which seeks dialogue informed by facts rather than myths, if at all possible; barring that development, at least to make clear the damaging nature of attacks on Catholicism that are false, unfair, and at times even scurrilous. The unity of Christians desired by Our Lord can only be advanced when all believers are grounded in the truth that sets men free, and by a willingness to love one another after the example of the Master Himself. These goals obviously have implications for dogmatic and pastoral theology alike, offering the potential for a healthy synthesis of faith and life.

The Present Situation

Fundamentalism began in the nineteenth century in opposition to liberal movements within Protestantism. Among these trends was a historically sensitive biblical scholarship that, under the strong influence of rationalism, called into doubt the whole supernatural content of Christianity (e.g., the inspiration of Scripture, Jesus' divinity, His virginal conception and bodily resurrection, miracles, salvation, the afterlife, and so on). Liberal Protestantism was by nature rationalist and secularist. Conservative Protestants who upheld the traditional understanding of fundamental Christian doctrines came to be known as "Fundamentalists." All of the mainline Protestant denominations found their congregations sharply divided between two camps, "Liberal" and "Fundamentalist."

Protestant Fundamentalists continued in the United States as a relatively despised group, both socially and intellectually. It is widely acknowledged that Fundamentalism has risen to great prominence on the American scene as a religious phenomenon (being the only sector of Protestantism to experience increased membership) as well as a sociopolitical force (e.g., in garnering support for the enactment of laws reflecting traditional and family values, or at least in providing a climate favorable to such legislation or policies). Also acknowledged is that Fundamentalism during the past two decades in this country (and in Latin America) has relied largely on disenchanted Catholics as the primary target of their proselytizing program. This fact is attested in their own sources and in objective surveys, but also in statements of various bishops, national hierarchies (in both North and South America, and increasingly on other continents), and even in Vatican documents.

What is relatively novel in the Fundamentalist outreach to Catholics is a specifically Marian dimension, used in one of two ways. The first approach is an outright attack on Marian doctrine and devotion, made in the hope of convincing the hearers to consider Catholicism a pagan cult of goddess worship that must be abandoned for the salvation of one's soul. The second method engages the Marian component to attract and keep Catholics who would otherwise refuse to be a part of Fundamentalist communities. The latter is a most significant development, both theologically and pastorally. Theologically, this is important for Fundamentalism because this *modus operandi* violates the absolute refusal in classical Fundamentalism to accord to Mary any role of intercession or mediation. Pastorally, it is a problem for Catholicism because the faithful will be less guarded with such proselytizers, since the line of demarcation is now less clear.

The technique of employing Marian devotion to lure Catholics to Fundamentalism is documented with increasing frequency in the literature (e.g., allusions in pastoral letters and in articles in the Catholic press). What are the implications for Fundamentalist theology? What is an appropriate pastoral response for the Catholic Church?

This Study

The purpose of the study is to determine how massive the problem of Fundamentalist proselytism of Catholics really is, and to discover the place of Mary in the Fundamentalist program of action in the effort to draw Catholics.

The study is limited to an investigation of the problem in the contemporary United States, with due attention given to a more global dimension, especially as that offers a suitable context. The project is further limited in that only denominations or groups properly considered Fundamentalists will be regarded.

The uniqueness of the study is made plain by a simple computer search that reveals not a single thesis, book, or even article on the interrelatedness of Fundamentalism, proselytism, and the place of Mary — although some documentation deals with this triad only in passing. The significance of the study is found in the theological and pastoral dimensions already cited, namely, that the use of Marian symbolism by Fundamentalists (especially in an apparently positive manner) creates a new climate for Fundamentalism and the Catholic Church alike, with serious implications for both.

As former Chairman of the National Conference of Catholic Bishops' (NCCB) Committee on Pastoral Care of Migrants and Refugees, Anthony Cardinal Bevilacqua initiated a study of Fundamentalist advances within the Catholic immigrant community. Recently he told me: "Although proselytism is particularly acute within traditional Catholic immigrant groups, it is a serious problem for the Church in general. The Marian dimension is a novelty and a complication, about which more accurate, more scientific and more analytical information is just beginning to surface. Therefore, serious research along these lines is both needed and welcome."[1]

Similarly, a communication from the Most Reverend Silvano Tomasi, former Secretary of the Pontifical Commission for the Spiritual Care of Migrants and Itinerants in Rome and now nuncio to Ethiopia (and the staff member originally responsible for commissioning what has emerged as the report of Sister Eleace King), also reflected on this present project:

> . . . An effort to highlight factual and well-documented information on Christian Fundamentalism is a critical service today. It will provide a comparative perspective on a cross-cultural phenomenon of major significance and, above all, it will help in understanding its socio-economic and religious causes.
>
> The special focus on the place of Mary in Fundamentalist proselytism will add a unique component to this study by showing the interplay of the requirements of pastoral strategies for growth and consequent theological adaptations.
>
> For any constructive dialogue with Fundamentalist Christians and for the development of appropriate pastoral care to Catholics coming from a tradition of a more devotional expression of their faith, an accurate and systematic study of the type you propose will certainly be valuable.[2]

The enormity of the theological and pastoral situation for the Church comes across in the alarm sounded by the Catholic bishops of Latin America. At their 1992 meeting in Santo Domingo, Dominican Republic, the bishops stated: "The problem of the sects has taken on dramatic proportions and has become truly preoccupying above all because of the growth of proselytism."[3]

Methodology

First, standard historical and theological sources were consulted, synthesized, and analyzed. In order to situate Fundamentalism in its proper context, it was necessary to move from the present time back to its origins, but also to its sources in sixteenth-century Calvinism and other Protestant traditions. Reference to the sociology of religion was also needed in order to understand the mentality and means of proselytism. Of necessity, all this information would provide a broad panorama against which a contemporary phenomenon could be considered.

At a second level, empirical data and anecdotal evidence were gathered from various sources and subsequently appraised; these included personal witnesses, public opinion surveys, and similar instruments used to detect developments and trends in society.

Chapter 1 introduces the topic with the statement of the problem and the limitations of the study as to place, time frame, and denominations covered. Terms are also defined.

Chapter 2 is concerned with Fundamentalism as a movement and a theology, with reference to its origins and various aspects of the movement today. Particular attention is given to its theological principles, especially in comparison and contrast with those of the Catholic Faith.

Chapter 3 deals with the place of Mary in classical Fundamentalism in itself and in contradistinction to its theological forebears in the Protestant Reformation. Highlighted, too, are more popular works of Fundamentalist preachers, inasmuch as these works have a direct impact on Catholics and other potential converts.

Chapter 4 examines the psychology and methods of proselytism in general and of Fundamentalism in particular. Specific attention is paid to the strategies of proselytizers, as well as to Catholic Church responses to their efforts, at the local, regional, and even universal levels. An important distinction is made between proselytism and evangelization.

The place of Mary in the mission of the proselytizers is the concern of Chapter 5. It is here where the uniqueness of our study is most striking. The Virgin Mary, so the research reveals, always has some role in Fundamentalist attacks on Catholicism. Traditionally this role has been negative: Marian devotion is usually pointed out as the single most glaring proof of Catholic idolatry and pseudo-Christianity. Lately, however, Fundamentalists have softened their tone so as not to "turn off" would-be converts. Mary is allowed a place, however superficial, in Fundamentalist proselytizing so that the convert's transition from "Romanism" to "Bible Christianity" is more subtle. The Catholic is weaned off "Mariolatry" gradually, step by step, until his faith lacks any Marian component to speak of: Mary as Mother and intercessor is reduced to Mary as merely an example to be imitated (but not venerated) or, still less, as a mere discardable vehicle for the Incarnation. Simultaneously, other Catholic beliefs and practices are whittled away, so that in the end, even the Catholic veneer is discarded. The program of this new breed of proselytizers is critical to appreciate, since it constitutes a rupture with the whole Fundamentalist tradition.

Our study ends with a summary of the principal findings and conclusions, as well as several recommendations for ongoing theological development and for pastoral work. An extensive bibliography is provided.

Definition of Terms

For the sake of clarity, the following terms are defined:

1. Churches: "Religious bodies in a relatively low state of tension with their environments."[4]

2. Cult: "An unconventional religion," to be understood in this book "in a technical rather than a pejorative sense."[5]

3. Evangelical: "While in the United States 'evangelical' connotes a theological conservative who emphasizes the Bible, personal salvation, and evangelism, in Latin America *evangelico* can refer to any non-Catholic Christian. The term (in Latin America) includes Mormons and Jehovah's Witnesses, whom most Evangelicals regard as false sects, as well as Protestants whose exegesis is unsuitably liberal."[6]

4. Evangelization: "Refers primarily to the proclamation of the Gospel of Jesus Christ to those who are not yet familiar with the Christian Faith or those who are no longer practicing their Faith."[7]

5. Fundamentalist: "Connotes doctrinal rigidity and is employed, somewhat promiscuously, against any Protestant inclined to quote

Scripture as his or her final authority. When used with more precision, it refers to conservative Protestants who show more concern for defending the purity of their churches. . . ."[8]

At their Fourth General Conference (Puebla IV), the Catholic bishops of Latin America defined Christian Fundamentalism as follows: "The fundamentalist sects are religious groups which insist that faith in Jesus Christ alone saves, that the sole basis of faith is Sacred Scripture interpreted in a personal and fundamentalist way thereby excluding the Church, and that the end of the world and the next judgment are imminent."[9]

6. *New Evangelization:* "The term . . . suggests that certain conditions apparently require the radical repetition of earlier evangelization."[10]

7. *Pentecostal:* ". . . refers to ecstatic forms of Protestantism defined in terms of special gifts bestowed by the Holy Spirit. Whereas only a minority of North American missionaries are Pentecostal, most Latin American Evangelicals are."[11]

8. *Popular Religiosity/Catholicism:* "The religious expression of our great majorities whose faith has not been cultivated enough," characterized by "a high regard for devotions (e.g., processions and novenas) and ecclesial marginality."[12]

9. *Proselytism:* "Improper attitudes and behaviors in the practice of Christian witness. Proselytism embraces whatever violates the rights of the human person, Christian or non-Christian, to be free from external coercion in religious matters, or whatever, in the proclamation of the Gospel, does not conform to the ways God draws free men to Himself in response to His calls to serve in spirit and in truth."[13] Concretely, "the effort to attract followers for an institution, using psychological pressure and imposition, persistently going after the person."[14]

10. *Sects:* "Religious bodies in a relatively high state of tension with their environments."[15] ". . . new organization(s) of a conventional faith (conventional, that is, in the society under observation)."[16]

11. *Secularization:* ". . . regarded as the master trend in modern times: a decline in the plausibility of supernatural beliefs that would culminate in the disappearance of religion."[17] The situation in which

"the importance of religious significance has vanished from more and more areas of life."[18]

Endnotes

1. Letter from Anthony Cardinal Bevilacqua to author, May 6, 1993.

2. Letter from Silvano Tomasi to author, May 6, 1993.

3. Puebla IV, *Nueva Evangelización, Promoción Humana, Cultura Cristiana* [*New Evangelization, Human Promotion, Christian Culture*] (Bogotá: Ediciones Paulinas, 1992), n. 139.

4. Roger Finke and Rodney Stark, *The Churching of America, 1776-1990* (New Brunswick, New Jersey: Rutgers University Press, 1992), 40-41.

5. Ibid., 295.

6. David Stoll, *Is Latin America Turning Protestant? The Politics of Evangelical Growth* (Berkeley: University of California Press, 1990), 4.

7. Karl Lehmann, "The Meaning of a New Evangelization of Europe," *Communio* (Winter 1992): 541.

8. Stoll, 4.

9. Puebla IV, n. 140.

10. Lehmann, 544.

11. Stoll, 4.

12. S. Galilea, *The Challenge of Popular Religiosity* (Quezon City, Philippines: Claretian Publications, 1988), 10.

13. "Christian Witness and Proselytism: A Study Document," *The Ecumenical Review* (January 1971): 9.

14. S. Galilea, *Catholics and the Sects* (Quezon City, Philippines: Claretian Publications, n.d.), 5.

15. Ibid., 41.

16. Ibid., 295.

17. Finke and Stark, 42.

18. Lehmann, 544.

CHAPTER 2

Fundamentalism in Perspective

The religious sect[1] that developed as a reaction to Liberalism took its name from a series of pamphlets known as *The Fundamentals*, written between 1910 and 1915. These works contained the basic teachings of the Christian Faith, with those who strictly adhered to these teachings becoming known as "Fundamentalists." Several of these "basics," or "fundamentals," were encapsulated in the 1878 Niagara Creed (see Appendix 1), which opens as follows: "So many in the latter times have departed from the faith, giving heed to seducing spirits, and doctrines of devils; so many have turned away their ears from the truth, and turned unto fables; so many are busily engaged in scattering broadcast the seeds of fatal error, directly affecting the honor of our Lord and the destiny of the soul, we are constrained by fidelity to Him to make the following declaration of our doctrinal belief, and to present it as the bond of union with those who wish to be connected with the Niagara Bible Conference."[2]

The apologetics[3] of the sect would lead one to believe that Fundamentalism is apostolic Christianity previously forced into hiding (presumably following the legalization of Christianity by the Emperor Constantine and the subsequent development of Catholicism). Supposedly existing under the surface for centuries, it emerged at the time of the Reformation, embracing the theology of John Calvin. However, it did not exist independently of other Calvinist sects (e.g., the Anabaptists, Baptists, and Congregationalists) differing among themselves while claiming Calvin as their common forefather.

The emergence of Fundamentalism as a separate sect was the result of nineteenth-century upheavals in theology and the sciences.

In theology, a new "higher criticism" of Scripture, heavily influenced
by a rationalism that could admit no supernatural realities, aimed at
"demythologizing" the Bible and Christian doctrine, thereby reducing the Christian message to a "social gospel." In the sciences,
Darwin's theory of evolution and modern psychoanalysis were causing quite a stir.[4] The acceptance of these modern developments was
seen by certain Christians "as a compromise with new forms of rationalism and secularism that were threatening the historical message of
the Church."[5]

The most visible and public manifestation of Fundamentalism's
discomfort with modern life and developments occurred in the famous Scopes trial of 1925, with William Jennings Bryan serving as
the spokesman for religious conservatism. Norman F. Furniss puts it
this way: The Scopes trial "opened the eyes of newspaper readers to
the fact that thousands, even millions, of Americans espoused a faith
leaving no room for acceptance of the remarkable achievements of
the past half-century, Americans who not only deplored the challenges
to their orthodox beliefs but were determined to crush those challenges by law and ecclesiastical court."[6]

Although the Fundamentalist movement itself was born as a result of the increasing liberalism of the nineteenth century, its roots are
Calvinistic. Consistent with the other Reformers of the period, Calvin
(1509-1564) considered the Scriptures to be the sole source of divine
revelation. According to Calvinist theology, man has no free will and is
instead predestined by God for salvation or damnation. Faith and good
works are signs that one is saved; recklessness and sin, an indication of
the opposite. For Calvin, union with Christ is a result of faith and the
work of the Holy Spirit. Thus he admits no possibility of a Church
under the guidance of the Holy Spirit that acts as an instrument of salvation. The Calvinistic view of the sacraments differed, therefore, from
that of Catholicism. Calvin recognized only two sacraments (as having
their basis in the Scriptures), namely, Baptism and the Lord's Supper.
With Catholicism, Calvin could affirm that Baptism produced effects
in the recipient: it remitted past sins and made the justice of Christ
one's own; but he departed from Catholicism by maintaining that future sins are also remitted. More strikingly un-Catholic, however, was

his conception of the Lord's Supper commemoration. The partaking of the bread and cup were merely a sign of that union with Christ accomplished by faith and the work of the Holy Spirit; Christ was not to be thought of as objectively present in the Communion elements, nor was the Last Supper commemoration to be considered, as the Catholic Mass, a re-presentation — a making present to us here and now — of Christ's Sacrifice and its saving effects.

Just how pervasive Calvinism was in the history of Fundamentalism becomes apparent by even a cursory review of the identities and associations of the "Founding Fathers." From 1878 to 1900, conferences to advance the movement were organized. In the early days, they were led by men such as: James H. Brookes, a Presbyterian and alumnus of Princeton Seminary and the pastor of the Walnut Street Presbyterian Church in St. Louis; William J. Eerdman, pastor of Presbyterian and Congregational churches and one of the founders of the Moody Bible Institute, as well as an editor of the *Scofield Reference Bible* and father of Charles R. Eerdman, who became a professor of theology at Princeton; William Go Moorehead, another Presbyterian, who served as professor and president at Xenia Seminary and was an editor of the *Scofield Reference Bible*, too. The only significant exception seems to have been Adoniram Judson Gordon, a Baptist, who was a close associate of Dwight L. Moody. Sandeen notes that "the 1878 Premillennial Conference marks the beginning of a long period of dispensationalist cooperation with Princeton-oriented Calvinists. The unstable and incomplete synthesis which is now known as Fundamentalism at this point first becomes visible to the historian."[7]

Princeton produced such impressive scholars as Archibald Alexander Hodge, Benjamin B. Warfield, and J. Gresham Machen — developers and advancers of the famous "Princeton theology," which they insisted was nothing new but merely a defense of the thought and system of John Calvin. However, "in this belief they were deceived, both the methodology and the conclusions of their theology differing clearly from the work of Calvin himself and the standard of the Westminster Confession."[8] The catalogue of key figures certainly reads like a *Who's Who* of Presbyterianism in general and Princeton Seminary in particular. David Stoll makes the point that "it is less appreciated that much of the intellectual elite of Fundamentalism has been Presbyterian."[9]

This "Calvinist connection" cannot be overemphasized, since even contemporary leaders like the Reverends Jerry Falwell and Pat Robertson have clearly and publicly identified themselves as Calvinist in orientation. Furthermore, Robertson has even argued that the United States Constitution is "based on Calvinist principles."[10]

The classical Protestant, and especially Calvinist, worldview was convulsed in the nineteenth century. The German philosopher Immanuel Kant (d. 1804), after devoting his *Critique of Pure Reason* to demolishing the ability of human reason to discover truth speculatively, attempted in his *Critique of Practical Reason* to build it all up again on a moral foundation.

Kant maintained that it is impossible to know objective reality (i.e., things as they really are, as opposed to how one perceives them to be). Underlying this argument is the observation that "objective truth is always filtered through subjective experience and perception, and thus scientific knowledge is always shaped by the cultural and historical context in which it emerges."[11] Kant's theory of knowledge, or epistemology, was bound to have repercussions on the world of science. The traditional idea that Scripture provided the truth in light of which scientific data was to be analyzed — which is the basic model presented by Francis Bacon (d. 1626) — was directly challenged.

Kant dealt a blow to traditional morality and particularly to Calvinist soteriology (the theology of salvation) as well. For Kant, morally right actions originate only in a good will; and a good will is one that acts, not from natural inclination or from external laws and the threat of consequences, but from *duty*. If any act is to be moral, one must first ask whether or not he would want to make the principle or maxim on which this act rests into a universal law binding on everyone. An act is morally wrong if one would make an exception for himself, thus contradicting the law in his own favor. In Kant's view, therefore, the subject imposes the moral law on himself. This "autonomy of will" flatly contradicts the Calvinist doctrine of predestination.

Charles Darwin's theory, making its formal debut in 1859 with the publication of his *On the Origin of Species by Means of Natural Selection*, became the symbol for all that was wrong with modern science when he proposed a scheme of changing, emerging, and disappearing species. This led to his conclusion that even man was a part of this evolving order, thus contradicting the Genesis account of man as a special creation.

Later on, the fledgling science of psychoanalysis began to suggest that the human personality was not formed in the act of creation by God, but rather by the interactions and traumas of childhood. Response to external stimuli and learned behavior had replaced the idea for the believer that the internal struggle was between God and Satan.

Scripture seemed to be under a double assault. First was the attack against the Baconian view of science and its relation to Scripture. The greater blow was a critical analysis of biblical texts that examined literary forms and historical contexts, in an attempt to date the books. The scholars involved concluded that the Bible was less than it seemed to be. As Robert Gnuse puts it: "By the nineteenth century, the best minds of Protestant Europe had turned their backs on the old orthodoxy for a new liberal theology which did not affirm the concept of biblical authority. Led by the theology of Friedrich Schleiermacher, a new age of theology had begun."[12] Instead of the revealed Word of God, the ideas in Scripture became part of a history of ideas about the nature of the world and human relationship to the divine. ". . . If time-bound authors with time-conditioned intentions had composed the Judaeo-Christian epics, then perhaps the words of the Bible are to be considered as something less than an exact and fully authoritative divine revelation. Perhaps they are only perceived as such, accepted by believers but elusive of any absolute proof. Such implications of nineteenth-century biblical criticism would prove unsettling to the church-going Bible-believer."[13]

The challenges to the established order, however, did not proceed only from science and theology.

With the new waves of immigrants, particularly Catholics and Jews, those who held classical Protestant beliefs could no longer assume their views were shared by their neighbors. The religious pluralism, coupled with the changes in science and theology (to which many mainline Protestant sects attempted to adapt), provided the background against which the Fundamentalists thought it necessary to break their connection with mainline Protestantism. George Marsden, professor of history at Calvin College, has offered perhaps the best definition of Fundamentalism as the "twentieth-century movement closely tied to the revivalist tradition of mainstream evangelical Protestantism that militantly opposed modernist theology and the cultural change associated with it."[14]

The challenges from science, biblical studies, and society required a response from religious leaders. The most drastic response took the form of Pentecostalism. Participants in this expression of the revivalist tradition prayed to be emptied of sin and filled with the Spirit, imitating the account of the day of Pentecost from the Acts of the Apostles. Almost all Protestant sects used revival meetings as a means of evangelization, particularly in the cities as the population grew. It served to make Christianity an important factor in family and civic life as prosperity increased in urban areas. The appeals from the preacher and the testimony of those present were charged with emotion. The art of revivalism was developed by Charles G. Finney who "was the first to articulate the goal of revivalism as 'winning souls' and the first to set out a step-by-step method for achieving that goal and calculating its success."[15] Finney likewise urged the avoidance of complicated theological categories, so as to be comprehensible to the average person. Nancy Ammerman judges that "both the results (individual decisions about salvation) and the message (plain truths about the Bible) were therefore democratized and taken outside the realm of institutional religion."[16] In other words, the communal and/or hierarchical approach was subsumed into an egalitarian method, far beyond what even the Protestant Reformers had ever envisioned.[17] However, the Pentecostals went so far as to claim speaking in tongues and physical healings as their hallmark. This further removed them from mainline Protestant denominations, as well as from previous revivalist sects.

The Fundamentalists used conferences, along with the revivals, to explore the teaching of the Bible as a vehicle of evangelization.

The conferences were places and occasions to share ideas against the modern attack on the Scriptures. From these conferences grew Bible Institutes, e.g., the Moody Bible Institute (established 1886), whose purpose was "aimed at training ordinary Christians to be effective evangelists in the cities where they lived."[18] Books, journals, and newspapers provided the source of identity and solidarity among those dedicated to the Word of God. The *Scofield Reference Bible*, printed by the Oxford University Press in 1909 and having taken shape from two generations of Bible conferences, became the Fundamentalist reference point. Large numbers accepted Scofield's interpretations with the same docility as the literal Scriptures they revered, a point to which we will return for greater elucidation.

Having successfully evangelized in the cities, Fundamentalism was on the rise. Skirmishes occurred between 1920 and 1925, particularly in the Northern Baptist and Presbyterian communities, as Fundamentalists fought for control of the denominations in the face of the continued onslaught of Modernism. During this period, much internecine warfare was being conducted between adherents of Liberalism and more traditional or conservative points of view, with the result that denominational lines were blurred in many instances, causing realignments to occur more according to liberal/conservative stances than denominational affiliation, leading Fox to refer to the phenomenon as "trans-denominational."[19]

The Congregationalists had already conformed to the new theological and social mores. At this same time, Fundamentalists battled the teaching of Darwinism in the public schools through the enactment of state laws. In Tennessee, however, the trial of John Scopes provoked a backlash of public opinion against the Fundamentalists. This was the first indication that their beliefs would not be embraced as the solution to the theological and social chaos of the time, but this did not stop William Jennings Bryan from declaring over and over again, "It is better to trust in the Rock of Ages than to know the age of the rocks; it is better for one to know that he is close to the Heavenly Father, than to know how far the stars in the heavens are apart."[20]

Ammerman summarizes the Fundamentalist reaction to scientific developments: "Now that they were outsiders, their view of mainstream culture and religion changed. As insiders, they had been concerned with modernism as a perversion of the true faith to be purged from religious life. Now they proclaimed that the denominations were hopelessly apostate, no better (and perhaps worse) than the secular world. . . . They had fought evolution as a dangerous idea to be purged from the schools. Now they saw the entire culture dominated by non-Christian influences. They became convinced that all of society had come under the sway of ideas that excluded God, ideas they saw as forming a pattern and an ideology that they eventually termed 'secular humanism.' "[21]

Perhaps understandably, a certain anti-intellectualism often accompanied Fundamentalism's opposition to unilateral rationalism. One of the more vulgar and aggressive Fundamentalists alleged that "half of the literary preachers in this town are A.B.'s, Ph.D.'s, LL.D.'s, and A.S.S.'s."[22]

Against the hostile forces, the Fundamentalists relied on the *Scofield Reference Bible* and *The Fundamentals* (with Volume I published in 1910), to ensure that they did not lose the Christian heritage of which they perceived themselves the guardians. Although the number of "fundamentals" varies, most commentators commonly identify five: (1) the inspiration and infallibility of Scripture; (2) the divinity of Christ, including the virgin birth; (3) the substitutionary atonement of His death; (4) His literal resurrection from the dead; and, (5) His literal return in the Second Advent.

These five were "adopted by the General Assembly of the Presbyterian Church in 1910 and reaffirmed in 1916 and 1923,"[23] which development demonstrates the hold Fundamentalism gained in Presbyterianism in the first quarter of this century. Fundamentalists rightly maintained that liberal Protestantism's "denial of the supernatural inspiration of the Bible and the deity, atonement, and resurrection of Jesus Christ was tantamount to a denial of everything that the Church (Catholic or Protestant) had always held to be Christian throughout the centuries. Machen argued that what the Liberals were proposing was, not a modernization of Christianity, but the elimination of it in favor of a brand-new religion. Liberals were now waving a Bible that they did not believe had its origin from God, proclaiming a Christ who they were not sure ever lived, or died for the sins of humanity, or rose again!"[24]

Precisely which liberal positions so rankled the Fundamentalists? American liberalism at the turn of the nineteenth and twentieth centuries seemed to espouse the following positions:

    1. God's character is one of pure benevolence — benevolence that is without standards.

    2. There is a divine spark in every man.

    3. Jesus Christ is man's Savior only in the sense that He is man's perfect Teacher and Example.

    4. Just as Christ differs from other men only comparatively, not absolutely, so Christianity differs from other religions not generically, but merely as the best and highest type of religion that has yet appeared.

    5. The Bible is not a divine record of revelation, but a human testament of religion; and Christian doctrine is not the God-given word which must create and control Christian experience.[25]

Returning to the fundamentals properly so called, we find Edward Dobson commenting that "although some have expanded this list [of fundamentals] to include such issues as a literal heaven and hell, soul-winning, a personal Satan and the local church, nevertheless the doctrinal character of Fundamentalism still centers around the five fundamentals listed."[26] That having been said, Zachary Hayes cautions: "Despite the common impression that Fundamentalists share a common, uniform position across the board, there is a significant diversity of viewpoints among Fundamentalists, even on issues that Fundamentalists themselves consider to be very important."[27] A case in point would be the diverse and rather mutually exclusive approaches to millennialism within Fundamentalism.[28]

Certainly many other people, Catholics included,[29] had concerns about liberal directions taken either in their churches or in society at large. What made (and makes) Fundamentalism something unique? "Fundamentalism . . . differs from traditionalism or orthodoxy or even a mere revivalist movement. It differs in that it is a movement in conscious, organized opposition to the disruption of those traditions and orthodoxies."[30] The notion of Fundamentalism as a movement is essential to grasp, for it explains why it has continued to exist long after the original controversy was settled, for better or worse.[31] Combativeness has also seemed to be a hallmark from its very inception, as Curtis Lee Laws, editor of *The Watchman Examiner*, urged his readers in 1920 to be prepared to "do battle royal" for their beliefs.[32] Or, as the editors of *Fundamentalisms Observed* put it: Fundamentalists are *"fighting back . . .* they *fight for . . . fight with . . . fight against,"* and they *"fight under"* Almighty God (emphasis in original).[33]

Fundamentalism in Its American Context

Aware of allegations to the contrary, Marsden feels compelled to remind all that "Fundamentalism was primarily a religious movement."[34] He then goes on to admit that "to understand Fundamentalism we must also see it as a distinct version of evangelical Christianity uniquely shaped by the circumstances of America in the early twentieth century," identifying the necessary focus as the discovery of "how individuals who were committed to typically American versions of evangelical Christianity responded to and were influenced by the social, intellectual and religious crises of their time."[35]

Faithful to the tenets of their Faith, then, some Fundamentalists tried to remain in their respective denominations as a witness to traditional beliefs. Others simply broke away and founded new conservative communities. Independent churches became the norm for such sects in the 1930s.[36] To provide an education consonant with their beliefs, they established Bible colleges "designed to give their students a broad base of learning — from the sciences to history and mathematics — carefully kept within the guidelines of an inerrant Scripture."[37] Their beliefs were further sustained by the houses that had published for some time the books, journals, and newspapers that had been so critical to gain a hearing for the movement. Now, as more conservatives openly broke with their former denominations, there was a new market for still more religious material of this type. The printing houses produced all that was necessary to educate new members of the increasing number of Fundamentalist sects. Particularly influential were the Bible conferences organized by Dwight L. Moody, as well as the work of the American Bible League, and that all-important pamphlet series known as *The Fundamentals*.[38] The revivalists, as has been noted, were always active in evangelization. They used all effective means to preach their message, which included radio broadcasts. It is not surprising, then, that Fundamentalists, in addition to their printing houses used radio programs.[39] "In the 60s Protestant conservatives began building major television empires."[40] This gave them access to a wide audience, beyond the local congregation in a revival tent or those on a subscription mailing list. Perhaps more importantly, these media provided the means for the continuation of the evangelical worldview in a time when society and (even) the rest of religion seemed hostile toward it. The Fundamentalists had succeeded in creating a culture of their own.[41] This should not be perceived as odd or unique to American Protestant Fundamentalism, for "Fundamentalist faiths are comprehensive, taking in the whole of life."[42]

It could be said that the Fundamentalist sect has three stages to its history. First, from the late-nineteenth century until the Scopes trial in 1925, a period characterized by a fierce orthodoxy and defense from the current of Modernism. Following the loss of public support for their positions in 1925, the movement again seemed to go underground. During this second period, however, it organized structures to reach their own adherents, to cross denominational lines, and even to venture into the general society; these structures rivaled those of most mainline religions for evangelization. The third period began roughly a generation ago when Fundamentalism began to emerge in the United States once again.

This third phase of development was fueled by the chaos that reigned in the 1960s. Society, again unsure where to turn for answers, was ripe for plucking by Fundamentalists. Continuing to spread their message by the mass media, they encountered great success. Beginning in the 1970s, they added to their arsenal of evangelization tactics a powerful political lobby, best symbolized by the Moral Majority. The division still exists among Fundamentalists between those who perceive their role as guardians of orthodoxy, separate from the ranks of unbelievers, and those who wish to work for the rebuilding of Christian values and culture overall.

The psychological question must finally be raised, since many observers assert a direct linkage between membership in a Fundamentalist congregation and particular personality deficiencies. For example, Peggy L. Shriver quite bluntly declares: "Because an insecure ego can be supported by the scaffolding of a Fundamentalist faith, it is not surprising that many people who are 'marginal' to society are drawn to Fundamentalism."[43] The Reverend Thomas F. Stransky is less willing to approach the phenomenon from this perspective, or at least to do so exclusively: "It seems naively prejudicial to over-psychologize Fundamentalism by claiming that it is only the symptom of socio-religious and personal problems of insecurity — the perennial claim of anti-religionists about 'the opiate of all religions' and 'the lust for certitude.' "[44] He also notes that the element of "future shock" has not been entirely absent from Catholic life in the era following the Second Vatican Council (1962-65), with the attendant liturgical and doctrinal deviations in many places, a point hit upon explicitly by the Reverend Lawrence Boadt: "These 'conservative' Catholics thus share the same concerns that gave rise to Fundamentalism within liberal Protestantism at the turn of the century."[45] While not overplaying the psychological element, Ammerman does highlight the fact that Fundamentalism offered "answers and order, love and stability."[46]

The Fundamentalist sect has been shaped by a number of theological, cultural, ideological, organizational, and political forces. As a body, Fundamentalists have been among the best in creating the structures (conferences, educational institutions, biblical commentaries, etc.) necessary to support their beliefs and spread the Word in hopes of converting hearers of the message. Spelling out their creativity, Fox recounts how "in 1919 the Fundamentalist movement took a major step with the establishment of the militant World's Christian Fundamentals Association. It began publishing a quarterly review and conducted annual rallies in North America for a decade. Around

1920, the title 'Fundamentalism' came into common use. It was used as a badge of honor in spreading and defending the 'fundamentals.' . . ."[47]

Believing in the certainty of their message, then, Fundamentalists continue to present their vision of a good society. Many seem to have found comfort in that certainty and followed them.

This is quite apparent in the political realm. When Falwell established his Moral Majority to represent traditional moral values in the public forum in 1979, he was so successful (at least in his own estimation but also in that of many dispassionate observers) that he declared his mission effectively accomplished by 1989, leaving behind a mood that has taken away the reproach from the word "conservative" in politics. As Boadt astutely remarks, "The Catholic bishops (in America) find it difficult to muster widespread support within their Church for unpopular political stands, while the Fundamentalists have put together a very powerful and well-organized campaign mustering numerous allies beyond their official church membership for their chief areas of concern."[48] It should be mentioned, however, that political involvement and action were hardly the original intent of Fundamentalists who, often enough, anticipated an imminent Rapture, thus considering political activity as useless and counterproductive.[49] This realization has caused Fox to hold that "the Fundamentalists have no use for a social gospel"[50]; one would, however, have to contest his use of the present tense. The truth of the matter, though, is more complex, as Ammerman thoughtfully declares: "Fundamentalists in North America could be found in both camps — waiting for the Rapture and lobbying in the White House. In both cases believers were drawing on a distinctive view of the world that had emerged about a century earlier. They were willing to argue that certain beliefs were 'fundamental,' and they were willing to organize in a variety of ways to preserve and defend those beliefs."[51]

With the increasing secularization of the nation, "the courts and schools and legislatures seemed to be daring Fundamentalists to come out of their separatist institutions to defend their right to exist."[52] The political agenda of the Moral Majority or Christian Right dealt with "family values," ranging from opposition to abortion, "gay rights" and pornography to a desire for the reintroduction of prayer in government schools. An interesting side effect of their active entrance into the pro-life camp was rubbing elbows, frequently for the first time, with Catholics, whom they had been generally trained to regard as "allies of the Antichrist."[53] But they also made "strange bedfellows" with feminists on pornography, with Mormons against the ERA, and with Jews in support for the State of Israel. Falwell, in particular, saw this as both necessary and desirable, in order to be effective participants in the political process of a pluralistic society.[54] Just how powerful the Moral Majority ever was is open to debate, but they certainly took the credit for conservative political victories, whether deserved or not.[55]

The primary instruments for their message, both religious and political, were radio and television, with the latter being very costly, to be sure. Nonetheless they also discovered that television could be a most productive source of fund-raising, with the following result: "They not only raised money to stay on the air and preach the gospel; they also raised money for whatever enterprises their imagination and charisma could create and sustain. Like the urban revivalists before them, these preachers built quasi-denominational complexes of institutions to extend their mission. There were colleges (CBN University, Liberty University, and the like), hospitals (most notably Oral Roberts's City of Faith Hospital), publishing houses, missionaries, and even amusement parks (Heritage USA being the most prominent)."[56]

Clearly, then, "Fundamentalists are quite selective in what they oppose and what they accept in modern culture."[57]

Contemporary Fundamentalism

Questions requiring answers to flesh out the identity of contemporary Fundamentalism are: Who are the Fundamentalists today? Where are they? What is their agenda?

Stransky says that "most Catholics think that the majority of Evangelicals are Fundamentalists." "Not so," he declares, observing that "of the forty-two to forty-five million American Christians who call themselves Evangelicals, roughly 4.5 million of them designate themselves as Fundamentalists."[58] He continues: "Catholics should be careful in labelling some Christian groups. The largest Protestant body in the USA is the Southern Baptist Convention. Within its membership are both Fundamentalists and those who want to be considered Evangelicals-without-Fundamentalism — the reason for the liveliness of their yearly convention."[59] He concludes by conceding that some Baptist groups are strictly Fundamentalists, like Bob Jones University and Falwell's Liberty Baptist College, while various Evangelical groups on secular campuses (like Campus Crusade for Christ, Intervarsity, etc.) are not necessarily so, although some local leaders are. The Missouri Synod of the Lutheran Church is also generally identified as Fundamentalist in thrust.[60]

Of course, one must realize that there are indeed people who are, in reality, Fundamentalists but who resist the label for a variety of possible reasons.[61] In terms of Church structure and organization, one can easily become confused as to who is and is not a "Fundamentalist," especially when the point of comparison is "Evangelical" versus "Fundamentalist," particularly for the first half of this century. It would probably be a fair assessment to suggest that all Fundamentalists would see themselves as Evangelicals, while not all Evangelicals would regard themselves or want themselves to be perceived as Fundamentalists.[62] Fox also observes that "more recently, representatives of these congregations have taken a more sophisticated stance in seeking to shed the Fundamentalist badge by identifying themselves with international conservative Protestant groups, e.g., the World Evangelical Fellowship."[63]

Because our study is based on the premise that Fundamentalism was and is essentially a theological phenomenon, the theology of the movement will be given special attention in a separate section, rather than here. For the moment, however, it is good to include this discovery of Benton Johnson and colleagues: "In our study, the single best predictor of church participation turned out to be *belief* — orthodox Christian belief, and especially the teaching that a person can be saved only through Jesus Christ. Virtually all our baby boomers who believe this are active members of a church. Among those who do not believe it, some are active in varying degrees; a great many are not.

Ninety-five percent of the drop-outs who describe themselves as religious do not believe it. And amazingly enough, fully 68 percent of those who are still active Presbyterians don't believe it either [emphasis in original]."[64]

Marsden, the most articulate spokesman for Fundamentalism, admits that Fundamentalism has much in common with other movements (e.g., Pietism, Evangelicalism, Revivalism, Millenarianism, Holiness Pentecostalism), but insists that *the* distinguishing characteristic was — and is — its total opposition to Liberalism, the theological movement of the late-nineteenth and early-twentieth century and, by extension, to its progeny today.[65] He also stresses that "the phenomenon that I have defined as 'Fundamentalism' was overwhelmingly American in the sense that almost nowhere else did this type of Protestant response to modernity have such a conspicuous and pervasive role both in the churches and in the national culture."[66] The almost uniquely American angle needs to be highlighted, in addition to the effect it has had on the overall American culture.

To pick up on Marsden's point regarding "opposition to Liberalism," one should not miss the fact that three of the four major mainline denominations (Episcopalian, Presbyterian, and Methodist — all known for the very liberalism obnoxious to Fundamentalism) have experienced membership losses of one-third over the past two decades, with the decline in Lutheranism, the fourth, being less precipitous.[67] On the other hand, "biblically conservative nondenominational Christian fellowships, for example, are among the fastest growing, and their typical location is not in rural Appalachia but in major metropolitan centers."[68] While "the name Fundamentalist is not synonymous with 'conservative,' " it is "a subset of that larger whole."[69]

Having lost the government schools to secular humanism, the Fundamentalists turned their attention to the formation of a private school system. This was a radical departure for the movement, which had earlier idealized public schools and looked with disdain on parochial schools, especially since the lion's share of the latter was sponsored by the Catholic Church. Ironically, during the same period when Catholic elementary and secondary schools were being closed at the rate of one a day, Fundamentalist academies were being opened.[70]

Why such sudden interest? Quite plausible is this explanation: "Between 1965 and 1983, enrollment in evangelical schools increased sixfold, and the number of schools reached about ten thousand. In addition, perhaps as many as one hundred thousand Fundamentalist children are being taught at home. Usually sponsored directly by one or more congregations, these schools draw primarily on the children of members. They offer parents the opportunity to surround their children with knowledge that is in harmony with their beliefs."[71]

But does the movement really have a future? Falwell believes so, for two reasons. First, Fundamentalism has a steady supply of clergy: "While the liberal seminaries are suffering from diminishing enrollments, the conservative schools are bursting at the seams." He reports "record enrollments" at places like Dallas Theological Seminary, Grace Theological Seminary, Southwestern Baptist Theological Seminary, as well as at the college level at Baptist Bible College, Bob Jones University, and Calvin College.[72] Yet again, Liberty Home Bible Institute has ten thousand students registered in a two-year program, while Moody Bible Institute annually enlists "over 100,000 people taking at least one course by correspondence."[73]

Second, Fundamentalism has reason to suppose that it will have congregations for the foreseeable future. Citing Gallup, Falwell speaks of the membership losses among mainline liberal Protestants as "staggering." Even more ominously, he declares that "the Presbyterian, Episcopalian, and United Church of Christ communions cannot long exist as viable church organizations nationally if the declines of the 70s persist in the 1980s,"[74] which they have well into the 1990s. With some hyperbole, he asserts: "On the other hand, the conservative churches appear to be in an up period, with the Southern Baptists and a variety of Fundamentalist groupings setting attendance and membership records almost hourly!"[75] One should not imagine, however, that the growth in Fundamentalism is a new development, for "Evangelical and Fundamentalist bodies have been growing faster than the more liberal denominations for at least seventy years."[76]

Beyond that, the attitudes of the general population are more in harmony with the holdings of Fundamentalism than with liberal Protestantism. For example, surveys have determined that "69 million people [in America] are hoping to go to Heaven because of their personal faith in Christ. Second, the vast majority of Americans believe the Bible is the Word of God and that it is a valid guide in moral and ethical issues. When one examines the religious beliefs of young people, families, young clergy, and the population in general, it is obvious that the American population has a strong personal commitment to orthodox, fundamental, evangelical Christianity. Skepticism, agnosticism, and atheism have little influence on this society. Fundamental Christianity is resurging as America begins the decade of the 1980s."[77]

And no empirical evidence exists to suggest that the present decade has witnessed any significant change to the contrary.

In sum, Fundamentalism has been shaped by a variety of influences — cultural, theological, political, and structural. While having a consistency of thought, the movement has also been remarkably flexible, adjusting to new developments with resiliency and relative ease. In all likelihood, the cement has been adherence to the bed-rock theological principles, to which we now turn.

Theological Principles

Not surprisingly, the basis of Fundamentalist theology are the five "fundamentals," enunciated in an organized fashion for the first time within the fourteen articles of the 1878 Niagara Creed, then developed in the series of pamphlets known as *The Fundamentals*.[78] To recap, they are: (1) The inspiration and infallibility of the Bible; (2) the divinity of Christ; (3) the substitutionary atonement of His death; (4) Christ's bodily resurrection from the dead; and (5) His literal return at the Second Coming. A Catholic reader, scanning the list, might be tempted to ask what the problems could be, since the Catholic Church affirms all five teachings. Suffice it to say now that the interpretation of these doctrines is often quite different, let alone the implications drawn from them.[79]

Also involved in the Fundamentalist corpus of doctrine in varying degrees at different times, but always present, is the element of millennialism. Furthermore, largely unspoken as a distinct principle — because presumed to be self-evident — is the Reformation doctrine of *sola Scriptura*, "Scripture alone," as the rule of Christian belief and practice.

It will be necessary, then, to comprehend just what Fundamentalists understand in regard to these seven theological pillars of their movement. It will also be worthwhile to engage in a "dialogue" with these views from the perspectives of both Catholicism and classical (Lutheran and Calvinist) Protestantism, when Fundamentalism diverges or converges in a particularly striking manner.

Before directly launching into the specifics of Fundamentalist theology, one must stress findings from recent studies that indicate how theological liberalism has affected the various Protestant denominations. Looking at it from a historical perspective, Finke and Stark assert that "to the degree that denominations rejected traditional doctrines and ceased to make serious demands on their followers, they ceased to prosper. The churching of America was accomplished by aggressive churches committed to vivid otherworldliness."[80]

Current data offer nothing to the contrary. In truth, Johnson and his colleagues confirm the conclusions of Finke and Stark. Johnson and others coin the expression "lay liberalism" to connote those individuals who pick and choose elements of faith in cafeteria fashion. This approach "supports honesty and other moral virtues, and it encourages tolerance and civility in a pluralistic society, but it does not inspire the kind of conviction that creates strong religious communities."[81] They continue: "One indication that lay liberalism is not an energizing 'faith' is the fact that its advocates told us they rarely attempt to convert anyone to their point of view."[82] Akin to this finding, one learns that "of all the various categories of churched and unchurched people that our study identified, only the Fundamentalists reported that they attend church more frequently than their parents did."[83] Johnson and his associates note that mainline churches "lost the will or the ability to teach the Christian Faith and what it requires to a succession of younger cohorts in such a way as to command their allegiance." They go on: "In response to the currents of modernity, denominational leaders promoted ecumenism and dialogue, but they did not devise or promote compelling new versions of a distinctively

Christian Faith. They did not fashion or preach a vigorous apologetics." They conclude: "If the mainline churches want to regain their vitality, their first step must be to address theological issues head-on. They must listen to the voices of lay liberals and provide compelling answers to the question, 'What's so special about Christianity?' "[84]

The Fundamentalists believe they have satisfactorily responded to that question in adhering to "the Fundamentals," now to be examined.

1 • Inspiration and Infallibility of Scripture ❖ It was no accident that the primary principle of Fundamentalism revolved around the inerrancy of the Scriptures. Using the new approaches inaugurated by Protestant scholars, the French Catholic priest and biblical scholar Alfred Loisy recalls that his early desire to eliminate "problematic" doctrines (e.g., the virgin birth) became feasible only upon taking the first truly bold step concerning Scripture itself: "What fell away from me at this juncture was the theological interpretation of Scriptural inspiration. I perceived that the sacred books were written as all books are written, only with less exactness and care than many. If the Holy Spirit had entered in, it could not be to transform them into historical sources of the first rank. This discovery was in no way disconcerting to me; on the contrary, my uneasiness of mind vanished in proportion as I advanced to a firm footing of critical certitude."[85]

The working principle of both liberal Protestantism and its theological counterpart in the Catholic Church, Modernism, was that modern science had rendered obsolete and ridiculous the traditional language of Christian belief. In sharp contrast to the liberals' biblical criticism, the 1878 Niagara Creed conceived of inspiration as follows: "We believe 'all Scripture is given by inspiration of God,' by which we understand the whole of the book called the Bible; nor do we take the statement in the sense in which it is sometimes foolishly said that works of human genius are inspired, but in the sense that the Holy Ghost gave the very words of the sacred writings to holy men of old; and that His Divine inspiration is not in different degrees, but extends equally and fully to all parts of these writings, historical, poetical, doctrinal and prophetical, and to the smallest word, and inflection of a word, provided such a word is found in the original manuscripts: 2 Tim 3:16, 17; 2 Pet 1:21; 1 Cor 2:13; Mark 12:26, 36; 13:11; Acts 1:16; 2:4."[86]

Therefore, when Fundamentalists speak about the inspiration and infallibility (or inerrancy) of the Sacred Scriptures, what they generally have in mind is "plenary-verbal inspiration": "This implies that in the original autographs all of Scripture is equally inspired and that inspiration extends to the very words themselves. The logical consequence of a God-breathed Bible was a document free from error in all of its statements and affirmations. This meant that the Bible was without error not only in theology but also in matters of science, history, geography, and the cosmos."[87]

The Princetonians (like Hodge, Warfield, and Machen, cited earlier), being true scholars, refused to rely on sentimentality for this doctrine; for they believed that "if the Bible was to be proven to be God's inspired Word, the demonstration must be made on the basis of reason through the use of external marks of authenticity — not inner convictions."[88] While adhering firmly to the concept of plenary inspiration (i.e., the absolute reliability of every fact — geographical, historical, etc.), they adopted a somewhat nuanced approach by couching their discussion in terms of "the original autographs."[89] This was a kind of escape hatch, allowing them to distance themselves from apparent "errors" in the sacred text, all the while maintaining that the original documents (wherever they may now be) were flawless. This recourse to original autographs was novel, for "this doctrine did not exist in either Europe or America prior to its formulation in the last half of the nineteenth century. It has become an essential ingredient in the theology of Fundamentalism."[90]

Less sophisticated believers and probably of a more anti-intellectual bent, eschewing reason either entirely or in the measure necessary to salvage their biblical presuppositions, would simply declare that when the "facts" of history (e.g., about which king ruled Israel at a specific moment), geography (e.g., about the location of certain places described in a biblical text), or science

(e.g., regarding the creation of the world) in question conflicted
with the Word of God, the actual errors were to be found in the
secular sphere.

Regardless of the route chosen, troubling questions still emerge.
For instance:

◆ Did Moses write the Pentateuch?

◆ Were Adam and Eve historical persons?

◆ How does one explain the apparent contradictions between the creation stories in Genesis 1 and 2?

◆ Was Jonah really swallowed by a whale?

◆ Are the infancy narratives genuine historical documents?

◆ How many "Isaiahs" were there?

◆ Did Jesus multiply the loaves and fish, change water into
wine, and work other miracles?

The liberal theologians and biblical scholars against whom the
Fundamentalists initially reacted simply dismissed the above questions as irrelevant, falling back on "myth" for the most part. The
mentality of the average Fundamentalist is summed up in the line on
the bumper sticker that proclaims: "God said it. I believe it. That
settles it." Needless to say, such a profession of faith raises more
questions than it answers, leading a skeptic to ask: When and where
did God pronounce on a given topic? In what is Christian faith rooted?
For whom is the issue settled, and in what manner? With good reason, then, many have labeled this method of biblical interpretation as
"simplistic."[91]

The Catholic Church, however, beginning with the Fathers (and
especially St. Augustine), has attempted to navigate carefully between
the two extremes. Hence, Augustine was not adverse to interpreting
the data of Genesis as religious poetry offering religious truth, noting
(in *De actis cum Felice Manichaeo*) that God's purpose in giving us
the Book of Genesis was that "He wanted to make Christians, not
mathematicians."[92] Similarly, in the Galileo controversy, Cardinal
Baronius could argue that in inspiring Holy Scripture "the Holy Ghost
intended to teach how to go to heaven, not how the heavens go."[93]

While Pope St. Pius X took strenuous measures against Modernism in the first decade of the twentieth century, the Roman Magisterium did not put a halt to certain types of biblical interpretation, so long as doctrinal integrity was safeguarded. Certainly, that is what comes across in the various "warnings," or *monita*, of the Pontifical Biblical Commission in the first half of the twentieth century, as well as in Pope Pius XII's *Divino Afflante Spiritu* (1943) and *Humani Generis* (1950).[94]

In more recent years, the Pontifical Biblical Commission's document "On the Historical Truth of the Gospels" has been viewed as a most balanced statement, faithful to the Catholic Tradition yet open to the insights of contemporary scholarship.[95] The Second Vatican Council's Dogmatic Constitution on Divine Revelation, *Dei Verbum*, has obviously become the *magna carta* for Catholic biblical scholarship. Just a few citations convey the flavor of the entire dogmatic constitution.

On inspiration: "For Holy Mother Church, relying on the faith of the apostolic age, accepts as sacred and canonical the books of the Old and New Testaments, whole and entire, with all their parts, on the grounds that, written under the inspiration of the Holy Spirit, they have God as their author, and have been handed on as such to the Church herself."[96]

On inerrancy: "Since, therefore, all that the inspired authors, or sacred writers, affirm should be regarded as affirmed by the Holy Spirit, we must acknowledge that the books of Scripture firmly, faithfully, and without error, teach the truth which God, for the sake of our salvation, wished to see confided to the Sacred Scriptures."[97]

The original Protestant Reformers put forth no unique theory of biblical inspiration or inerrancy.[98] Therefore, their silence indicates basic agreement with previous and received Catholic opinion, approaches, and teachings in that area.

In reality, the Fundamentalists engaged in this discussion for the first time in the polemical atmosphere engendered by Rationalist and Enlightenment thought. The "Princeton method" sought to effect some sort of reconciliation with modern science, while the more popular tack was merely to call science itself into question, or even to forge a "creation science" whose purpose was to validate biblical data, especially since "the Fundamentalist gives no room for development in the understanding of Divine Revelation."[99]

2 • *The Divinity of Christ* ✧ "The deity of Christ is the most essential fundamental of all," insisted Dobson without fear of contradiction.[100] And rightly so. Warfield, who wrote the article on Christ's divinity for *The Fundamentals*, argued this from two angles. First, he said, Jesus claimed to be God, accepted the homage associated with that claim, and was so held by the apostles and the early Church (the "objective" level). Second, Warfield attached great importance to the believer's inner conviction and personal experience (the subjective level): "The supreme proof to every Christian of the deity of his Lord is his own inner experience of the transforming power of his Lord upon the heart and life."[101]

Even the most committed believer in Christ's divinity would have to admit that neither argument is compelling for one favorably disposed, let alone a questioner or a scoffer. For example, many liberals at the time taught that, in point of fact, Jesus did not teach His own divinity; rather, belief in His divinity was a fabrication of the primitive Church — for noble or ignoble purposes. More blasphemous types would not hesitate to agree that Jesus did, in all likelihood, believe He was divine but then go on to present this as a sign of His megalomania or insanity. Yet others would say that the doctrines connected with Christ's divinity as they developed at the general Councils of Nicaea (325) and Chalcedon (451) would be unrecognizable to the apostles. And surely the contention that the lives of people have been changed by this belief is hardly evidence for the veracity of the teaching, but only for what that teaching can do to a person's psyche — for better or worse.

It is fascinating to discover that the Christology to which the Fundamentalists adhered was (and still is) that of the Church Councils. It did not seem to occur to them that they were violating their own principle of *sola Scriptura* in this case, or that *sola Scriptura* could not take them far enough in a time of crisis. The truth is that they refused to acknowledge that they were truly dealing with theological categories for which the biblical evidence was rather sparse. Equally interesting is that the only place in which the Virgin Mary figures in Fundamentalism is in the context of the Lord's divinity. The Marian doctrine involved was the virginal conception of Jesus in Mary's womb. It was deemed foundational for two reasons. First, it reinforced the concept of miracles. That is, its historicity "proves" that God is not bound by the laws of nature, thus vindicating all other miracles recorded in Sacred Scripture and, along with them, the principle of biblical inerrancy. The second reason was proffered by James Orr, who treated this topic in *The Fundamentals*, concluding that the virgin birth was not an option, but an absolute necessity: "Doctrinally, it must be repeated that belief in the virgin birth of Christ is of the highest value in the right apprehension of Christ's unique and sinless personality."[102]

On the divinity of Christ, the Fundamentalists were (and are) in concert with the faith of the early Church, the Protestant Reformation, and the Catholic Church, too.

3 • The Substitutionary Atonement of Christ's Death ✧ "The liberal theologians had developed new theories regarding the death of Christ. They were propagating the idea that the death of Christ was merely that of a martyr and provided nothing more than a moral influence on society."[103] Fundamentalists saw this as a denial of the essence of Christianity. Indeed, the entire gospel is summed up in the passion, death, and resurrection of Christ, for "the whole mandate of the Church in society centered around" this truth.[104] The uniqueness of the Church, therefore, depends on the uniqueness of Christ. Inasmuch as the world has known countless moral teachers, Jesus cannot be unique in that regard; rather, His uniqueness is found in His ability to atone for the sins of mankind — something no one before ever did or claimed to do.

As far as Catholicism is concerned, the Council of Trent's (1545-63) explanation of the significance of Christ's death would be completely acceptable to any Fundamentalist (at least in terms of a surface reading and appreciation): "The meritorious cause [of justification, i.e., of setting the sinner 'right' before God] is the beloved only-begotten Son of God, our Lord Jesus Christ Who, 'while we were sinners' [Rom 5:10], 'out of the great love with which He loved us' [Eph 2:4], merited for us justification by His most holy passion on the wood of the cross and made satisfaction for us to God the Father."[105]

Having noted, however, the basic acceptability of Trent's position on justification to most Fundamentalists, one is required to mention that this is another example of how Fundamentalists have moved away from their Reformation roots. The Reverend George Jamieson, a Reformed theologian (and a "liberal"), registers his disagreement with original Calvinist thought (but also would be uncomfortable with Fundamentalists of his day, even though their position was a modification of Calvin's) on this issue thus: "And now as regards that view of Calvinism, which makes everything pertaining to our salvation purely objective to us (and this is what the dogma of substitution, against which I am contending, greatly encourages), I have to say that this is not the view of the Church to which you as well as I belong, in that the Church makes our justification, adoption, and sanctification depend on 'effectual calling.' ... The Church assuredly *makes our salvation dependent upon a moral change wrought in us* — that moral change being a conviction of sin and misery, a knowledge of Christ, a renewal of the will, and an embracing of Christ as our Redeemer" (emphasis in original).[106]

For Calvin, the matter of the atonement was inextricably bound to his "thought of the sovereign will of God."[107] The Reverend J. K. Mozley, a dean at Cambridge, explains further: "Calvin proceeds to argue that the merit of Christ depends entirely on the free grace of God, to which it is related as accessory to principal. The central thesis of the chapter, which is then defended from Scripture, may be found in the words, 'There is nothing to prevent the justification of man from being the gratuitous result of the mercy of God, and, at the same time, to prevent the merit of Christ from intervening in subordination to this mercy.' "[108]

Mozley states that "Calvin goes beyond every one of his predecessors in teaching that Christ 'bore in His soul the tortures of a condemned and ruined man.' "[109] Mozley comments: "One is not surprised that (the Jesuit Cardinal Robert) Bellarmine spoke of this as 'a new and unheard-of heresy.' "[110]

Not without reason, then, do many Fundamentalist preachers give great play to graphic depictions of the Lord's passion and death, as well as to images of an angry Father demanding blood appeasement. But many popular Catholic spiritual writers have also sought to impress their readers and listeners in similar fashion over the centuries. In the main, it is probably accurate to say that modern Fundamentalist spirituality is strongly Calvinistic, without an appreciation or acceptance of Calvin's theological depth and sophistication, as well as the extraordinary position it really was. Therefore, most Fundamentalists are, in all likelihood, more consonant in their belief on the atonement with the Council of Trent than they are with Calvin.

In other words, Trent's straightforward explanation is better understood and accepted by today's Fundamentalists than Calvin's very involved discussion of the matter. It seems that nineteenth-century liberals, in an effort to affirm the role of man's cooperation with grace in the process of salvation, reacted in Semi-Pelagian fashion to Calvin's "pure" doctrine of the atonement, which was never entirely assimilated by Fundamentalists, anyway. The Semi-Pelagian heresy taught that man can perform some acts profitable to salvation without God's grace ("God gives me the grace to desire my salvation; now I must do my part"). The Catholic doctrine as articulated at Trent, on the other hand, holds the basics in an appealing and creative tension: even our cooperation with grace is itself under the influence of grace (hence one can pray for an increase of grace, but not simply for grace, because the impulse to pray is itself grace). This is not to argue, however, that contemporary Fundamentalists are aware of the teaching of Trent, let alone consciously subscribe to it.

4 • The Bodily Resurrection of Jesus ✧ Liberalism's representatives "were advocating a spiritual, not a literal resurrection. They claimed that Jesus did not physically and bodily come out of the grave, but rather His spirit and influence came out of the grave. They believed that Christ rose in people's hearts."[111] At the very same time that the Fundamentalists were engaged in mortal combat within their various denominations to defend the historical fact of the Resurrection, the Holy Office (now called the Congregation for the Doctrine of the Faith) stressed the reality of the event in its 1907 decree, *Lamentabili*, by condemning propositions that taught that: "The resurrection of the Savior is not properly a fact of the historical order but a fact of the purely supernatural order, which is not and cannot be demonstrated, a fact which the Christian consciousness derived gradually from other sources." Or again, that "faith in the resurrection of Christ has been from the beginning not so much faith in the fact of His resurrection as in the immortal life of Christ with God."[112] Another line of fire consisted in no outright denial of the Resurrection, but a major redefinition of the doctrine, such that the focus was taken off Christ and placed on His disciples' faith, a tack common to both Catholic Modernists and Protestant Liberals.[113]

Again, Fundamentalism and the Roman Magisterium (even though individual Catholic theologians have dissented) hold to the centrality and historicity of the Resurrection, understanding it in the same basic manner.

One interesting side issue revolves around the connection between belief in the physical resurrection and the validity of the biblical witness: "The Scriptures clearly taught a bodily resurrection from the dead. The Scriptures substantiated that Christ appeared in a literal body to His disciples. To deny the resurrection was to deny the clear accounts of Scripture, the confirmation of many witnesses, and the theological necessity of the resurrection."[114]

5 • A Literal Return of Christ in a Second Coming ✧ The ancient creeds are unanimous in asserting faith in the second coming of Christ "to judge the living and the dead." Fundamentalists saw in this "the culmination of all history. On the other hand, the liberals who questioned the death of Christ and denied the resurrection of Christ were in no position to advocate the return of someone they were not sure had lived, died, rose again."[115] In point of fact, the liberals flatly repudiated any faith in a Second Coming.[116] Why this would be so is explained by Bernard Ramm: "The Enlightenment discarded the common Christian eschatological beliefs about the return of Christ, the end of the world, final judgment, heaven and hell. . . . ." He goes on to say: "In a word, the Enlightenment both within and outside the Church initiated the downfall of Christian eschatology, a task thoroughly completed at the end of the nineteenth century."[117]

While Catholic theology has always devoted attention to "the four last things" (death, judgment, heaven, and hell), it has never been preoccupied with the Parousia in the same way as Fundamentalism. The Reverend Alfred McBride, O. Praem., puts it this way: "Though Catholics do not speak of the rapture, they do subscribe to a glorious and final manifestation of Christ at the end of time. The Catholic view of the millennium is that Christ's kingdom of love, justice, peace, and salvation has already become available to believers through grace, faith, active membership in the Church, active participation in the sacraments, and a Christian moral life."[118]

In truth, much of Fundamentalism is identified in view of its teaching on the Lord's Second Coming. However, "this particular tenet of Fundamentalism is still the most debated and divergent,"[119] with factions choosing quite different interpretations of the meaning of the doctrine and thus arriving at quite different interpretations of the Christian life. Therefore, it is important to analyze how the Second Coming has become the centerpiece of Fundamentalist theology and spirituality, in so many ways, but considered under the title of Dispensationalism.

In this connection, T. L. Frazier wisely suggests that a fruitful discussion of Mary's Assumption could be carried out in the context of the Fundamentalist interest in the rapture. Reflecting on his own pilgrimage on that score, he writes: "I began to see it was very similar to the Evangelical doctrine of the rapture where, at the end of time, Christ snatches living Christians off the face of the earth, glorifies them, and transports them both body and soul into heaven. The same idea of being physically snatched away into heaven before the general resurrection lies behind both the Assumption and the rapture."[120]

6 • Dispensationalism ✧ The doctrine of Dispensationalism, part and parcel of Fundamentalism's "apocalyptic view of history,"[121] is intimately tied to that of Christ's literal and bodily Second Coming and is grounded in a view of salvation history that considers seven "dispensations," or ages of God's activity with man. Zachary Hayes summarizes them thus:

1. The dispensation of innocence (Gen 1:28–3:6).
2. The dispensation of conscience (Gen 4:1–8:14).
3. The dispensation of civil government (Gen 8:15–11:9).
4. The dispensation of Promise (Gen 11:10–Ex 18:27).
5. The dispensation of Mosaic Law (Ex 18:28–Acts 1:26).
6. The dispensation of grace (Acts 2:1–Rev 19:21).
7. The dispensation of the millennium (Rev 20).[122]

Dispensationalists, holding to the Bible as first and foremost a book of prophecy, believe that God's promises to Abraham and David must be fulfilled. Inasmuch as they do not think that has yet happened either in the first coming of Christ or in the time of the Church, they reason that it must be destined for accomplishment in some future age, which is the millennium.

Contemporary dispensationalists (among whom would be numbered Hal Lindsey, Jerry Falwell, Jimmy Swaggart, and Pat Robertson) also come to a most interesting political position, namely, unwavering support for the State of Israel, which they regard as the clearest sign of God's making good on His promises[123] and causing them to be proponents of what Sandeen calls "enthusiastic Zionism."[124]

It should also be mentioned that the interests of the dispensationalists represent a distinct minority view in the grand sweep of Christian theology, with the Protestant Reformers silent on the issue and only a handful of usually heretical and fanatical sects subscribing to detailed positions on Christ's glorious return and the implications for humanity in general and the Church in particular.

From very little scriptural evidence, a rather complicated theory of dispensationalism has been constructed, with proponents maintaining their particular point of view with as much tenacity as they do with the virginal conception or bodily resurrection of Jesus. The irony, of course, is that so much effort is expended on a matter on which

Jesus Himself confessed relative ignorance,[125] and from people who decry adding to the biblical data or subtracting from it.

At any rate, one must have at least an acquaintance with the several schools of dispensationalist theology. At the heart of the matter is the promise of a reign of peace at the time of the Lord's Second Coming. Differences of opinion, however, emerged among dispensationalists about the time of that coming and the reign of peace. Divided into premillennialists, postmillennialists, and amillennialists, all shared an intensely pessimistic view of the world's future, combined with a hope in God's immanent and direct intervention in human life.[126] Thus, past patterns, based on the promises and prophecies, were projected into the future.

The premillennialists expected Christ to establish the promised millennium by His own might at the time of His Parousia. The postmillennial believers still accepted the notion — common even among Protestants — that the Church would prepare the way for the millennium and that Christ Himself would return only at the end of that period. The amillennialists taught that the millennium would be an exclusively internal reality, with no external manifestations.

The belief in millennialism is rooted in the passion of dispensationalists for biblical literalism. "Literalism in the early nineteenth century usually refers quite specifically to the interpretation of prophecy and contrasts with the figurative or symbolic manner of interpretation."[127] This, in spite of the fact that, as Ammerman counters, it was exactly the drive to base their eschatological hopes in the Word of God and to justify their theological and political agenda that caused them to deviate most dramatically from a literal interpretation of texts and to rely on the use of symbol and metaphor to give substance to their prognostications.[128]

Nonetheless, from their literalism (at least as they perceived it to be so), it becomes clear that only a minority of millennialists could be dispensationalists, not to mention the necessary exclusion of the amillennialists out of fidelity to the same criterion of literalism. Owing to their own biblical interpretation, they rejected any concept of a Church as understood according to the great Tradition. Using the biblical example of the case of the leaders of Israel and the golden calf, and then holding forth the liberal religious leaders of their day, they eschewed any hierarchical structure as leading to apostasy. According to dispensationalist teaching, "the true church can never be an organization, but must remain a spiritual fellowship of individual Christians."[129] This is so much the situation that Sandeen does not hesitate to declare that "the ecclesiology of dispensationalism is so individualistic that each individual becomes his own church."[130] Having thus eliminated the postmillennialists from their ranks, the dispensationalists can only be premillennial believers, as Ammerman has cogently demonstrated.[131] These were then seen to be God's elect — small in number and without power.

The premillennialists are broken into two groups of those with a historicist or futurist bent, depending on whether one thinks the prophecies have been and are being fulfilled in the Church or must still await the personal return of Christ. Those of the futurist persuasion are further divided into pre-tribulationism, mid-tribulationism, and post-tribulationism, based on their convictions as to when the rapture will occur.[132] For our purposes, further discussion is not needed, but surely one can see that a rather intricate system of thought has been developed around this article of faith.

It is precisely within the context of discussing dispensationalism that Sandeen feels compelled to remind all that "the Fundamentalist's assertion of his own orthodoxy and conservatism cannot be accepted uncritically. Both dispensationalism and the Princeton theology were marked by doctrinal innovations and emphases which must not be confused with apostolic belief, Reformation theology, or nineteenth-century evangelism."[133] Needless to say, Sandeen bristles at the suggestion that any of this can be squared with "their claim to be defending the truths of an historic faith."[134]

7 • *Private Interpretation of Scripture* ✧ If one is seeking a concise statement of the Fundamentalist understanding of the relationship between the individual believer and the sacred text, the counsel of A. T. Pierson is representative: "The humblest reader might, without any other guide than the Bible itself, by careful, prayerful searching, come to know the Word, exploring its contents till he became another Apollos, mighty in the Scriptures."[135] He also took aim at higher criticism, the darling of liberal theology, by declaring: "Like Romanism, [it] practically removes the Word of God from the common people by assuming that only scholars can interpret it; while Rome puts a priest between a man and the Word, criticism puts an educated expositor between the believer and his Bible."[136] He is, of course, reacting to the notion of the Church as Scripture's proper interpreter and "home," encapsulated in the formula of Vatican II thus:

> Sacred Tradition and Sacred Scripture, then, are bound closely together, and communicate one with the other. For both of them, flowing out from the same divine well-spring, come together in some fashion to form one thing, and move towards the same goal. . . .
>
> Sacred Tradition and Sacred Scripture make up a single sacred deposit of the Word of God, which is entrusted to the Church. . . .
>
> But the task of giving an authentic interpretation of the Word of God, whether in its written form or in the form of Tradition, has been entrusted to the living teaching office of the Church alone. Its authority in this matter is exercised in the name of Jesus Christ. Yet this Magisterium is not superior to the Word of God, but is its servant. . . .
>
> It is clear, therefore, that in the supremely wise arrangement of God, sacred Tradition, sacred Scripture, and the Magisterium of the Church are so connected and associated that one of them cannot stand without the others. Working together, each in its own way under the action of the Holy Spirit, they all contribute effectively to the salvation of souls.[137]

Thus, concludes the Reverend Avery Dulles, S.J., "the Church emphatically rejects any interpretation that is contrary to the general consent of the Fathers."[138]

Falwell maintains that this individualistic attitude has been shared by all sectarians throughout Christian history: "It may be definitely said that these movements had a basic distrust of human reason and the corporate consensus of religious ecclesiasticism. They placed the Bible above creeds, councils, papal edicts, philosophical arguments, and religious tradition. The one unifying factor in all these movements, without a doubt, is their common adherence to the basic authority of Scripture as the only dependable guide for faith and practice."[139]

Dulles comments that "the Protestant formula — in this sharp expression of it — bypasses Tradition, and affirms that the Bible not only contains the entire Revelation, but that it is a self-interpreting document. It is not only the Constitution but the Supreme Court in the republic of faith."[140]

But exactly what did the sixteenth-century Reformers have in mind when they cried out, "*sola Scriptura*" ("Scripture only")? Did it mean the individual Christian interpreting Scripture in his or her own way?

It would appear that Martin Luther launched out on that path until confronted with the same insubordination directed toward him that he had accorded the Pope. At which point, he felt compelled to modify his position significantly: "I learn now that it is not enough to throw many passages together helter-skelter, whether they are fit or not. If this is to be the way, then I can easily prove from the Scriptures that beer is better than wine."[141] Jaroslav Pelikan does not hesitate to say that "Luther could not have been the exegete he was without the help of the Church's Tradition. The Tradition gives him a footing on which he could and did move and shift, but which he never lost."[142]

Similarly, John Calvin condemned a free-floating and totally subjective form of Bible interpretation: "I acknowledge that Scripture is a most rich and inexhaustible fountain of all wisdom; but I deny that its fertility consists in the various meanings which any man, at his pleasure, may assign."[143] In point of fact, Harry Stout says with complete assurance:

> The inclusion of theological commentary was not original with the Geneva Bible. Martin Luther's German translation included it as did Calvin's French. Indeed what would have been

novel in the sixteenth century would have been the preparation
of a popular translation *without* comment. Protestant churchmen
believed they were already taking risks simply in making Bibles
available to the masses and encouraging their active use. Such an
endeavor was unprecedented and its effects were unpredictable.
To provide this Word raw, with no interpretive guidance, would
be socially and spiritually reprehensible. It would encourage readers to think they were also their own interpreters of Scripture
when, in fact, they lacked the linguistic tools necessary to interpret the "real" Scriptures preserved in the original tongues and
ancient manuscripts. While the people could and must read their
Bibles, they could not interpret them independent of ministerial
guidance. The commentary, together with the sermon, was responsible for leading Bible readers into true spiritual awareness
[emphasis in original].[144]

Nathan Hatch holds that "it is equally clear that eighteenth-cen-
tury evangelicals like John Wesley and George Whitefield, Jonathan
Edwards and Isaac Backus did not think of viewing the Bible absolutely alone. . . ."[145]

Where and when, then, did the common perception arise that
each Christian could act as his own Pope or Council? John Nevin, a
"high-church" German Reformed theologian, in surveying the American denominational scene, concluded that this stress on individual
interpretation "stemmed from a popular demand for 'private judgment,' involved a wholesale dismissal of historical and systematic
theology, and stripped the institutional Church of all mystery and
authority."[146] Hatch notes Nevin's view that Americans "had carica-
tured the meaning of *sola Scriptura* . . . by interpreting it through
lenses of individualism and democracy," with the result of
"threaten[ing] to reduce *sola Scriptura* into a new kind of charter that
would encourage reveling in private opinion more than submitting to
a common authority."[147]

In discussing the change in approach from the Reformers to the
Fundamentalists, Hatch suggests: "This shift occurred generally and
without fanfare, concealed, I think, because innovators could exploit

arguments as old and as trusted as Protestantism itself. Luther, Calvin, Wesley, and Backus had all argued for the principle of *sola Scriptura*; Elias Smith, Elhanan Winchester, William Smyth Babcock, Lucy Smith, and John Humphrey Noyes all argued that they were merely fulfilling that same mandate. Yet somewhere along the line, I would argue, a revolution had taken place that made private judgment the ultimate tribunal for the exposition of Scripture."[148]

He concludes his analysis tersely: "Instead of calming sectarian strife, trying to follow the Bible alone seemed to multiply denominations endlessly."[149]

A closer reading of the Fundamentalist situation, however, reveals that complete freedom of interpretation does not exist. Timothy Weber explains: "While assuring common Christians that they did not need scholarly help in Bible study, these teachers initiated them into a complicated system that most people could never maneuver without considerable assistance. In the final analysis, there is something incongruous about Fundamentalists who say that they can read the Bible by themselves, then pore over Scofield's notes in order to discover what the text really means."[150]

Weber goes on to note that the Fundamentalist claim regarding the perspicuity of the Bible to any Spirit-filled Christian was overplayed, so that the possibility of divergent interpretations was either denied or not tolerated.[151] Reacting to the paramount position of professional exegetes in Fundamentalism, Weber sums up the gap between Fundamentalist theory and practice in strong — even harsh — language:

> Early Fundamentalist leaders fought hard to keep the Bible accessible to ordinary believers but in the end made them nearly totally dependent on themselves. . . .
>
> The ultimate irony of the Fundamentalist approach to the Scriptures is that it has produced so little really independent Bible study. While Fundamentalists still claim that they are capable of doing it for themselves, most of them still derive their greatest "blessing" from hearing some notable Bible teacher tell them what the Bible really means.[152]

This insight is not Weber's alone. Kathleen Boone remarks: "It is ironic that commentary has become so influential in a movement purportedly devoted to the sole authority of the text."[153] Ammerman concurs: "Studies of Fundamentalists invariably point to the central role of pastors and Bible teachers in creating authoritative meanings out of the biblical text."[154] And with perhaps more than a tinge of sarcasm, she reflects: "Fundamentalists are confident that everything in Scripture is true, and if they have questions about a seemingly difficult passage, they know that prayer, study, and *a visit with the pastor* are guaranteed to provide an answer" (emphasis added).[155]

Somewhat more forcefully, Boone points out the fallacy and even hypocrisy of the Fundamentalist stance:

> Not *my* words, we are told, but the inerrant words of God, the literal sense of which one ignores at one's peril. Here, the potential for abuse must be recognized, a potential particularly acute in a discourse which portrays its pronouncements as the Word and will of God, denying the interpretive contributions of fallible humans. Protestants and Fundamentalists in particular have often accused the Roman Catholic Church of authoritarianism, but the Roman Church has at the very least been forthright about acknowledging the role of human beings in the constitution of authority — whether in the particular person of the Pope or in the communal authority of ecclesiastical tradition. One stands a far better chance of challenging a revealed authority than a hidden one, and one stands hardly any chance at all when that hidden authority is parading in the guise of Holy Scripture [emphasis in original].[156]

Barr grounds his opposition to the primacy of biblical commentary in Fundamentalism, and the concomitant appeal to the primacy of individual interpretation, in the scriptural admonition of 2 Peter 3:16, which teaches that the Word of God can be "twisted and distorted" by the uneducated and unbalanced. Barr recalls that 2 Peter 1:20 likewise clearly warns against private interpretation. The net effect of all this confusion, however, is the construction of a real — if unnamed and unacknowledged — teaching authority or Magisterium: "It is in Fundamentalism that particular regard is paid to the great individual personality, the great evangelist or radio pastor who virtually creates and runs his own church and is venerated for 'his' teaching."[157]

In other words, the Fundamentalists should have no real problem with the declaration of *Dei Verbum* (n. 10), which speaks of the necessity of a teaching authority for the authentic interpretation of Sacred Scripture. Of course, Fundamentalists consider this intensely problematic — even as they study their *Scofield Reference Bible* commentaries and refuse to consider alternative meanings for biblical texts if they conflict with cherished positions or hallowed interpretations. What makes it all the more interesting, if not downright amusing, is that these are the very people who castigate Rome's heavy-handedness in interposing herself between Christian and Bible — the same Rome that has defined no more than a handful of pericopes in a definitive manner.[158]

Finally, they would do well to heed the insights of Paul Tillich regarding the relation of Scripture and Tradition: "Evangelical biblicism, past and present, is unaware of it [dependency upon an ecclesiastical tradition] and produces a 'biblical' theology which actually is dependent on definite dogmatic developments in the post-Reformation period. Through historical scholarship, the difference between the dogmatic teaching of most American evangelistic churches and the original meaning of the biblical texts can easily be shown. Church history cannot be evaded; therefore, it is a religious as well as a scholarly necessity that the relationship of systematic theology to the ecclesiastical tradition be stated frankly and pointedly."[159]

Dulles also discusses "the manifest inadequacies of Fundamentalist exegesis as practiced in the first quarter of the twentieth century." He says: "The extreme biblicists in the American churches of Calvinist lineage imagined that it was possible for the individual believer, without any special training, to achieve an adequate understanding of God's message to mankind by a simple reading of the Bible." And what was the practical result?

But the doctrines proclaimed in the name of pure biblical teaching were so mutually contradictory and so incompatible with the findings of the natural sciences that the Fundamentalist stand was totally discredited, at least among intellectual believers. The extravagances of Pentecostalism, Seventh Day Adventism, and the Jehovah's Witnesses are a living demonstration of the perils of such naivete in exegesis. Private judgment in the exposition of the Scriptures leads ineluctably to sectarianism. Anyone who thinks he finds a new religious position in the Bible feels authorized to set up a new denomination. Just as Luther and Calvin opposed the Enthusiasts and Sectarians of their day, so conservative Protestantism in the twentieth century is emphasizing the authority of confessional traditions against the rabid individualism of the fanatics.[160]

Stanley Hauerwas, a United Methodist teaching at Duke Divinity School, has come to a similar position: "It is time for the Church to take the Bible away from the people. Insofar as they are individuals, we should not let them read it on their own." He places both Fundamentalists and advocates of "higher criticism" in the same camp, to the probable consternation of both, because they hold that the Bible "makes sense separate from the community that makes it make sense." He concludes: "When Scripture is divorced from worship, it cannot be but an idol."[161]

Some General Considerations

"Fundamentalism is a dynamic and ever-shifting force."[162] This assertion might cause some to raise an eyebrow in disbelief, since it could seem to the casual observer that Fundamentalism is static, if anything at all. But that would be entirely too facile an evaluation. If this brief overview has succeeded, the reader should have begun to appreciate the tremendous complexity of "the Fundamentalist phenomenon."

Wuthnow highlights this aspect with great clarity and insight, and is thus worth quoting at length:

Diversity is another element in Fundamentalism that will assure its persistence. To say, as some analysts do, that Fundamentalism can be defined in terms of its deep commitment to certain core teachings is simply wrong. If that were true, it should be the case that all Fundamentalists who believe in teaching X should also believe in teaching Y and Z. But we know that it is not the case. Millions who believe in inerrancy, for example, have no idea what Dispensationalism is. And millions who believe in Dispensationalism do not practice the charismatic gifts.

Fundamentalism is also more flexible than we generally think. At one time it focused its jeremiads on saloons; today it is deeply opposed to abortion; in the future it may protest something else. This flexibility makes it readily adaptable. Even its uses of the Bible and its understandings on salvation and eschatology exhibit more malleability than we ought to have supposed.[163]

Historian Randall Balmer has reflected on Fundamentalism's "staying power": "Evangelicalism will also persist, I think, because of its timeless appeal. It promises intimacy with God, a support community, an unambiguous morality, and answers to the riddles of eternity. . . . Evangelicalism simply will not go away. In the 1920s H. L. Mencken, no friend of the Evangelicals, remarked that if you tossed an egg out of a Pullman window almost anywhere in the country, you would hit a Fundamentalist. Pullman cars are obsolete in America today. Fundamentalists are still around."[164]

Endnotes

1. "Sect" is used here in a technical sense and should not be perceived as a pejorative term.

   Roger Finke and Rodney Stark maintain that "the sect-church process concerns the fact that new religious bodies nearly always begin as sects and that, if they are successful in attracting a substantial following, they will, over time, almost inevitably be gradually transformed into churches" (*The Churching of America, 1776-1990* [New Brunswick, New Jersey: Rutgers University Press, 1992], 42).

   A more detailed analysis of the word is given in Chapter 4.

2. Ernest R. Sandeen, *The Roots of Fundamentalism: British and American Millenarianism, 1800-1930* (Chicago: University of Chicago Press, 1970), 273.

3. Like "sect," the term "apologetics" is employed in a technical, nonpolemical manner, simply referring to that branch of theology that is concerned with the defense and explanation of doctrine. See Robert J. Fox, *Protestant Fundamentalism and the Born-Again Catholic* (Alexandria, South Dakota: Fatima Family Apostolate, 1991), 38-39.

4. See Eric W. Gritsch, *Born Againism: Perspectives on a Movement* (Philadelphia: Fortress Press, 1982), 40-41 passim.

5. Jerry Falwell et al., eds., *The Fundamentalist Phenomenon: The Resurgence of Conservative Christianity* (Garden City, New York: Doubleday & Co., 1981), 4.

6. Norman R. Furniss, *The Fundamentalist Controversy: 1918-1931* (New Haven, Connecticut: Yale University Press, 1954), 10.

7. Ernest R. Sandeen, *The Origins of Fundamentalism: Toward a Historical Interpretation* (Philadelphia: Fortress Press, 1968), 11.

8. Ibid., 12.

9. David Stoll, *Is Latin America Turning Protestant? The Politics of Evangelical Growth* (Berkeley: University of California Press, 1990), 5.

10. Nancy T. Ammerman, "North American Protestant Fundamentalism," in *Fundamentalisms Observed*, eds. Martin E. Marty and R. Scott Appleby (Chicago: University of Chicago Press, 1991), 53.

Inasmuch as this entire work, but especially this chapter by Ammerman, has been relied upon rather heavily, it may be well to explain this reliance by reference to several reviews of this volume that have appeared in a wide variety of scholarly sources: "A distinguished set of international scholars' contributions integrate a considerable variety of primary and secondary sources, and make extensive use of the terminologies of the field, which characterizes this voluminous work as a worth-reading document dealing with a complex issue. . . . The volume is the outcome of penetrating thinking — diligently researched" (Abu al-Hasan Salmaan, *Muslim World Book Review* 12 [1992]: 5).

"The volume is an astonishing and remarkable work. . ." (*ADRIS Newsletter* 21 [January/March 1992], 5).

These essays "constitute a rather encyclopedic wealth of information. . . . An invaluable work. . ." (T. M. Pucelik, *Choice* [July/August 1992]: 10).

"It is hard to see how *Fundamentalisms Observed* could be significantly bettered" (Chris Arthur, *Times Higher Education Supplement*, June 12, 1992, 12).

". . . required reading for every student of modern world history" (Jon Butler, *Wilson Quarterly*, Autumn 1992, 82).

The chapter on American Fundamentalism is singled out as "the valuable section in this volume by sociologist Nancy T. Ammerman" (Robert Wuthnow, "The World of Fundamentalism," *The Christian Century* [April 22, 1992]: 426).

This same section is also deemed "accurate, comprehensive, and concise" (John G. Stackhouse, "Are Fundamentalists All Alike?" *Christianity Today* [November 23, 1992]: 37).

Finally, one should not overlook the fact that this work has been listed among "Notable Books of the Year" for 1992, "Outstanding Academic Books" for 1993, and has won the 1991 award for Philosophy and Religion of the Association of American Publishers.

11. Ibid., 9.

12. Robert Gnuse, *The Authority of the Bible: Theories of Inspiration, Revelation and the Canon of Scripture* (New York: Paulist Press, 1985), 9.

13. Ibid., 12.

On the Catholic involvement with this crisis, see also Gnuse (8-13). For an official Catholic reaction, *Providentissimus Deus* (1893), *Lamentabili* (1907), Letter of the Pontifical Biblical Commission to Cardinal Suhard (1948), and *Humani Generis* (1950) are all helpful and are found in J. Neuner and J. Dupuis, eds., *The Christian Faith in the Doctrinal*

Documents of the Catholic Church (New York: Alba House, 1982), nn. 220-239. Of course, the final reconciliation of the conflict seems to have been reached with Vatican II's *Dei Verbum*.

14. George Marsden, "Fundamentalism as an American Phenomenon: A Comparison with English Evangelicalism," *Church History* (June 1977): 215.

15. Ammerman, 18.

16. Ibid.

17. See pp. 36ff of this chapter for a more detailed discussion.

18. Ammerman, 21.

19. Fox, 16.

20. William Jennings Bryan, *In His Image* (Freeport, New York: Books for Libraries Press, 1971), 93.

21. Ammerman, 27-28.

22. Richard Hofstadter, *Anti-Intellectualism in American Life* (New York: Alfred A. Knopf, 1963), 114.

23. Sandeen, *Roots of Fundamentalism*, xiv.
It is worth noting that a substantial portion of the Fundamentalist battle was being waged within Presbyterianism, so much so that Princeton Theological Seminary itself ended up divided, with a new institution of a more staunchly Fundamentalist orientation (Weston) begun in Philadelphia in 1936.

24. Falwell, 5-6.

25. George M. Marsden, "Defining American Fundamentalism," in *The Fundamentalist Phenomenon: A View from Within, A Response from Without*, ed. Norman J. Cohen (Grand Rapids, Michigan: Eerdmans Publishing Co., 1990), 23-24.

26. Edward Dobson, "Fundamentalism — Its Roots," *New Catholic World*, (January/February 1985): 5.

27. Zachary Hayes, "Fundamentalist Eschatology: Piety and Politics," *New Theology Review* (May 1988): 21.

28. See pp. 34ff in this chapter for a more detailed discussion.

29. On the relationship between Protestant Liberals and Catholic Modernists, the Reverend George Rutler has some salient observations: ". . . but the tension between Liberal Protestantism

and Catholic Modernism was the sort which exercises people
of different stations caught in the same lifeboat. The Modernists had tried to save the ship, and the Liberals had torpedoed
her; and their joint anxiety became unbearable when they saw
the ship sailing on, almost blithely. The Catholic Modernists
and the Liberal Protestants only spoke to each other to say the
ship would go over the edge nonetheless. The Pope wrote
Pascendi Dominici Gregis as his way of saying that the world
is round" (George W. Rutler, *Christ and Reason: An Introduction to Ideas from Kant to Tyrrell* [Front Royal, Virginia:
Christendom Press, 1990], 148-149). And yet again, he declares:
"Liberal Protestantism wanted a Gospel without a Church;
Catholic Modernism wanted a Church without a Gospel" (ibid.,
180).

30. Ammerman, 14.

31. See Sandeen, *Roots of Fundamentalism*, xiii.

32. Quoted in Ammerman, 2.

33. Marty and Appleby, ix-x.

34. George M. Marsden, *Fundamentalism and American Culture:
The Shaping of Twentieth Century Evangelicalism, 1870-1925*
(New York: Oxford University Press, 1980), 3.

35. Ibid.

36. Thus Robert Wuthnow in "The World of Fundamentalism" (427):
"The result was the proliferation of small sects. Separatist groups
of Presbyterians, Baptists, Methodists and Pentecostalists
emerged in abundance. Indeed, separatism itself came to be a
distinguishing feature of Fundamentalism."

37. Ammerman, 33.

38. Sandeen, *Roots of Fundamentalism*, xvii.

39. Finke and Stark note, for example, that "despite being banned
from every major radio network, Charles Fuller's 'Old Fash-
ioned Revival Hour' remained one of the most popular religious radio programs" (220).

40. Rosemary Radford Reuther, review of *Fundamentalisms Observed*, ed. by Martin E. Marty and R. Scott Appleby. In *The
New York Times Book Review* (January 26, 1992): 32.

41. To some degree, Fundamentalism was alternately being forced into a sectarian corner or moving itself there, becoming self-sufficient in every significant way. This became even more apparent in the twentieth century, as Fundamentalists built up a school system and a coherent political ideology. One can see similarities to the Catholic subculture in the United States prior to Vatican II, when a Catholic's every human need was able to be met through the Church, without need of an outside source.

42. Stephen Goode, "Exploring the Passion of Faiths," *Insight* (June 1, 1992): 15.

43. Peggy L. Shriver, "Guardians of Fundamentalism's Fortress," *New Catholic World* (January/February 1985): 15.

44. Thomas F. Stransky, "A Catholic Looks at American Fundamentalists," *New Catholic World* (January/February 1985): 13.

45. Lawrence Boadt, "Fundamentalism," *New Catholic World* (January/February 1985): 2.

    William Dinges, in asserting that Catholic Traditionalism is a form of Fundamentalism, argues that the Mass of the Roman Rite as revised after Vatican II holds a place comparable to evolution as a symbol of departure from orthodoxy. (See William D. Dinges, "Roman Catholic Traditionalism and Activist Conservatism in the United States," in *Fundamentalisms Observed*, ed. Martin E. Marty and R. Scott Appleby [Chicago: University of Chicago Press, 1991], 84-85.)

    James Hitchcock rebuffs the use of the term "Catholic Fundamentalists" and prefers "conservative Catholic activists." (See James Hitchcock, "Roman Catholic Traditionalism and Activist Conservatism in the United States," in *Fundamentalisms Observed*, ed. Martin E. Marty and R. Scott Appleby [Chicago: University of Chicago Press, 1991], 101.)

46. Ammerman, 39.

47. Fox, 15.

48. Boadt, 2.

49. See Ammerman, 1.

50. Fox, 18.

51. Ammerman, 1.

52. Ibid., 41.

53. Ibid., 45.

    In the not-too-distant past, it was common to find titles like the
    following appearing in Protestant periodicals in general and
    Fundamentalist periodicals in particular: T. W. Medhurst, "Is
    Romanism Christianity?" and J. M. Foster, "Rome, the Antago-
    nist of the Nation," both of which formed part of Charles
    Feinberg's second volume, *The Fundamentals for Today* (Grand
    Rapids, Michigan: Kregel Publications, 1958), 485-503.

54. See Ammerman, 46.

55. Ibid., 44.

56. Ibid., 14.

57. Robert Wuthnow, "Fundamentalism in the World," *The Chris-
    tian Century* (April 29, 1992): 456.

58. Stransky, 12.

59. Ibid.

60. See Ammerman, 47.

61. See James Barr, *Fundamentalism* (Philadelphia: Westminster
    Press, 1978), 2. Also see Ammerman, 37, and Falwell, 2.

62. See Ammerman, 4.

    For the purposes of this study, which is essentially theological
    in scope, Fundamentalists and Evangelicals are equated because
    "there is ultimately very little difference between the theologi-
    cal framework of Fundamentalists and Evangelicals" (Falwell,
    6).

63. Fox, 15.

64. Benton Johnson et al., "Mainline Churches: The Real Reason
    for Decline," *First Things* (March 1993), 15.

65. See Marsden in *Church History*, 215.

    Today the scope of "liberalism" would be expanded to include
    not only theological concerns but also all forms of political lib-
    eralism, especially where it collides with traditional biblical
    positions (e.g., abortion, homosexuality, etc.).

    Dealing with the identity of contemporary Fundamentalists,
    Marsden writes: "A Fundamentalist is an evangelical Protestant
    who is militantly opposed to modern culture. This definition re-

fers to Fundamentalism in its classical historical American sense, the Protestant movement that was so named in 1920. It also applies to those Protestants who call themselves Fundamentalists today" (George M. Marsden, "Defining American Fundamentalism," in *The Fundamentalist Phenomenon: A View from Within, A Response from Without*, ed. Norman J. Cohen [Grand Rapids, Michigan: Eerdmans Publishing Co., 1990], 22-23).

66. Ibid., 215-216.
67. See George Gallup and Sarah Jones, *100 Questions and Answers: Religion in America* (Princeton, New Jersey: Princeton Religion Research Center, 1989), 200-201.
68. Johnson et al., 13.
69. Ammerman, 2.
70. See Peter M. J. Stravinskas, *Constitutional Rights and Religious Prejudice: Catholic Education as the Battleground* (Milwaukee: Catholic League for Religious and Civil Rights, 1983), 20-21.
71. Ammerman, 42.
72. Falwell, 13.
73. Ibid., 14.
74. Ibid.
75. Ibid., 14-15.
76. Johnson et al., 16-17.
77. Ibid., 16.
78. Sandeen, *Roots of Fundamentalism*, 273-277 passim.
79. See Fox, 13.
80. Finke and Stark, 1.
81. Johnson et al., 16.
82. Ibid.
83. Ibid., 17.
84. Ibid., 18.
85. Alfred Loisy, *My Duel with the Vatican: The Autobiography of a Catholic Modernist* (New York: Greenwood Press, 1968), 87. In what is perhaps the most damning statement in his angry memoirs, Loisy admits: "What I was beginning to believe regarding the Bible, Jesus, the Christian principles and their ori-

64 REV. PETER M. J. STRAVINSKAS

gins, was the absolute negation of any supernatural character for religion whatever," pp. 102-103.
86. Ibid., 273.
87. Dobson, 6-7.
88. Sandeen, *Origins of Fundamentalism*, 13.
89. Ibid.
90. Ibid., 14.
91. Fox, 18.
92. William A. Jurgens, *The Faith of the Early Fathers* (Collegeville, Minnesota: Liturgical Press, 1970), volume 3, 88.

Also worth noting are similar comments of Augustine: "With the Scriptures it is a matter of treating about the faith. For that reason, as I have noted repeatedly, if anyone not understanding the mode of divine eloquence, should find something about these matters [about the physical universe] in our books, or hear of the same from these books, of such a kind that seem to be at variance with the perceptions of his own rational faculties, let him believe that these other things are in no way necessary to the admonitions or accounts or predictions of the Scriptures. In short, it must be said that our authors knew the nature of the skies; but it was not the intention of the Spirit of God, Who spoke through them, to teach men anything that would not be of use to them for their salvation" (*De Genesi ad Litteram Opus Imperfectum* in Jurgens 3:83).

Other early Christian writers were of a similar mind: "They [the Evangelists] often preserved the pneumatic truth in what some might call a somatic falsehood" (Origen's *Commentarius in Evangelium Joannis* in Jurgens 1:202).

"Occasionally in the Holy Scriptures terms are used in accord with what the opinion of the times would employ, and not in accord with what is really the truth of the matter" (St. Jerome's *In Jeremiam Commentarii* in Jurgens 2:213).
93. Donald DeMarco, "The Dispute between Galileo and the Catholic Church," *Homiletic and Pastoral Review*, June 1986, 50.
94. *Rome and the Study of Scripture* (St. Meinrad, Indiana: Grail Publications, 1962), passim.

95. Pontifical Biblical Commission, "Instructio de Historica Evangeliorum Veritate," *Catholic Biblical Quarterly* (July 1964): 299-312.

96. Vatican Council II, "*Dei Verbum*," ed. Austin Flannery, O.P. (Northport, New York: Costello Publishing Co, 1980), n. 11.

97. Ibid.

98. "Dogmatic models of propositional revelation are more typical of seventeenth century orthodox fathers of Lutheranism and Calvinism" (Gnuse, 27).

99. Fox, 17.

100. Dobson, 6.

101. Benjamin Warfield, "The Deity of Christ." (See Charles Feinberg, ed. *The Fundamentals for Today* [Grand Rapids, Michigan: Kregel Publications, 1958], 240.)

102. James Orr, "The Virgin Birth of Christ." (See Charles Feinberg, ed. *The Fundamentals for Today* [Grand Rapids, Michigan: Kregel Publications, 1958], 248.)
The Fundamentalist rejection of the perpetual virginity of Mary is handled in Chapter 3.

103. Dobson, 8.

104. Ibid.

105. Neuner and Dupuis, 558.

106. George Jamieson, *Discussions of the Atonement: Is It Vicarious?* (Edinburgh: William Blackwood and Sons, 1887), 113-114.

107. J. K. Mozley, *The Doctrine of the Atonement* (London: Gerald Duckworth & Co., 1962), 142.

108. Ibid., 145.

109. Ibid., 146.

110. Ibid.

111. Dobson, 8.

112. Neuner and Dupuis, 181.
These statements of the Church's Magisterium came about in response to the attacks on the Lord's resurrection from proponents of Modernism, the counterpart to Liberalism within the Catholic Church. For a good presentation of the situation within both Prot-

estantism and Catholicism at this time, see H.P.V. Nunn, *What is Modernism?* (New York: Macmillan Co., 1932), 69-124.

Likewise, Emile Poulat notes that in regard to the resurrection of Jesus, "Harnack particularly weighs his words" (*Histoire, Dogme et Critique dans la Crise Moderniste* [Paris: Casterman, 1962], 53). Loisy, on the other hand, appears more reckless; for him, "the Resurrection . . . could not have been directly and formally verified" (91).

113. See W. Maurice Pryke, *Modernism as a Working Faith* (Cambridge: W. Heffer and Sons, 1926), especially 9, 11, 17, 87, 151, 218ff.
114. Dobson, 8.
115. Ibid.
116. See Pryke, 226-231.
117. Bernard Ramm, *After Fundamentalism* (San Francisco: Harper and Row, 1983), 181.

Ramm provides a very complete analysis of this matter in his chapter on Christological Eschatology, 181-192.
118. Alfred McBride, O. Praem., *The Second Coming of Jesus* (Huntington, Indiana: Our Sunday Visitor, Inc., 1993), 161.
119. Ibid.
120. T. L. Frazier, "Assumptions about Mary." *This Rock*, May/June 1992, 13.
121. Fox, 25.
122. Hayes, 26.
123. See Hayes, 26.
124. Sandeen, *Origins of Fundamentalism*, 5.
125. See Matthew 24:36, an admittedly difficult passage. Catholic exegesis of this pericope runs the gamut from the approach of the Navarre Bible Commentary, which maintains that Jesus as God did in fact know the hour of His Parousia but chose to withhold that information from others for various reasons (see Navarre Bible, *St. Matthew* [Dublin: Four Courts Press, 1988], 198), to that of the original and revised *Jerome Biblical Commentary*. The Reverend John L. McKenzie offers a rather careful interpretation: "Yet what seems to be as clear an indication of time, apart

from an exact date, as one could wish is followed by a statement that not even the Son knows the day and the hour. Distinctions between the fall of Jerusalem and the Parousia have no basis in the text; and reservations on the ignorance of the Son likewise have no basis in the text. The words mean that Jesus did not know the time, and He did not add 'in my human nature' or 'with my experiential knowledge.' Perhaps it would have made no sense had he added such phrases, but in this case it would have been better to omit a completely unnecessary remark. We are, of course, not dealing with 'the very words' of Jesus; but it is hard to understand how the apostolic traditions would have preserved such a difficult saying if it did not rest on the memory of something Jesus had said. The first Christian writer to find this sentence difficult was Luke [21:32-33] and he solved his problem by omitting it. We cannot do this; and perhaps the only remark that can be made is that there is much about the relations of Jesus and the Father that we do not know" (in *Jerome Biblical Commentary*; Raymond E. Brown et al., eds. [Englewood Cliffs, New Jersey: Prentice-Hall, 1968], s.v. "The Gospel according to Matthew," 106).

Much less cautious is the Reverend Benedict T. Viviano, O.P.: "This verse states the principle that no one knows the exact time of the Parousia. . . . Since the Son (of God) is ignorant of the hour, this verse has a lower christology than v. 30. . . . Sharing our human condition, the Son shared also our partial ignorance" (in *New Jerome Biblical Commentary*, s.v. "The Gospel according to Matthew," 668).

While Fundamentalists would resonate well to the Navarre approach, they would find aspects of both *JBC* exegeses problematic, with the latter certainly posing serious problems for them. In truth, its unnuanced language would also raise difficulties from the perspective of Catholic doctrine, too.

126. Sandeen, *Origins of Fundamentalism*, 5.

127. Ibid., 7.

128. See Ammerman, 7.

129. Sandeen, *Origins of Fundamentalism*, 6.

130. Ibid.

131. See Ammerman, 6.

132. Timothy P. Weber, *Living in the Shadow of the Second Coming* (Chicago: University of Chicago Press, 1987), 8-12 passim.

133. Sandeen, *Origins of Fundamentalism*, 25.

134. Ibid.

135. A. T. Pierson, *Knowing the Scriptures* (New York: Gospel Publishing House, 1910), 2-3.

136. A. T. Pierson, "Antagonism to the Bible," *Our Hope* 15 (January 1909): 475.

137. *Dei Verbum*, nn. 9-10.

138. Avery Dulles, S.J., *Revelation and the Quest for Unity* (Washington, D.C.: Corpus Books, 1968), 71.

139. Falwell, 53.

140. Dulles, *Revelation and Quest*, 71.

141. Helmut T. Lehmann, ed., *Luther's Works* (Philadelphia: Fortress Press, 1970), 39:75-76.

142. Jaroslav Pelikan, *Luther the Expositor* (St. Louis: Concordia Publishers, 1959), 88.

143. A. Skevington Wood, *The Principles of Biblical Interpretation as Enunciated by Irenaeus, Origen, Augustine, Luther and Calvin* (Grand Rapids, Michigan: Eerdmans Publishing Co., 1967), 92.

144. Harry S. Stout, "Word and Order in Colonial New England," in *The Bible in America: Essays in Cultural History*, eds. Nathan D. Hatch and Mark A. Noll (New York: Oxford University Press, 1982), 22.

145. Nathan Hatch, "Sacred Scripture and the Novus Ordo Seculorum," in *The Bible in America: Essays in Cultural History*, eds. Nathan D. Hatch and Mark A. Noll (New York: Oxford University Press, 1982), 61.

146. Ibid., 60.

147. Ibid.

148. Ibid., 73.

149. Ibid.

150. Timothy Weber, "Fundamentalist Use of the Bible," in *The Bible*

in *America: Essays in Cultural History*, eds. Nathan D. Hatch and Mark A. Noll (New York: Oxford University Press, 1982), 114.

151. Ibid., 115-116 passim.
152. Ibid., 117.
153. Kathleen C. Boone, *The Bible Tells Them So: The Discourse of Protestant Fundamentalism* (Albany, New York: State University of New York Press, 1989), 81.
154. Ammerman, 5.
155. Ibid., 6.
156. Boone, 111.
157. James Barr, *Beyond Fundamentalism* (Philadelphia: Westminster Press, 1984), 6.
158. See Raymond E. Brown et al., eds., *New Jerome Biblical Commentary* (Englewood Cliffs, New Jersey: Prentice-Hall, 1990), s.v. "Hermeneutics," by Raymond E. Brown and Sandra Schneiders, n. 85, p. 1164.
159. Paul Tillich, *Systematic Theology I* (Chicago: University of Chicago Press, 1951), 37.
160. Dulles, *Revelation and Quest*, 74.
161. Willmar Thorkelson, "Scholar: Interpret Bible in Community," *The Lutheran* (October 1992): 36.
162. Fox, 16.
163. Wuthnow, 429.
164. Randall Balmer, *Mine Eyes Have Seen the Glory* (New York: Oxford University Press, 1989), 233-234.

CHAPTER 3

The Place of Mary in Classical Fundamentalism

To discover the place of Mary in classical Fundamentalism[1] requires one to move back to the Protestant Reformation, inasmuch as Fundamentalism regards itself as a direct descendant of that theological tradition. As John Mark Reynolds puts it, Fundamentalists "are historic Protestants."[2] Our first concern, then, is to determine the status of Marian doctrine and devotion among the Reformers. Second, it is necessary to see if Fundamentalism is in continuity with its Reformation pedigree.

The guiding hypothesis of this chapter is a modification of that of Charles Lees: "In modern dialogues between Catholics and their separated brethren, it is often ignored that, historically, the Protestant Reformers did not attack devotion to Our Blessed Mother; that such an attack came from their successors."[3] It is also the guarded conviction of David Wright that "the Churches that look back to the Reformers have on the whole been less affirmative about Mary than most of the Reformers themselves."[4]

The Protestant Reformation and Mary

Martin Luther ✧ The lion's share of a discussion on Protestantism and Mary must be centered on Martin Luther, inasmuch as he is commonly acknowledged as the "Father of the Reformation." Therefore, the question of the Reverend William Cole's magisterial article is quite to the point: "Was Luther a devotee of Mary?" The Reverend Thomas O'Meara sets a sober tone for this process of discernment: "During any discussion of Luther and the Blessed Virgin we must keep uppermost in our minds that there was development in his ideas, a change more or less drastic in each aspect of Marian theology. This development had its beginning in Catholicism; it passes through contradictions, struggles, and uncertainties, and terminates in a new Marian viewpoint, one which Luther decided was Christocentric, biblical, unexaggerated, and edifying."[5]

Cole cautions against imagining Luther's "being preoccupied with Mary. He was critical in the measure in which Mariological declaration conflicted with what he considered essential points: the primacy of grace, the transcendence of God, the unique Mediatorship of Christ, etc."[6] An important point to ponder is that, in the very heat of the debate, "in the resolutions of the 95 theses Luther rejects every blasphemy against the Virgin and thinks that one should ask for pardon for any evil said or thought against her."[7] Cole also stresses the necessity of using official Reformation documents, like the *Apology of the Augsburg Confession,* to make a formal determination regarding Luther's mind on this topic, adding to that the suggestion of taking into account Lutheran practices after the fact: ". . . [Luther's] custom of preaching Marian sermons on the Marian feasts continued in the Lutheran Church a hundred years after his death. Following the example of Luther, other great songwriters of the Reformation glorified the greatness of Mary's divine maternity. This lasting piety towards the Mother of God found an outlet in piety so that generally the celebrated pictures of the Madonna and her statues from the Middle Ages were retained in Lutheran churches. According to Heiler, it was only the spirit of the Enlightenment with its lack of understanding of the mystery of the Incarnation, which in the eighteenth century began the work of destruction."[8]

Picking up the fact of Luther's preaching on Marian feasts, Cole observes with some irony that "the Reformer preached more about Mary than Catholic priests do in this era of the Church's history."[9]

At a doctrinal level, one finds Luther's "acknowledgment of the perpetual virginity of Mary, that is, virginity before birth, in birth, and after birth, is explicit and he uses such formulas of Mariology as *de ventre clauso utero,* without the seed of man, ever-virgin."[10] It is worth taking note of Wright's observation that Luther accepts this teaching "as a received assumption rather than a securely biblical deduction."[11] In other words, Luther was not such an "absolutist" on the issue of *sola Scriptura*, as some might think. Wright also admits that of Luther's acceptance of Mary's perpetual virginity came a recognition of "the long-established universal belief in Mary's perpetual virginity, which was endorsed by all the Reformers virtually without qualification." And furthermore, this position even found its way into the marginal comments of the Geneva Bible of 1560.[12]

Quite remarkable, too, is that Luther "with considerable consistency down to the time of his death in 1546 accepted the immaculate conception of Mary."[13] As for Mary's Assumption, he "did not pronounce clearly on this subject, but was content simply to affirm it."[14] Wright adds to this list the fact that " 'Mother of God' is a frequent instinctive usage for Luther," down to "the last years of his life." He goes on to mention that "Zwingli also endorsed it explicitly," even if Calvin "never adopted the phrase."[15]

When we come to the question of the invocation of Mary (or any other saints), the matter becomes more complicated. In Luther's *Explanation of the Magnificat* in 1521, he begins and ends with an invocation to Mary, which Wright feels compelled to call "surprising."[16] In 1530, Article 21 of the *Augsburg Confession* states that "it cannot be proved from the Scriptures that we are to invoke saints or seek help from them,"[17] even though there is no explicit denial of the possibility of the saints' intercession for the members of the Church on earth, nor any opposition to such a holding. The reason for the denial of the practice is twofold: It is not taught in Scripture; and conversely, it is taught in Scripture that Christ is the "one mediator . . . the only savior, the only high priest, advocate and intercessor before God."[18] A bit later, in Luther's *Apology of the Augsburg Confession*, he presents a corollary deriving from the second point, namely, that it is essential and sufficient to invoke only Christ.[19] In the *Schmalcald Articles*, Luther seems to argue that even if the saints can and do pray for us, the common people need to have this drummed out of their piety, so that the entire cult of the saints will eventually fall, with all its abuses finally gone.[20] This is somewhat more nuanced than might appear at first blush. Is he, in fact, leaving open the door to some limited form of invocation, at least at the theoretical level? Siding with Stakemeier against O'Meara, Cole responds in the negative.[21] The motivation for Luther's apparent (but not definitive) ban on the invocation of Mary and the other saints is rooted in four principles, which will be treated in another section: (a) Scripture alone; (b) God alone; (c) Christ alone; and (d) grace alone.[22]

The question becomes even more muddled, however, when one seeks to learn how this prohibition was, or was not, incorporated into the daily life of Luther and his followers. For example, he directed that the *Magnificat* be sung daily in all churches. While struggling mightily with the *Ave Maria*, especially because he was troubled by those who failed to pray it correctly and with the proper attitude, Luther did concede that it could likewise form part of the prayer life of a true believer. He concluded, on the other hand, that the "extravagances" of the *Salve Regina* and *Regina Caeli* were "unevangelical."[23]

But Luther, if uncomfortable with the idea of invoking the saints in prayer, was rather strong in proposing Mary (and other saints as well) as models for emulation. He regularly praised Mary's virtues and held her (and all the saints) up for imitation, especially as regards her exemplary living of humility, chastity, and faith.[24]

Nor was Luther an iconoclast, for he strictly forbade the fanatical destruction of images and demanded at least a crucifix and a representation of Our Lady for his own use. He quite clearly did not see the Old Testament prohibition against images as having any application, so long as the images were not used in an idolatrous manner.[25] Most interesting of all, perhaps, is the realization that his burial chamber in the Wittenberg church, on whose door he had posted his ninety-five theses, was adorned with Peter Vischer's 1521 sculpture of the Coronation of the Virgin, with the inscription *Ad summum Regina thronum defertur in altum: Angelicis praelatia choris, cui festus et ipse Filius occurrens Matrem super aethera ponit.*[26]

This "archaeological" fact would seem to speak volumes about Luther's final thoughts on the place of Mary in the life of a Christian.

In noting Luther's absolute and unswerving adherence to the doctrines of Mary's perpetual virginity and Immaculate Conception, Wright suggests the reason as Luther's "holding more closely to the late medieval world of thought than Calvin."[27]

The very careful final verdict on Luther's Marian devotion is summed up as follows by Cole, relying on the traditional language of Roschini:

> I would submit that it is beyond all reasonable doubt that Luther *loved* and *venerated* (honored or praised) Mary personally and *imitated* the evangelical virtues he saw displayed in her life. Likewise, no one can doubt that he wished all Christians to follow him along these lines.
>
> As for *gratitude* and *servitude* to Mary, only in the most restricted sense can any argument be adduced that Luther either recommended or practiced these parts of Marian devotion.
>
> Finally, in spite of the fact that some scholarly opinion still maintains a contrary opinion, I would maintain that the Reformer eventually rejected any form of *invocation* [emphases in original].[28]

One last consideration might well be how contemporary Lutherans (and other Protestants) read and understand the Mariology of Luther and the other Reformers. Lutheran Sister Basilea Schlink seems to sum up the situation honestly when she writes about "how far the majority of us [Protestants] have drifted away from the proper attitude towards her, which Martin Luther had indicated to us on the basis of Holy Scripture." She links much of this difficulty to the rise of Rationalism, which "has lost the sense of the sacred. In Rationalism, man sought to comprehend everything, and that which he could not comprehend he rejected." This insight is key, since Fundamentalism arose, in large measure, as a reaction to the influence of Rationalism on traditional Protestantism. She continues: "Because Rationalism accepted only that which could be explained rationally, Church festivals in honor of Mary and everything else reminiscent of her were done away with in the Protestant Church. All biblical relationship to the Mother Mary was lost, and we are still suffering from this heritage."

She then concludes in remorseful fashion: "When Martin Luther bids us to praise the Mother Mary, declaring that she can never be praised enough as the noblest lady and, after Christ, the fairest gem in Christendom, I must confess that for many years I was one of those who had not done so, although Scripture says that henceforth all generations would call Mary blessed (Luke 1:48). I had not taken my place among these generations."[29]

The Reverend Raniero Cantalamessa notes that "after the [Second Vatican] Council, theologians from various Protestant denominations — Lutherans, Calvinists, Anglicans, Evangelicals — made similar declarations."[30] Certainly, the Lutheran-Roman Catholic Dialogue on Mary is at least tacit, if not explicit, admission of this as well, in addition to the works of many theologians cited later in this chapter.

John Calvin ✧ "To look at Protestantism today would make one think that, of all the Reformers, Calvin had inveighed most violently against Mary. The Churches stemming from Geneva have no Marian feast (except in European communities which have accepted a liturgical reform), no word at all about the Mother of Christ. . . . Calvin's position, however is not that extreme."[31]

Calvin's approach to Mariology is a bit more radical than Luther's, but in its main lines, is not much different,[32] although he senses a greater urgency to hem it in with more qualifications. For example, while adhering to Mary's perpetual virginity, "his more careful biblicism could insist on only Mary's refraining from intercourse before the birth of Jesus (i.e., her virginity *ante partum*). On the other hand, he never excluded as untenable the other elements in her perpetual virginity, and may be said to have believed it himself without claiming that Scripture taught it."[33]

In this connection, William J. Bouwsma makes the point that "among matters on which he [Calvin] discouraged speculation were the order of angels . . . and the perpetual virginity of Mary."[34]

With reference to the title "Mother of God," we learn that Calvin disapproved of its use because "it promoted superstition." Wright continues by bringing the line up to date by saying that "what many

Protestants identify as Mariolatry persuades them not to call her 'Mother of God.' "[35] What is interesting is that Calvin never "even cited the Greek term *Theotokos*"[36] (literally, "God-bearer"). On the *Ave Maria*, Calvin commented that it should be seen as "no more than a word of congratulation."[37]

Did Calvin have anything specifically positive to say about Mary? Yes, he "commonly speaks of Mary as 'the holy Virgin' (and rarely simply as 'Mary,' preferring 'the Virgin,' etc.)." Calvin "rarely depicts Mary expressly as a sinner" although he did object "to her specific exclusion from the reach of original sin by the Council of Trent."[38] For instance, Calvin considers the failing (sin) of Mary at Cana to have been her desire "to exceed humanity and to make herself an intermediary, which is to forget that grace is totally from God and at His disposal."[39] Bouwsma recounts the charming story that "when Mary rebuked the boy Jesus for His truancy, Calvin apologized for her. 'The weariness of three days was in that complaint,' he explained."[40] It seems that, often enough, Calvin went to particular lengths to assert that "Calvinists are not foes of Mary, but [that] they feel that they have given her true honor, whereas others have taken from God and given to Mary. Throughout Calvin's sermons on the Scriptures, there are occasional references to the dishonor rendered to Mary and to God by her various titles and by Roman theology."[41]

In Book III of his *Institutes*, Calvin deals with the mediation of Christ and the intercession of saints. His approach is rather carefully nuanced, with no outright condemnation or denial but with more concern about abuses, about the possible obscuring of the unique intercession of Christ, or about the attribution of divine powers to the saints.[42]

In formal doctrinal statements of the Reformed tradition, we find two of the Ten Conclusions of Bern (1528) particularly relevant:

> 6. As Christ alone died for us, so He is also to be adored as the only Mediator and Advocate between God the Father and us. For this reason, it is contrary to the basis of the Word of God to direct worship to be offered to other mediators beyond the present life.

8. It is contrary to the Word of God, contained in the books of the Old and New Testaments, to make images for use in worship. For this reason, they are to be abolished, if they are set up as objects of worship.[43]

Similarly, the Westminster Confession of 1646 says the following: "Religious worship is to be given to God, the Father, Son, and Holy Ghost; and to Him alone; not to angels, saints, or any other creature; and since the Fall, not without a Mediator; nor in the mediation of any other but of Christ alone."[44]

The Reverend Thomas O'Meara sums up Calvin's Marian thought thus: "[His] comments on Mary center on a constant theological image — the transcendence of God: Mary must not obscure Christ. Mary must not be Mother of Divine Grace because grace is at God's disposal through Christ alone. And yet, we cannot say that Calvin was an iconoclast. In retaining belief in the perpetual virginity of Mary, in encouraging our imitation of her many virtues, in holding her to be free from most sin, he showed a certain balance. He should not have inspired the complete absence of the Mother of God in his spiritual descendants."[45]

Ulrich Zwingli ✧ What comes across in a brief survey of the Marian thought of Zwingli is that "generally on Mary [he] is nearer to Luther than one might expect," which is to say that he is "more Catholic" on this matter than Calvin.[46]

On the perpetual virginity of Mary, Zwingli not only holds to it, but defends it scripturally, with reference to the "shut gate" of Ezekiel 44:2. He apparently feels compelled to find biblical grounding for this teaching, lest he yield on *sola Scriptura*; thus Zwingli "believes he has shown that Mary's permanent virginity rests on biblical fact, not human decree."[47] This doctrine had added significance for him as well; he considered it crucial that "Mary herself had to be free of any pollution of normal child-bearing — which hints strongly at the logic that leads to her own immaculate conception."[48] On the *Ave Maria*, one finds that "Zwingli defended its use, but as praise, not prayer,"[49] which many might take as a purely fictional distinction. Finally, as regards the Assumption: "In Zwingli's Zurich . . . even the feast of the Assumption of Mary was apparently specifically retained — and Zwingli's successor, Bullinger, once confessed that Mary's 'sacrosanct body was borne by angels into heaven,' although he declined to take a firm stand on either her bodily assumption or her immaculate conception."[50]

Similarly, "Zwingli likewise often called Mary 'pure, holy, spotless,' without offering an unambiguous commitment to either her immaculate conception or sinlessness."[51]

Anecdotal evidence suggests a very careful approach to Mariology at the level of practice. "His delicate Mariology was expressed in an early sermon *On the Perpetual Virginity of Mary* (1522) and came to light in the Zurich liturgy which retained the *Ave Maria*. . . ."[52] Furthermore, it would seem that Zwingli had no fundamental objections either to statues or to pilgrimages, since "he joined a pilgrimage to Aachen [site of a famous Madonna] in 1517."[53] By 1530, however, under the sway of Oecolampadius, a different story had emerged as all such Marian manifestations had been banned.[54]

The Reform in England[55]

Wright feels comfortable in asserting, without fear of contradiction, that "the English Reformers probably to a man shared [the] conviction of Mary's perpetual virginity."[56] Hugh Latimer, Miles Coverdale, and Robert Barnes all accepted this doctrine, as did Thomas Cranmer himself, who taught it as biblically founded. "They all proved it by Ezekiel chapter 44. Had they not judged it to be in Scripture, they would never have made it binding."[57] Latimer also expressed strong support for Mary's Immaculate Conception.[58] Charles Miller notes: "As regards the practice of invocation of the saints, and the Virgin Mary in particular, Herbert Thorndike (1598-1672), for instance, allows prayers to God which 'desire His blessings by and through the merits and intercession of His saints' precisely because in his view its practice is based on a theological perspective which 'all Christians from the beginning' have espoused implicitly or explicitly."[59] The recent address by the Reverend Roger Greenacre of Chichester Cathedral confirms the preceding broad sweep of Marian devotion and doctrine in Anglicanism.[60] At the same time, one must acknowledge that "all invocations to Mary were removed from the Book of Common Prayer in England."[61]

A Summary of Reformation Mariology

"Mary was not a central or prominent issue in the sixteenth-century Reformation," declares Wright.[62] But why? First of all, because most of the Marian doctrines were taken for granted and accepted. The Reformers' Marian concerns were more related to devotion than doctrine: "The Reformers' teachings about Mary were to a considerable measure a critique of piety and liturgy."[63] O'Meara offers this careful summary evaluation of the situation: "It was the times with their changes in intellectual and cultural outlook, it was the very history of the Reform with its forgetfulness of the fullness of its Lutheran and Calvinist inheritance, which caused a Christian religion to come into existence without any place for Christ's Mother. We should remember that this was not the view of the Reformers, nor is it intrinsic to Protestantism."[64]

Fundamentalism and Mary

Having reviewed the principal Protestant Reformers' positions and attitudes toward Mary and the doctrine and devotion connected to her, it is now appropriate to examine similar areas within Fundamentalist theology. It is important, however, to divide this topic into two segments: the first being that group of Fundamentalists who are serious theologians, and the other being apologists at best or anti-Catholic polemicists at worst. Our reflections are rounded out with reference to basic theological principles of Fundamentalists that demonstrate a more positive evaluation of the place of Mary on their part. This task can probably best be accomplished by proceeding along the lines of a "review of the literature."

Theological Works

The primary reference to Mary in Charles Hodge's nineteenth-century three-volume work in systematic theology[65] occurs within the context of First Commandment prohibitions, coming under the title of "Mariolatry." After an opening paragraph of praise for the Mother of Jesus, Hodge launches into an unremitting assault on what he calls "the deification of the Virgin Mary [by] the Church of Rome," identifying it as "a slow process." He sums up that process: "The first step was the assertion of her perpetual virginity. This was early taken and generally conceded. The second step was the assertion that the birth, as well as the conception of our Lord, was supernatural. The third was the solemn, authoritative decision by the ecumenical council of Ephesus, A.D. 431, that the Virgin Mary was the 'Mother of God.' "[66]

He does agree, however, that "there is a sense in which the designation [Mother of God] is proper and according to the analogy of Scripture."[67] He identifies the fourth step of Marian "deification" as "the dedication in her honor of numerous churches, shrines, and festivals; and in the introduction of solemn offices designed for public and private worship in which she was solemnly invoked."[68] Writing just after the promulgation of the dogma of the Immaculate Conception, Hodge takes particular aim at this teaching, citing its nonacceptance by Sts. Augustine, Anselm, Bernard, and Thomas Aquinas.[69] He also castigates Catholicism for its interrelated notions of Tradition and the development of doctrine.[70] In summarizing the results of the definition of the Immaculate Conception, he says: "She was thus placed, as to complete sinlessness, on an equality with her adorable Son, Jesus Christ, Whose place she occupies in the confidence and love of so large a part of the Roman Catholic world."[71]

F. F. Bruce contributed the chapter on "The Person of Christ: Incarnation and Virgin Birth" to Carl Henry's *Basic Christian Doctrines*.[72] In a seven-page discussion of this topic, Mary is presented in only the most incidental of ways. The stress throughout is on the truth that "God did a new thing in the earth when His Son became incarnate, and the virginal conception was part and parcel of that new thing."[73] There is also a heavy emphasis on the miraculous nature of this event. Hence, Barr's conclusion that "in Fundamentalism, there is much emphasis upon the virgin birth because it is thought to be a test case of miracle."[74] No treatment of the person of Mary or even her faith occurs. He does not entertain in any way the vexing question (from the Fundamentalist perspective) of Mary's perpetual virginity, let alone any other Marian matters.[75]

The two-volume work of systematic theology by H. Orton Wiley, representing the Church of the Nazarene, in his reflections on Christology, takes cognizance of Mary, so that in her "human submissiveness and trust found its highest Old Testament expression." He goes on: "It was in Mary, therefore, that the protoevangelium given in Eden came to its fulfillment through the grace of the covenant."[76] With some measure of inaccuracy, he declares that "Protestantism . . . uniformly rejected the *Theotokos*, regarding the expression, 'Mother of God' as objectionable and misleading."[77] In a most dispassionate manner, he treats the doctrine of the Immaculate Conception within the context of original sin, giving its history and noting its dogmatic definition in 1854 by Pope Pius IX.[78] He makes no mention (either affirming or denying) of the virginity of Mary beyond the point of Christ's birth; the Assumption is not treated at all.

David Wright's introduction for his own *Chosen by God*,[79] an attempt to deal with Marian issues in a serious manner, begins with the less-than-congenial talk about the "scriptural nakedness" of Catholic Marian statements.[80] He does urge Evangelicals to "resist the temptation to indulge in Marian muck-raking," all the while moving on to the assertion that "Mariology labors under a crushing weight of religious crudity, vulgarism, and sheer crass superstition." Suspecting that someone might think he has not quite "resist[ed] the temptation to indulge in Marian muck-raking," he assures the reader that his introduction is comparatively restrained and that he has "scarcely scratched the surface."[81] That having been said, Wright avers that "at the same time, some of our [Evangelical] Churches must start calling Mary blessed for her part in the incarnation."[82] He cites a passage from the Catholic theologian Hans Urs von Balthasar: "Mary . . . belongs to the innermost circle of that human 'constellation' around Jesus which is of theological significance. To regard her merely as a mother in the physical sense, without a spiritual relationship to her child, is untheological because it is inhuman."[83]

He views Von Balthasar's evaluation in a positive light, yet immediately cautions: "But it is Von Balthasar's second sentence that leads us to one of the nerve-centers of Mariological debate. If we accept that Mary's motherhood was not exhausted by her giving birth to Jesus, how much further does it extend?" He answers his own question: "I discern no mileage in a renewed Evangelical appreciation of Mary for her 'motherhood' of the Church, because its logical and exegetical bases are so flimsy."[84] He concludes his opening remarks with a quotation from Ferguson's *Chasing the Wild Goose:* "The Iona Virgin, set with wonderful irony in the heart of the old masculine bastion, points us to a person who is neglected and feared by left-brained Protestantism, and exalted into a pseudo-goddess cum anti-sex symbol by the unhealthy wing of Catholicism. Mary needs to be liberated from the grizzly [sic] hang-ups and defensive positions of centuries, to be revealed as what the biblical tradition shows her to be: the person who par excellence opened herself in lowliness to One Who brings new life out of acknowledged impotence."[85]

Revealing his own ambivalence and apparent desire to move out of some of that "left-brained Protestantism" without simultaneously moving into the exaltation of Mary as "a pseudo-goddess," he ends with the trenchant remark: "I will settle for that."[86]

Wright's essay on "Mary in the New Testament," unlike the major ecumenical work of the same title, can be described as carping at best, failing to take seriously alternative data or possibilities.[87] In discussing whether or not there were "brothers and sisters of Jesus," he agrees that "this question has added piquancy for Evangelical Protestants because the sixteenth-century Reformers were united in answering it in the negative, even when, as in Calvin's case, no interest was apparent in what has always been assumed to be the flip side of the question — namely, the perpetual virginity of Mary."[88] He spends much time on Pope John Paul II's 1987 encyclical *Redemptoris Mater*[89] and his biblical method that, according to Wright, "requires . . . careful analysis, because at first sight the letter pays a great deal of attention to Scripture. It certainly cites numerous verses, and yet at the same time gives the overall impression of a private, privileged circle of understanding impervious to biblical challenge."[90] He sarcastically refers to the Pope's handling of the Cana pericope as "display[ing] some extraordinary exegetical ingenuity."[91] Strangely for one with Evangelical/Fundamentalist tendencies, he seems to side with that school of thought that suggests that the *Magnificat* "was not originally about Mary at all."[92] This stance can only be chalked up to a prior disposition to strip the New Testament of any significant Marian dimension.

In developing the topic of the virginal conception of the Lord, Wright scores those who seek "parallels in occurrences of partheno-genesis" as "totally misguided, since we are dealing with a miracle and not a freak of nature."[93] Like many other Fundamentalists, Wright's primary interest in this phenomenon is that it is a "sheer miracle."[94] He comes up with an alternative nomenclature for the virginal con-ception, speaking of it as Christ's "Spirit-conception."[95] At first blush, that carries some appeal until one realizes that its principal motive might be to marginalize Mary yet more, reducing her to nothing more than the biologically necessary receptacle for the God-Man's intra-uterine life. He cites with approval the Reverend Raymond Brown's conclusion on the historicity of the virginal conception of Jesus that "it is easier to explain the NT evidence by positing historical basis than by positing pure theological creation."[96]

He takes great pains to ensure that no one establish a linkage between pagan heroic births and that of Jesus Christ. He argues: "It is inconceivable that early Christians drew their ideas from pagan my-thology. . . . The view that pagan ideas had somehow been baptised into Judaism and hence found their way into Christianity is also very unlikely."[97] His position is important, given the fact that many of his theological fellow-travelers, on the contrary, declare that Christian Mariology can only be understood in connection with paganism.[98]

In a somewhat irenic spirit, Wright admits that *Redemptoris Mater*'s use of images of Mary as "the true believer, the perfect model for the Church . . . may have something to teach Protestant commen-tators, who have probably pitched the balance between the Mary of the nativity stories and the Mary of the later life of Jesus completely in reverse."[99] He is also willing to entertain the prospect that all the problems may not be exegetical but may have to be "thrown back on more fundamental disagreements of a theological nature (for example, on the relation between Christ and His Church, or on the place of human cooperation in the accomplishment of salvation). . . ."[100]

The Reverend David Crump's essay "The Virgin Birth in New Testament Theology" shares the basic orientation of Wright, especially in its failure to appreciate Mary as more than a mere receptacle or vehicle for the Incarnation:

> . . . we see that there are no grounds for the exaltation of Mary as the mother of Jesus. She is unique only in her election (Luke 1:28, 30), not in her person. The one text in all of Scripture which might offer some sort of basis for Mary's commemoration is Luke 1:48.
>
> . . . However, Mary's self-reflection is circumscribed by Jesus Himself within this very Gospel. On the first occasion (so far as we know) of someone's actually calling Mary "blessed" Jesus quickly cuts short such aggrandizement of His mother with a lesson on the value of true discipleship. . . .[101]

He concedes, however, that "if Mary was a 'blessed mother,' it was only because she became an obedient disciple of her Son; it had nothing to do with her virginity."[102] Of course, the Church has always held that the corrective issued by Our Lord should not be viewed as a slighting of Mary, precisely because she was in truth "an obedient disciple of her Son." Virginity, in and of itself, does not guarantee holiness of life.

The contribution of Tony Lane (a lecturer in Christian doctrine at London Bible College) to Wright's volume is valuable for its nuanced approach and for its consideration of the theology of the Church Fathers, which considered the virgin birth "to be both possible and fitting."[103] He has a good appreciation of patristic thinking and of the implications of certain doctrines. For instance, he warns against a too-facile demand for a virginal conception on the basis that it guarantees a sinless Child. Such ideas, he says, "are therefore vulnerable to the countercharge that we also need a sinless Mother to explain the sinless Child. This easily leads to the doctrine of Mary's immaculate conception."[104] He is also much impressed by Barth's grasp of the significance of the virgin birth, seeing "the distinctive point about [it]" consisting in "what is lacking." He goes on: "This is not primarily the sex act, nor even the sinful element in it, but rather *active* human participation" (emphasis in original). Lest the point be missed, he highlights the key aspect, namely, humanity's "merely receptive" stance before God.[105] This is, as we have seen before, a recurring and favorite theme.

Lane discusses the Eve-Mary connections developed by Irenaeus, holding that this effort was "probably the innocent search for parallels."[106] He keenly observes that "it does not require much imagination to see how this can be developed to the point where Mary is today seen as '*co-redemptrix*' with Christ and her *fiat* (Luke 1:38) is seen as a vital part of the salvation of humanity." He concludes: "Thus the virgin birth has served, in Roman Catholic theology, to pave the way to Mariology. Those who cannot accept the Mariological doctrine will naturally not consider this to be part of the genuine significance of the virgin birth."[107]

In reflecting on outcomes of an adherence to the virgin birth, he cites Barth's remark to the effect that "it might have been better for the Christian doctrine of marriage had there been no virgin birth." He argues, however, that "the virgin birth does not really exalt celibacy unless it is supplemented with the further doctrine of Mary's perpetual virginity." Very fairly, he concedes that "this doctrine is found already in the second century and was well established by the third century."[108] In a carefully presented summation of the topic, Lane says: "That the virgin birth is less central is supported by the paucity of reference to it in the New Testament and by the fact that very little theological use is made of it there. But 'less central' is not to be confused with 'unimportant.' Its inclusion in the creeds clearly implies that it was felt to be important. The Church should proclaim the virgin birth because it happened, because it is scriptural, and because it is a pointer to Christ and to His work."[109]

Dialogue is eminently possible and desirable with theologians who can produce such assessments.

In his chapter "Mary, Mother of God?" Wright mixes attempts at objectivity with slurs, perhaps not even intended or perceived. He

86 — Rev. Peter M. J. Stravinskas

opens with this sober evaluation: "It is tempting for Christians who seek to base all their beliefs on Scripture to attack the exaggerated reverence for Mary in Catholic Christianity at its weakest points. . . ." He continues: "But Mary's role in Catholic Christendom is by no means so vulnerable as to be shaken by fire directed at these sitting targets, nor so shallowly rooted as to be in danger of collapse if some of its more extravagant excrescences were cut back."[110]

In all likelihood, Wright would be surprised were someone to indicate that a Catholic might take offense at his reference to "extravagant excrescences" or to his mention on the same page of "galloping Marianism." What is clear, however, is that the author does not exhibit the naïveté of some Fundamentalists,[111] who proceed as though Catholic Mariology is nothing more than a pitiful house built on sand. He also demonstrates how deep-seated the difficulty is by observing how a most ancient title for Our Lady could have such partisan usage: "To be explicit, rarely if ever do Methodists, Presbyterians, Congregationalists and many Anglicans and Lutherans speak of Mary as 'mother of God.' " By contrast with these Protestant groups is the practice of Catholic and Orthodox Christianity: "The committed and fervent use of this title is, however, perhaps the most significant common element in the Marianism of Anglo-Catholicism, Orthodoxy and Roman Catholicism."[112] What is his problem (and that of the many he represents theologically)? Very simply, a concern lest "a Mariological term [be] the ultimate test of Christological orthodoxy," which would, in his estimation, "turn history on its head."[113] He finds "Mother of God" more irksome than *Theotokos* itself or even "God-bearer" because the latter formulations admit of "a certain singularity," whereas the former "has demonstrated its ability to extend its reach and to encompass the relationship between Mother and Son not only throughout His earthly life but even beyond it."[114] Of course, all of this misses the very human point made by Cantalamessa: "Once a mother, a mother forever."[115]

Wright also finds himself in concert with Barth, who wrote: "As Christians and theologians, we do not reject the description of Mary as the 'Mother of God,' but in spite of its being over-loaded by the so-called Mariology of the Roman Catholic Church, we affirm and approve of it as a legitimate expression of Christological truth. . . . The description of Mary as the 'Mother of God' was and is sensible, permissible and necessary as an auxiliary Christological proposition."[116]

Willing to make allowances for Barth's acceptance of the title and having agreed to the critique of "a master," he feels compelled to add his own *caveat:* "We note his [Barth's] earnest concern to confine the designation to a precise Christological focus." He does grant that Mariology emerged "out of Christological roots."[117] That statement of his, however, is intended more to demonstrate the subordination of Mariology to Christology (a valid enough point) than to establish a genuine linkage.

To justify his own skittishness regarding the use of "Mother of God" or even *Theotokos*, Wright makes much of the fact that St. Augustine and other Church Fathers never used the title. He also defends Nestorius's refusal of the title on the grounds that he thought "it risked making Mary herself divine."[118] Following up on that line of thought, Wright asks some probing questions: "What may properly be said of the Mother-Son relation beyond the incarnate life of the Son? Is an eternal intimacy between them to be asserted, on the basis of an (alleged) intimacy in their earthly relationship? Is the Son dependent still on His Mother, and does He still honor and revere her as a human son should his human mother? Can she influence Him the way a mother can her child? Is humanity taken up into the eternal Godhead not only in Christ, Who never ceases to be the God-Man, but also in Mary? Or does Scripture set certain bounds to the maternal role of Mary?"[119]

Maintaining that "Mother of God" suggests affirmative answers to the above questions, Wright concludes: "Everything that Christ did and was, does and is, must also be in some fashion connected with Mary, because, on this understanding, Christ is inseparable from His Mother."[120] He sums up the entire discussion: "And they [Evangelicals] are likely to remain properly nervous of calling Mary 'the Mother of God.' The 'privileges of Mary' grounded in her 'divine maternity' have in Catholic Tradition at times seemed to threaten even an expansion of the Trinity into a quaternity. Biblical Christians are right to be cautious and reserved."[121]

The reader will observe how petulant Wright becomes at this point, with his use of expressions in quotation marks, falling back on the discredited red herring of Mary's forming part of a divine "quaternity," and opposing "Catholic Tradition" to "biblical" Christianity.

In many ways, this most articulate of Evangelical theologians exemplifies the problem of his school of thought: When lucid discourse has run its course, one begins to fall back on name-calling and alarmism. Wright's total exasperation and incomprehension surface when he cites a passage from E. L. Mascall: "The Christian returning from his Communion can repeat in a totally new sense the words of Adam, 'The woman gave me and I did eat.' "[122] Wright refers to Mascall as "an eminent theologian" and can term the citation nothing less than "startling." With only a little exaggeration, he continues: "When Evangelical Christians have recovered their breath before statements such as this one, which are by no means the utterances of the lunatic fringes of Marianism, they will rightly be provoked to think harder — but still biblically — about the Mother of Christ."[123] What Wright cannot understand is that Mascall obviously sees not only the Eve-Mary parallel, but the Mary-Church connection as well, so that a Christian does indeed receive Holy Communion from the woman, Mary-Church. Not surprisingly does one discover a related insight from Irenaeus, namely, that one who cannot comprehend the birth of God from Mary cannot appreciate the Eucharist, either.[124]

Richard Bauckham's "The Origins and Growth of Western Mariology" is a good and objective overview of the topic. Quoting the Lateran synod of 649 on the perpetual virginity of Mary, he acknowledges that "thereafter the standard formula used was 'virginity before, in and after giving birth.' "[125] He agrees that taking up *Theotokos* into the language of theology "proved a spur to Marian devotion."[126] He offers a fair assessment of the trajectory following therefrom: "In Luke's narrative of the annunciation, Mary could be seen to have made the incarnation possible by her free consent to be the Mother of God's Son. Mary's obedience in faith comes to be seen as a lynch-pin on which the whole history of salvation hangs. Without her cooperation there would have been no incarnation and no redemption."[127]

What does Bauckham see as implications of the divine maternity? "The first is the idea that the human being who fulfilled such a role must have been, by God's grace, the most perfect of all human beings (other than Jesus Himself). The woman who was to give birth to the Son of God must have been endowed by God with perfect holiness."[128] "This principle," he says, "was already at work in the period of the Fathers."[129] "The second implication of Mary's 'divine maternity' may be usefully mentioned here, though it is not yet found explicitly in the Fathers. It is the notion that this role in salvation-history makes her co-redeemer, one who cooperated with God in the work of human redemption." He comments: "Here perhaps lay the greatest dangers of Mariological excess."[130]

On the matter of the invocation and mediation of saints, Bauckham calmly and confidently declares that "simple prayers to the saints began quite early in Christian history." He even offers a rationale for this practice: "Just as one would ask a fellow-Christian to pray for one, so it seemed natural, at the tomb of a martyr, for example, to ask the martyr in heaven to intercede for one." He then quotes the third-century *Sub Tuum Praesidium* as the earliest Marian prayer available.[131] He holds that "the developed cult of the saints was in danger of paganizing Christianity with a proliferation of figures of religious devotion." He goes on: "In the popularity of the mediation of Mary, there was doubtless also the desire for a heavenly mother-figure, to replace the mother goddesses of pagan religion and to balance the sometimes all too male, authoritarian images of God." In discussing the spiritual motherhood of Mary toward Christians, he explains that "it focuses attention not simply on Mary's role in the history of salvation in the past, but on her present role in heaven. . . . On this, the cult of Mary, with all its medieval extravagances, depended."[132]

Bauckham views the doctrine of the Assumption in the light of "the stories of Enoch and Elijah in the biblical tradition, and on later Jewish ideas about the assumption of other great figures of the bibli-

cal history, though the stories of Mary's assumption do not claim that
she escaped death, only that her body and soul have already been
reunited after death."[133]

Bauckham evinces high regard for St. Anselm, even speaking of
"three fine and very theological prayers to Mary" composed by the
saint.[134] He sees Anselm's Mariology as rather healthy: ". . . the cult of
Mary was not necessarily connected with a failure to grasp the significance of the incarnation. With Anselm it was quite the opposite." With
great insight and sensitivity, he analyzes the situation as follows:

> He [Anselm] shows how the growing medieval emphasis on
> the humanity of Christ stimulated interest in Mary His Mother:
> Jesus our human Brother makes us children of His human Mother.
> It is not too much to say that many medieval Christians felt that, in
> becoming brothers and sisters of Jesus, they were adopted into His
> human family. They became not only adopted children of Jesus'
> divine Father, but also children of His human Mother, and even in
> a sense, as the medieval interest in all the other close and distant
> relatives of Jesus (biblical and apocryphal) suggests, specially re-
> late to the rest of His human family. In the medieval imagination,
> the Holy Family on earth remained the Holy Family in heaven,
> uniquely associated with the divine Trinitarian "family" of Father
> and Son. Thus Mariology was part of an imaginative appropriation
> of the meaning of the incarnation as God's identification with us in
> our humanity through becoming one of a human family. This as-
> pect of Mariology seems to exist in tension with an emphasis, which
> we shall notice was also strong, on the human accessibility of Mary
> by contrast with the remoteness of her Son.[135]

This analysis is seconded by Greenacre as he links Mariological
development to the interest of the medievals (and Anselm in particular) in the sacred humanity of Christ.[136]

Knowing that some "biblical Christians" are horrified at the
notion of having Mary stand in the breach for a less-than-approach-
able Jesus, Bauckham very fairly reminds them "of that degenerate
form of Protestant atonement doctrine which contrasts the just Father

and the merciful Christ,"[137] so that it is clear that theological excesses are not the sole province of any one tradition.

Summing up his grand sweep of Mariological history and bringing it to the present moment, Bauckham provides this critique: "To the authorities and theologians of the last three decades, it has been left to moderate the admitted excesses of Marian devotion, to reinterpret the traditional dogmas to some extent, and to balance Mary's cooperation in the work of salvation with an emphasis on her role as a model of Christian faith and obedience. Indeed, the truth of the former is coming to be seen to lie wholly in the latter."[138]

In "Mary in Recent Catholic Theology," the Reverend Julian Charley offers a stern critique of Pope John Paul's *Redemptoris Mater*, especially its use of Scripture. While admitting that "it is unfair to lift out a number of sentences in this way as if they typified the whole document" and that "much of it contains good and helpful exegesis," he nonetheless complains that "the overall impression is a picture of Mary that bears little resemblance to what we find in the New Testament. It is far more than a mere difference of emphasis upon the New Testament materials. Mary is extolled to a height that conveys almost semidivine status, despite all the protestations to the contrary."[139] He highlights "three particular difficulties" for Evangelicals as they behold Mariology:

> First, Catholic interpretation of Scripture reads into the Marian texts far more than strict exegesis would allow. Subsequent developments are claimed to be implicit in the Scriptures. Secondly, it follows that the Marian dogmas, which are asserted to be God-given revelation, raise the whole question of the teaching authority of the Church. The magisterium claimed authority to verify these subsequent developments as a matter of faith. Finally, it is hard to envisage how the unique position and glory of Christ as Savior of the world can be maintained for ordinary believers, when the veneration of Mary is given such prominence. Despite all protestations to the contrary, to the effect that a true devotion to Mary points to Christ, the scales seem to be tipped the other way.[140]

In a dialogue with Charley, one could respond that (1) Protestant exegesis appears to find too little in the biblical text; (2) he is quite correct in locating one "difficulty" in the issue of authoritative teaching; and (3) given his proclivity and that of others of a similar mindset for phrases like, "despite all protestations to the contrary," one must ask: Is it not important to take people at their word, unless and until the opposite can be proven?

Charley does conclude his essay, however, on a somewhat irenic note: "Too often this whole area of theology and piety has been regarded by Protestants as forbidden territory. Progressive agreement on the New Testament data is an important milestone, such as the Catholic/Lutheran study claimed. In the words of J.M.R. Tillard, 'Mary is for all Christians the reminder of the profound meaning of their vocation.' And what could be more beneficial than that?"[141]

"Appreciating Mary Today" by Peter Toon is an interesting effort to find common ground on which to "appreciate Mary today." He ends his essay saying: "Having offered what is, I hope, a warm, scriptural appreciation of Mary, I still cannot escape the feeling that there is more to say than I have said and more than we Evangelical Protestants normally say, even in our most generous moods and compassionate moments." Waxing autobiographical, he writes: "I felt this, for example, recently in the retreat center called Maison Rivière in Sherbrooke, Québec. It is run by Roman Catholic Sisters, who are most caring and who have a deep devotion to the one they call 'our Lady.' I looked at books by a variety of authors on Mary, sat in the chapel, walked in the garden, and listened to the singing of the nuns, and as I did so, the question was deeply impressed on my mind: Am I missing something?"[142]

That event caused him to reflect yet more on his apparent, innate inability to say and do more in regard to Mary, against all logic, in his judgment:

> I must confess that I am deeply impressed by the way in which some of my favorite writers — Bernard, Francis de Sales, Anselm, and moderns like Hans Urs von Balthasar — have both

a profound love for our Lord and a special love for Mary. Take for example this extract from a prayer of Anselm:

> Surely Jesus, Son of God, and Mary His Mother, you both want, and it is only right, that whatever you love, we should love too. So, good Son, I ask you through the love you have for your Mother, that as she truly loves you and you her, you will grant that I may truly love her. Good Mother, I ask you by the love you have for your Son, that, as He truly loves you and you Him, you will grant that I may love Him truly.[143]

And then in a most wistful manner, he writes: "I ask myself: Why cannot I pray in this manner? Is there something lacking in my theological and spiritual appreciation that prevents me from regarding Mary in this way? And as yet I have found no satisfactory answers to my questions."[144] But he may have come upon one answer, albeit unwittingly, as he tendered this summary evaluation: "In the joyful celebration of Mary, we hear, confess, and believe the truth that God has taken the initiative for our salvation. Mary is a continuing witness to the divine initiative. She expressed '*sola gratia*,' 'by grace alone,' in a dynamic and compelling way."[145] Cranfield has highlighted this concept in a striking manner:

> The virginal conception attests the fact that God's redemption of His creation was by grace alone. The *sola* of *sola gratia* is seriously meant and must be seriously acknowledged. Our humanity, represented by Mary, here does nothing more than just accept — and even that acceptance is God's gracious gift. That is the real significance of the *kecharitomene* of Luke 1:28. Our fallen humanity's role is here strictly limited. The male sex, which has been characteristically the dominant, powerful, aggressive element of humanity, is altogether excluded from this action (and must we not see included in this exclusion all dominant, powerful, aggressive manifestations of female *homo sapiens* as well?). All our pride and self-reliant initiative set aside, our humanity's part is here simply to be made the receptacle of God's gift, to be

enabled to submit to be the object of God's mercy: *Ecce ancilla Domini: fiat mihi secundum verbum tuum.*[146]

It is significant that *Christian Research Journal* chose to publish a two-part series on "The Mary of Roman Catholicism," by Elliot Miller.[147] Like much of the newer Fundamentalist literature on Mariology, it seeks to avoid the shrill and polemical, except when certain neuralgic issues surface; it likewise takes *Redemptoris Mater* as a starting point for the discussion. Miller opens the discussion by suggesting that in the period immediately following Vatican Council II, theologians determined that ecumenism would call for "a more restrained posture on Mary."[148] Whether or not the decline in Marian devotion was primarily influenced by ecumenism is open to debate, but Miller's real point is that, with the accession of Pope John Paul II to the Chair of Peter, "Mary is now 'back in style,' "[149] which realization so distresses Miller that "the time has come for a Protestant response."[150] He says: "The purpose of this two-part series is to explain in detail why Protestants consider the Catholic Mary to be unhistorical and un-biblical. While this may appear anti-ecumenical, it is ultimately the opposite. For if issues and concerns such as those raised here are not openly addressed, dialogue and communion between Catholics and Protestants (at least Evangelicals) will inevitably reach an impasse."[151]

He should be taken at his word and be seen to have the precise attitude of *Unitatis Redintegratio*, which castigates a refusal to deal with substantive matters and "a false irenicism" that glosses over genuine differences.[152] Errors regarding history exist in the mind of the author; for example, that the Council of Chalcedon, rather than Ephesus, is responsible for the title of *Theotokos.*[153] Theologically, there is little ability to take nuances into account. This latter problem assumes major proportions when we study the works of Fundamentalists of even less theological acumen and less goodwill.

On Mary's perpetual virginity, Miller accepts the fact that by the Second Council of Constantinople (A.D. 553) that doctrine was in place, although he does try to justify a failure to accept the teaching with appeals to early Christian theologians such as Tertullian. He argues that the perpetual virginity of Mary "eventually won out, thanks to the rise of asceticism and monasticism."[154] While that is one possible explanation, another viewpoint — and the considered opinion of both the present writer and the Reverend Boniface Ramsey, O.P.[155] — maintains that asceticism and monasticism came about largely due to a belief in Mary's perpetual virginity. Miller fails to consider biblical and patristic data that support this doctrine, let alone the firm adherence of the Protestant Reformers themselves.

He provides a fairly accurate review of the history of the doctrine of the Immaculate Conception. And he is certainly to be commended for not falling into the usual Fundamentalist technique of declaring the dogma an "invention" of Pope Pius IX.[156] He does not, however, advance the discussion in any meaningful manner, relying on all the standard Fundamentalist objections and not adequately dealing with Catholic responses.

On Mary's Assumption, what is perhaps most interesting is Miller's obvious willingness to deal with Tradition, even if the history of it all does not impress him in the final analysis. He does contradict himself at one point, declaring that there is "no mention of the Assumption in either Scripture or Tradition,"[157] even though he has just spent a full page surveying patristic texts on that topic! He concludes the first installment with the honest statement that "the real issue in this disagreement between Catholic and Protestant theology is the oldest issue: authority." He goes on to say that no real Christian unity can occur from the Protestant side, so long as Catholics "recognize an authority equal to Holy Scripture."[158] Even allowing for his less-than-precise encapsulization of the problem, one must appreciate the truthfulness of the assertion.

In the second part, Miller deals with Mary's spiritual motherhood and her status as co-redemptrix and mediatrix. Not unexpectedly, he rejects all of these outright, even while noting that the latter two are surely not defined dogmas and, at best, are "subordinate, secondary, dependent."[159] He is clearly impressed by the argumentation of Frank Sheed in these areas, deeming him to be "among the foremost Catholic apologists" and referring to his presentation of these teachings as having "a disarming effect because there is a strong element of truth in it."[160] Ultimately, however, he refuses to be swayed. He ends the discussion by declaring that "the Church appears to have painted itself into a theological corner. In trying not to detract from Christ, its theologians have so defined the role of Mary as to make it entirely dispensable: Everything we need we get from Christ." He is thus caused to ask, "If that's the case, what is the point or importance of Mary's mediation?"[161] He would do well to reflect on the insight of his fellow-Evangelical Tony Lane (cited earlier), who realizes that just because a doctrine is not central or primary should not lead one to regard it as unimportant.[162] He maintains that Catholic piety on these approaches to Mary "illuminates the fact that the Church's in-adequate view of Christ's mediation is directly related to its distinc-tive doctrine of justification."[163] Again, he has hit upon a basic issue.

In treating the question of Marian veneration and invocation, he reduces all to the level of the ridiculous by falling back on the silly and common Fundamentalist argument that goes thus: "And even if they [Mary and the other saints] could hear some prayers, how could Mary hear *all* [emphasis in original] of the hundreds of thousands of prayers that undoubtedly are addressed to her every minute of the day?"[164] He is not being contentious; he simply is exhibiting the Fundamentalist inability to fathom an eternity de-void of human constraints.

Miller does concede that "it is regrettably true that some Protes-tants — no doubt in reaction to Catholic excesses — have almost forgotten Mary. This is no more the will of God than it would be for Christians to ignore Moses, John the Baptist, or the apostles Paul, Peter, and John." But he can bring himself to say no more than this: "In other words, while Mary is not exalted above every other created being in the Bible, she *is* [emphasis in original] one of the most im-portant figures found in it. 'Blessed among women,' she is the pre-eminent feminine model of faith and obedience — worthy of honor and admiration." But then comes the disclaimer: "Just as much can be gained from contemplating and imitating the life and faith of a Paul, Elijah, or Samuel, so with Mary."[165] He finishes with an appeal that "our Catholic brethren will fully embrace what God has made available to them through their great High Priest, [so that] they will no longer feel a need for prayer to Mary, or any other created be-ing."[166] Although *This Rock* magazine viewed the Miller series as an "attack on Mary,"[167] I would not completely concur, especially due to the rather restrained language and tone, in contrast to some of the tracts yet to be examined. Father Mateo does, however, engage Miller in helpful dialogue, leading him to consider additional data, particularly coming from biblical and Protestant sources.

An outgrowth of Miller's articles was his decision to produce a book on the topic with Kenneth Samples,[168] although consideration will only be given here to new approaches or material not substantially treated in the series of the *Christian Research Journal*. In the foreword, Norman Geisler remarks on the necessity of this work because, "in going beyond Scripture in her teachings about Mary, Roman Catholics have threatened Scripture as the sole authority for the faith."[169] He goes on to see in Catholic Mariology an assault on the Protestant doctrine of *solus Christus*, "Christ alone," which of course can be understood in an orthodox Catholic fashion. And in less-than-ecumenical style, he castigates the Catholic dogma of the Assumption as "little more than baptized paganism," even while acknowledging that "Mary has hardly been given her God-appointed respect in most Protestant circles as the 'favored one' of the Lord (Luke 1:28). While many Catholics overexalt Mary, many Protestants do not even see her correctly as the most blessed among women (Luke 1:42)."[170]

Miller and Samples introduce their venture by claiming that Pope John Paul II's presentation of Mary as the source of Christian unity "could be viewed as a paradox because his two predecessors, John XXIII and Paul VI, had deliberately de-emphasized Mary for the sake of promoting unity with their 'separated brethren.' "[171] They offer no evidence for the position, however. They also want to make it clear that when they speak of the "cult of the Virgin," as they do in the title, they are "using here the definition of 'cult' which indicates obsessive devotion to or veneration for a person, principle, or ideal."[172] Further on, they helpfully admit that "at the Second Council of Constantinople (A.D. 553), the Church used the phrase *ever-virgin* (Greek: *aeiparthenos*)" with reference to Mary.[173] In light of the earlier statements of Geisler, it is notable that they are willing to accept something beyond Scripture as a source of authority or at least as providing valid information.

Strangely, Miller and Samples want to ground Marian devotion in "pagan soil," all the while conceding that, by the time such development had occurred, "nobody considered themselves [sic] pagan."[174] Of course, this posture of theirs is somewhat necessary, since agreeing to an earlier-than-medieval date for this brings it all too close to the apostolic Church. At the same time, creating more distance forces the less-than-convincing conclusion to which they seem required to come.

Many inaccuracies demonstrate some lack of control over Catholic sources (e.g., the identification of Xavier Rynne as Xavier Range on page 142). As in Miller's earlier articles, there is no serious endeavor to engage the Protestant Reformers in their own Mariology; in fact, there seems to be a conscious decision to avoid such a possibility. In a positive vein, the two Fundamentalist theologians write that they "have avoided using the term *worship* in regard to Catholic devotion to Mary out of respect for the fact that ever since the Second Council of Nicaea (A.D. 787), the Catholic Church has officially taught that there are three degrees of devotion to be practiced by Christians," going on to list the categories as *latria, dulia,* and *hyperdulia*.[175] That does not stop them, however, from alleging that Mary has, regardless of that theological fact, "been worshipped by millions all over the world, especially in the Latin countries, and the Church has done very little to discourage it."[176]

Miller and Samples also seem to exhibit a peculiar fascination with Marian apparitions, devoting half the book to this matter. In a welcome nod toward dialogue, they allow the Reverend Mitchell Pacwa, S.J., the opportunity to respond to their volume, albeit in only a few pages and then with a rebuttal following. As an overall assessment, it is probably fair to say that the authors have generated more light than heat, and have made a good contribution to a Protestant reconsideration of Mariology and to ecumenical exchange.

"The Evangelical Mary" by the Reverend John de Satgé exhibits a very different and much less nervous attitude toward the Mother of the Lord than that of Miller and Samples; it is also much more scholarly.[177] His basic thesis may be summed up as follows: ". . . a proper relationship with our Lord's Mother safeguards the conditions essential for evangelical religion, the heart of which is to know Christ as your Savior."[178] Reflecting the style of St. Anselm, found so appealing to Toon, noted above,[179] De Satgé explains: "If evangelical religion is not to be merely metaphor or sentiment or coziness, it must say things about the Savior which mean that though He is fully human and our Brother, He is a great deal more besides. And those are the very things that lead us to call His Mother the Mother of God. The things which Catholics say about Mary safeguard the things which Evangelicals say about her Son."[180]

He explicitly rejects the position that, since Marian devotion can become distorted, it must be shunned completely: "Proper Marian devotion, on the contrary, opens up further reaches of experience to the searching and the succor of the Gospel."[181] Of course, in many ways, he does not represent the mainstream of Evangelical thought. Holding for nonnegotiable doctrines, he is not tied to a specific context: "My Protestantism is relative, not absolute. If evangelical religion can exist in another theological frame, I have no special concern for Protestant theology."[182] Putting an even finer point on it all, he declares: "Once the Catholic Church has reordered its house, the time for protest is past and the evangelical should go home as soon as may be. I believe that, in Marian matters at least, that point has been reached. The task before those who believe as I do is to help our fellow-heirs of the Reformation appreciate that which they had previously denied."[183]

An extraordinary statement, to be sure. But he goes yet further:

> It seems to me that our Lady stands in the life of her Son's people as a gracious hostess, making one free of large rooms which hitherto had been closed or dark and forbidding. She is supremely fitted to do this, being wholly one of us and wholly yielded to God, the Mother of God who through grace is the daughter of her Son.
>
> May evangelicals who rejoice in her Son's Gospel take their

proper share in calling her "blessed," who accepted so fully that
grace by which they live.[184]

Gottfried Maron's "Mary in Protestant Theology"[185] offers a very
careful and insightful overview of history and theology within the Reformed tradition in regard to Mary. He hits upon the dogmatic definition of the Immaculate Conception as something of a turning point, but
not one-sidedly. Rather, he argues that "since that time it has met with
both sharp repudiation and friendly agreement in close succession."[186]
Trying to find common ground, he honestly stakes out the potential
territory: "In the strict sense, *there cannot be a Protestant 'Mariology'*
as an independent topic, because Mary has not value in herself, and can
only be rightly seen in relation to her Son. A Protestant doctrine of
Mary must therefore first of all be Christologically based and centered."[187] That is certainly a legitimate point of departure and light-
years ahead of other types of discussions.

The Reverend J. A. Ross Mackenzie explores "Mary as an
Ecumenical Problem."[188] Echoing many of the sentiments of De
Satgé, Mackenzie reminds his Protestant brethren: "To be true to
the Reformation does not mean to echo in our day the legitimate
protests of Luther and Calvin and those who came after them. 'No
Popery' and 'No Mariolatry' may make popular battle cries, but
to be truly 'reformed' does not mean to be like the generals who
are always fighting the last war. It means to listen afresh to the
Word of God as a reality higher than any of our traditions, as that
which judges us and our past, and calls us into a new future. A re-
examination of the meaning of Mary may well form part of this
larger *metanoia* which Protestants, at their best, have always
sought."[189]

However, popular preachers of Evangelicalism or Fundamentalism, to whom we now turn our attention, have a very different idea
and agenda.

Popular Preaching and Apologetics

The Reverend Jimmy Swaggart summarizes his understanding
of the place of Mary in Christian life and doctrine in this manner:

In all the Early Church, no statement is reported of an apostle referring to Mary as the "Mother of God." There is no hint of prayers being offered to her, nor admonitions given to the saints to honor her beyond what the Bible suggests as normal deference.

Surely, if this great fabrication were valid, we would have at least a *word* [emphasis in original] from the Early Church concerning Mary. The silence is deafening![190]

One immediately notes the combativeness of the style but also the inability to appreciate history or development of doctrine, in even the most minimal way. His fellow-Evangelicals of a more professional bent would certainly wish to distance themselves from him. And one would have to ask for his definition of "Early Church" or else to question his grasp of exactly what was taught and believed in that period.

Perhaps the premier anti-Catholic writer of this century, Loraine Boettner, minces no words in his estimation of Catholicism's "worship" of Mary.[191] The following passage is worth quoting in full to give some flavor to the allegations, but also to demonstrate the kind of theological reflection that goes into such statements:

The Roman Catholic Church officially denies worshipping Mary. Officially she says that Mary is only a creature, highly exalted, but still a creature, in no way equal to God. Yet she tells us that Mary hears the prayers of millions and that she constantly gives attention to her followers throughout the world. It may well be that, as Rome says, she does not *intend* idolatry. But the intention and the practical working out of the system are two different things. We must insist that it is worship, and that therefore it is *idolatry* as practiced by millions of people who kneel before Mary's statues and pray and sing to her. Most of these people know nothing at all of the technical distinctions made by their theologians between adoration and worship. It certainly is idolatrous to give her the attributes of omnipresence and omniscience and to give her titles and functions which belong to God, as when

by the late Pope Pius XII, she was officially designated the "Queen
of Heaven," and "Queen of the World," and when prayers are
made to her for salvation [emphases in original].[192]

Once again we witness the coalescence of several characteristics: First, the refusal to take seriously the Church's insistence on the
worship of God alone; second, the apparent failure to understand
Catholic theological terminology (e.g., that "adoration" and "worship" are synonymous, and that the word he is searching for is "veneration"); third, the desire to put the worst face possible on Catholic
piety, along with a fertile and mischievous imagination that perceives
all Catholic laity as illiterate and superstitious peasants. Swaggart
who, in many ways, took up the mantle of Boettner some years later,
echoes the same type of talk: "Catholics are taught (although they
will deny this) that Mary is to be given worship equal to God — and
higher than that afforded the angels and saints. She is to be addressed
as 'My Mother.' Even casual observation of Catholics reveals that
both conversations and services bring forth more references to the
'Blessed Virgin' than to the three Persons of the Holy Trinity [em-
phasis in original]."[193]

Boettner continues in a more theological vein by arguing that
Catholic Mariology labors under an incorrect exegesis of John 19:
"The natural meaning of those words is that they were addressed to
Mary and to John as individuals, that from that time forward Mary
should look upon John, the beloved disciple, as her son, as the one
who in her life would take the place of Jesus, and that John should
assume the duties of a son and care for Mary with filial affection, that
he should comfort her in her loneliness, as a true son would. And that
Mary and John so understood those words is clear from the immediately following verse, which reads: 'And from that hour the disciple
took her into his own home' (vs. 27)."[194]

When Boettner (not unlike some Catholic theologians in other
periods) holds for "the natural meaning of those words," as he does
for various passages that refer to the Lord's "brothers and sisters" on
the very same page, he does not see that he cannot have it both ways.
If, indeed, "the natural meaning" of "brothers and sisters" is to be

taken, why would Christ entrust His Mother to someone outside the family when siblings were available?

But Swaggart does not even see as much as Boettner does in the Johannine passage, holding that it merely "talks about how Mary stood at the foot of the cross and observed with great sorrow the death of her Son — her Savior and our Savior — the Lord Jesus Christ."[195] And apparently no more than that.

Boettner continues his attack on what he calls "so much of the myth and legend [that] has [sic] been added to Mary's person" in Catholicism, alleging that the Church has turned Mary into a weak, submissive individual, without offering any proof for the charge. He maintains, however, that "when most mothers would have been in a state of collapse [on Calvary], Mary persisted through a long and agonizing ordeal which only the most valiant spirit could have endured."[196] Had he taken the trouble to read any number of Marian meditations done by the Church Fathers or various spiritual writers over the centuries, he would have learned that many others arrived at that evaluation before him. Of course, one might also ask if he or any who share his perspective would ever preach the encomium to Mary, which he wrote. But what is the real issue here?

Rome's purpose in exalting Mary and in thus rendering her weak and ineffectual, according to Boettner, is nothing less than malevolent: "The most important service rendered by this caricature of the Blessed Mary is that of maintaining the control of the Roman clergy over Roman Catholic women. For the promotion of the Church program, it is absolutely essential that they remain spineless, mindless, 'meek and mild,' as Mary is pictured, willing to accept dumbly a half-life in which their role is merely to bear [children] and to drudge."[197]

His diatribe is unabated: "In an alternative to her child-bearing services for the glory of Rome, the Catholic woman is offered the privilege of becoming a holy drudge within the Church, namely, a nun in a convent. Here again the Blessed Virgin plays a key role, that of recruiting officer." This makes sense, he says, since the nun is "almost a replica of the Blessed Virgin."[198] When all the nastiness is cleared away, one is left wondering if the author's concern is genuine

theological discourse or providing a veneer of theology to countenance bigotry.

Swaggart expends much energy denying to Mary the title "Mother
of God." He writes: "No, Mary is *not* the Mother of God. Mary was
the Mother of the human being, Jesus. Mary served a biological function that was necessary to bring about a unique situation" (emphasis
in original).[199] Aside from the fact that Swaggart's language suggests
rejection of the orthodox Christology defined at the Council of
Chalcedon in 451 (e.g., Jesus referred to as a "human being"),[200] he
also indulges in the frequent Fundamentalist technique of reducing
Mary's role in the Incarnation to that of sheer biology.[201] He goes on:
"The unbiblical worship of Mary has its perverted foundation in the
insupportable misnomer, 'Mother of God.' The *correct* scriptural description of Mary is the simple biblical expression, 'Mary, the Mother
of Jesus' [Acts 1:14]" (emphasis in original).[202] This surely appears
like a lack of familiarity with the history of Christian doctrine, whereby
Nestorius was condemned precisely for the same kind of argumentation offered by Swaggart.[203] Here he completely parts company with
the more intellectual branches of his religious family, like Hodge and
Wright.[204] He seals his discussion of the divine maternity thus: *"If
this* had *happened, we would have a quadrinity instead of the Trinity"* (emphasis in original), [205] reminiscent of Wright.[206] Of course,
Swaggart is once more indebted to Boettner in this regard, as he holds
that Catholic use of this title has made "Roman Catholics come to
look upon Mary as stronger, more mature, and more powerful than
Christ. To them, she becomes the source of His being and overshad-
ows Him."[207] Boone wastes little time on such a topic, noting that a
Fundamentalist would simply "denounce the very idea of Mother of
God as papist poppycock."[208]

In treating the doctrine of the Immaculate Conception, Swaggart
judges that "when the Catholic attributes the immaculate conception
to Mary, they [sic] are conferring divinity upon her by this claim." He
proceeds to give the definition of "worship" from Webster's Dictionary and concludes, with little basis in the dictionary definition, that
"the Catholic Church has, in effect, declared her divine and thus renders her worship that *should* be reserved only for deity" (emphasis in

original). Then switching gears, he declares: "By their [sic] constant reference to her, worship is afforded."[209] But he has not really touched on the Immaculate Conception, requiring him to pick up that theme again some pages later:

> By her own words Mary refuted the Catholic doctrine of the immaculate conception: "And my spirit hath rejoiced in God my Savior" (Luke 1:47).
>
> This statement totally discounts the theory of an immaculate conception and the Catholic contention that Mary was ever without sin. If God was her Savior, then she must have needed salvation, which presupposes some history of normal sin. *No Scripture even* hints *that Mary was sinless* [emphasis in original].[210]

This is rather standard fare among Fundamentalists regarding the Immaculate Conception, particularly the citation of the Lucan verse, with the attendant interpretation. Nowhere does Swaggart demonstrate the most remote knowledge of the Catholic notion of prevenient grace. He seems to think that the entire issue is sealed with the following statement: "This false cult of Mary worship is another effort by Satan who knows that one cannot completely accept Christ as long as one retains heretical concepts of Mary. Incidentally, Luke's statement in 1:28 quotes Gabriel's words as being, 'Blessed art thou *among* women.' It does not say, 'Blessed art thou *above* women' " (emphasis in original).[211]

It is worth noting that Swaggart obtains the above almost entirely from Boettner, without offering attribution.[212]

On the matter of Marian mediation, Swaggart states it succinctly: "There is no need for additional mediators or motivators." He puts an even sharper edge on it all: "We blaspheme when we imply that Jesus Christ would not satisfactorily accomplish His eternal job without persuasion from His earthly mother."[213] Sarcasm aside, it is clear that no concept of human mediation can be entertained. This discomfort with human mediation is likewise found in Swaggart's mentor, Boettner: "Despite all protestations to the contrary, the fact is that the worship, intercession, and devotions that are given to Mary obscure the glory of Christ and cause the Church to set forth a system of salvation in which human merit plays a decisive part. While asserting the deity of Christ, Rome nevertheless makes Him subservient to the Virgin, and dispenses salvation at a price through the agency of the priest. This most blessed of women, the Mother of Jesus, is thus made His chief rival and competitor for the loyalty and devotion of the human heart. In Romanism, Mary becomes the executive director of deity, the one through whom the prayers of the people are made effective."[214]

The institutional Church, the ministerial priesthood, and the Virgin Mary are all seen as threats to Christ, rather than associates of His (by His own free and sovereign will) in the work of the redemption of the human race.

The venom of Boettner comes to the fore on nearly every page. He refers to Catholicism's "full-fledged system of Mariolatry" and concludes his analysis thus: "How complete, then, is the falsehood of Romanism that gives primary worship and devotion to her [Mary]!"[215] He has special words of opprobrium reserved for St. Alphonsus Liguori, who, "more than any other person, has been responsible for promoting Mariolatry in the Roman Church, dethroning Christ and enthroning Mary in the hearts of the people." He goes on: "Yet instead of excommunicating him for his heresies, the Roman Church has canonized him as a saint and has published his book [*The Glories of Mary*] in many editions."[216]

When Boettner deals with prayer to Our Lady, he reduces everything to the level of the ludicrous: "There is nothing in the Bible to indicate that any departed human being, however good, has any further contact with affairs in this earth, or that he can hear so much as one prayer from earth. How, then, can a human being such as Mary hear the millions of Roman Catholics, in many different countries, praying in many different languages, all at the same time? Let any priest or layman try to converse with only three people at the same time and see how impossible that is for a human being to do. How impossible, how absurd, to impose on her the works which only God can do! Since Mary is not omnipotent nor omniscient, such prayers and worship are nothing less than idolatry — that is, the giving of divine honors to a creature."[217]

The shallowness should be apparent, for Boettner has hemmed in eternity with temporal limitations. In heaven there is no past, present, and future (these are human constructs); there is only the eternally present, the "now."[218]

The same author claims that "in Romanism probably ten times as much prayer is directed to [Mary] as to Christ." Where does he get that statistic? From the fact that "the most popular prayer ritual of Roman Catholics, the rosary, has ten prayers to Mary for each one directed to God." Boettner intends this analysis to be taken seriously as he winds up the treatment with great satisfaction: "Mary is unquestionably the chief object of prayer."[219]

Desiring to adhere to the scriptural data on Mary, Boettner charges that "Roman tradition has so altered the picture of Mary that the Mary found in the New Testament and the Mary found in the Roman Catholic Church are two different and conflicting persons."[220] Attempting to follow his own advice, he decides that Jesus "was ever careful to call Mary 'woman,' never 'Mother.' "[221] His literalism has made him conclude that because Mary is addressed by Jesus only twice in the Gospels and there called "woman," therefore, that is what the Lord must have called her all the time! His contemporary disciple Swaggart fails similarly in the opposite direction when he says that Mary was a "little teenaged maiden."[222] Where does the Bible say that Mary was "little" or "teenaged"? Of course, poetic expressions are quite valid and normally none of this matters, unless one is committed to taking the Scriptures literally and to the principle of adding not an iota to the received text.

Amazingly, Boettner summarizes the entire Marian discussion by declaring that "as evangelical Protestants we honor Mary." He also warns against "neglect[ing] to give Mary the distinguished and honored place which the Scripture itself accords her."[223] Having read his Marian musings, one can legitimately wonder what place he thinks that might be.

Some of the most vicious material on Mary, however, comes from the pen of Joseph Zacchello, who claims to have been a Catholic priest. Some of his work would be no more than humorous, were it not intended to be a serious contribution to the salvation of Catholics from pagan idolatry. One instance of this comes out in his calculations of the number of "Hail Mary's" recited in any given day by Catholics the world over. Using the Catholic population of his time, estimating that one "Hail Mary" takes at least ten seconds, assuming that half the world's Catholics say at least one "Hail Mary" a day, and allowing for even more through rosaries, litanies, etc., Zacchello decides that this "low estimate" would require Mary "to listen to 46,296 petitions every second of time from one end of the year to the other, or, in other words, have to listen to 46,296 petitions at one and the same time, simultaneously." All of this is supposed to challenge Catholics to consider if they still are willing to say that Mary "is only a creature" if she can pull off a feat such as described by Zacchello.[224]

Then, moving on to the use of Marian sacramentals, Zacchello asks: "How is it that priests meet with many and unforeseen accidents and deaths, even being shot to death in church while performing their priestly duties, if the wearing of the scapular of the Blessed Virgin, which all priests and good Catholics wear, is 'a badge of her special protection'? Why do good Catholics have accidents, some of them fatal? 'By their fruits you shall know them' — the rosary, the scapular."[225]

One final line of attack on Mary taken by Fundamentalist polemicists revolves around the allegation that Marian devotion is rooted in pagan goddess worship. Swaggart maintains that the source of Madonna-like images is to be found in Babylon:

> The image of mother and child had been a primary object of Babylonian worship for centuries before the birth of Christ. From Babylon, this spread to the ends of the earth. The original mother figure in this tableau was Semiramis — the personification of unbridled lust and sexual gratification. And once we start to study the worship practices of heathen nations, we find amazing similarities embraced over wide areas and through long periods of time.
>
> These nations all trace their common worship from Babylon

— before its dispersion in the days of Nimrod. *Thus, worship of Mary is Babylonian in origin. There is absolutely no suggestion of such worship in Scripture* [emphasis in original].[226]

As should be clear by this point, this insight is not the product of Swaggart's own mind; it comes, without attribution, from the work of Boettner.[227]

One fascinating angle highlighted by Ralph Woodrow is the purported reason for the holding at Ephesus in 431 of the ecumenical council that declared Mary *Theotokos*, "Mother of God." He explains: "At Ephesus? It was in this city that Diana had been worshipped as the goddess of virginity and motherhood from primitive times! She was said to represent the generative powers of nature and so was pictured with many breasts. A tower-shaped crown, a symbol of the tower of Babel, adorned her head."[228]

In case the connection is not immediately apparent, he continues: "When beliefs are held by a people for centuries, they are not easily forsaken. So Church leaders at Ephesus — as the falling away came — also reasoned that if people would be allowed to hold their ideas about a mother goddess, if this could be mixed into Christianity and the name Mary substituted, they could gain more converts."[229]

Woodrow also has an interesting theory on Marian iconography: "The Egyptian goddess of fertility, Isis, was represented as standing on the *crescent moon* [emphasis in original] with stars surrounding her head. In Roman Catholic churches all over Europe may be seen pictures of Mary exactly the same way! The accompanying illustration below (as seen in Catholic catechism booklets) pictures Mary with twelve stars circling her head and the crescent moon under her feet!"[230]

One wonders if Woodrow[231] would be willing to indict not only the Catholic Church on this score but also the author of the twelfth chapter of the Book of Revelation. Similarly, one must observe how adamant Barth was in arguing against attempts at establishing connections between paganism and Christianity:

It is not to be recommended that we should base our repudiation on the assertion that there has taken place here an irruption from the heathen sphere, an adoption of the idea, current in many non-Christian religions, of a more or less central and original female or mother deity. In dogmatics you can establish everything and nothing with parallels from the history of religions. The biblical witness to revelation itself worked with "heathen" ideas and germs of ideas; indeed it had to do so, as the world in which it aimed at getting a hearing was a "heathen" world. The assertion may be ever so correct in itself: but leave your Catholic opponent at peace in this respect. Such an assertion cannot possibly be a statement of Evangelical belief. It cannot, therefore, be a serious question for Catholicism.[232]

Some Summary Reflections

As we come to the end of this section, we find some interesting points of continuity and discontinuity between and among the three groups we have surveyed, namely, the original Protestant Reformers, their Fundamentalist descendants of a more serious theological bent, and their Fundamentalist heirs whose efforts are more directed to popularizations than true professional reflection.

Those in the first group took seriously Mary and her place in the Church. In point of fact, for the most part, they did not challenge Catholic Mariology, except in terms of piety or devotional practices. Luther, the most "Catholic" of them, appears to have accepted all the traditional Marian doctrines, including the as-yet-undefined teachings on the Immaculate Conception and Assumption. Certainly, they all adhered to Mary's perpetual virginity and all thought that Mary should be held in honor in Christian life and worship, as evidenced by their maintenance of several Marian feasts, prayers, and hymns. They were concerned with abolishing what they perceived to be the Marian excesses of the medieval Church and not with taking an axe to the entire tree. The primary source of irritation seems to have come from the Catholic invocation of Mary, with a view toward obtaining her intercession.

Theologians of the second group, beginning with the Fundamentalists of the last century, took a quantum leap away from the Marian doctrines of their Reformation fathers. The reason is hard to ascertain, except for the conjecture that many of those doctrines were already either marginalized or eliminated in the Reformation communities to which the Fundamentalists had belonged before their departures into new denominational settings. Some contemporary Fundamentalist theologians tend to exhibit a more open and tolerant attitude toward Mariology and are disposed to engage in intelligent theological discourse on the subject. Others are as adamantly opposed to it as were the original Fundamentalists, many of whom insist that they are simply being faithful to the Reformation tradition — all testimony to the contrary notwithstanding.

One might be tempted to ignore or denigrate the final gathering of Fundamentalists as being alternately theologically innocent and naïve or else virulent and vicious, if not a bit of both options. Not to consider them in a profound way would be to commit a colossal error, since they seem to be the very ones who are most in touch with "real people," both their own and Catholics whom they seek to attract to their "pure" version of Christianity. Their influence is pursued in much greater detail in Chapter 5.

Some common threads can be found among the various Protestants as they encounter Marian doctrine and devotion. The first stems from a theology of revelation, linked to an absolutist understanding of *sola Scriptura* (generally much more extreme than found in the first Reformers), which makes Mariology inadmissible, since it cannot be easily found in the written Word of God. The second views the Marian dimension as unacceptable because of the principle of *solus Christus*, again, more radically interpreted than in the Reformation era. A final concern surfaces over alleged pagan connections between Mariology and goddess worship — an association not drawn by Luther, Calvin, or Zwingli; for it reveals tremendous anxieties about appropriate ways to incorporate anthropological, historical, and cultural elements into the Christian Faith. At this level in particular, it is also interesting and important to observe how much these writers and preachers rely on each other, simply parroting whole sections of one another's works uncritically.

Endnotes

1. At the outset, it is important to note the following:

(a) Classical Fundamentalism in this work refers to that theological movement that has its roots in the nineteenth-century reaction to liberal Protestantism, beginning within Presbyterianism and hence possessing a Calvinist heritage. It quickly crossed denominational boundaries, sallying into any community where the basics of Christian doctrine were under fire.

(b) As already mentioned in Chapter 2 (note 62), the present research supports the assertion that "there is ultimately very little difference between the theological framework of Fundamentalists and Evangelicals" (Falwell, 6). Therefore, Evangelicalism is taken as a theological *locus* acceptable to Fundamentalism, congenial to it, and generally cited by Fundamentalist theologians with approval.

2. John Mark Reynolds, "Are Fundamentalists Really So Bad?" *New Oxford Review* (October 1992): 5.

3. Charles Lees, "Archbishop Gawlina, Martin Luther and the Magnificat," *Mary Today* (March/April 1965): 26.

4. David F. Wright, *Chosen by God: Mary in Evangelical Perspective* (London: Marshall Pickering, 1989), 123.

5. Thomas O'Meara, *Mary in Protestant and Catholic Theology* (New York: Sheed and Ward, 1965), 113.

6. William J. Cole, "Was Luther a Devotee of Mary?" *Marian Studies* (1970): 110.

7. Ibid., 116.

8. Ibid., 101-102.

9. Ibid., 182.

10. Ibid., 115.

11. Wright, 172.

12. Ibid., 169.

13. Cole, 121.

14. Ibid., 123.

15. Wright, 167.

16. Ibid., 178.

17. John H. Leith, ed., *Creeds of the Churches* (Louisville: John Knox Press, 1982), 78.

18. Ibid.

19. See Theodore G. Tappert, ed., *The Book of Concord* (Philadelphia: Fortress Press, 1981), 230f.

20. See "The Smalcald Articles," *Martin Luther's Basic Theological Writings*, ed. Timothy F. Lull (Minneapolis: Fortress Press, 1989), 508-509. This reading of Luther's position is reinforced by the contribution of Gerhard O. Forde to the Lutheran-Catholic Dialogue. See "Is the Invocation of Saints an Adiaphoron?" *The One Mediator, the Saints, and Mary*, eds. H. George Anderson, et al. (Minneapolis: Augsburg Fortress Press, 1992), 327-338.

21. Cole, 158.

22. Ibid., 172.

23. See ibid., 183-190.

24. See ibid., 133ff.

25. See ibid., 190-191.

26. Ibid., 193-194. The gist of these lines means that Christ Himself exalts His Mother above all creation.

27. Wright, 176.

28. Cole, 201.

    A summary view of Luther's Marian teaching by Eric W. Gritsch for the Lutheran-Catholic Dialogue would seem to give added validity to Cole's judgments. See "The Views of Luther and Lutheranism on the Veneration of Mary" in *The One Mediator, the Saints, and Mary*, eds. H. George Anderson, et al. (Minneapolis: Augsburg Fortress Press, 1992), 235-241.

29. Basilea Schlink, *Mary, the Mother of Jesus* (London: Marshall Pickering, 1986), 114-115.

30. Raniero Cantalamessa, *Mary, Mirror of the Church* (Collegeville, Minnesota: Liturgical Press, 1992), 131.

31. O'Meara, *Mary in Protestant and Catholic Theology*, 126.

32. See Williston Walker, *John Calvin: The Organiser of Reformed Protestantism* (New York: Schocken Books, 1969). It is significant, for example, that in this most comprehensive analysis

of Calvin's life and thought (nearly five hundred pages in length), only one reference is made to the Blessed Virgin, and not as a point of contention.

33. Wright, 173.

34. William J. Bouwsma, *John Calvin: A Sixteenth-Century Portrait* (New York: Oxford University Press, 1988), 275.

35. Wright, 130.

36. Ibid., 167.

37. Ibid., 179.

38. Ibid., 175.

39. O'Meara, *Mary in Protestant and Catholic Theology*, 133.

40. Bouwsma, 123.

41. Ibid.

42. See John T. McNeill, ed., *Calvin: Institutes of the Christian Religion* (Philadelphia: Westminster Press, 1960), 874-887.

43. Leith, 130.
    In reality, there is a great deal of nuance and restraint in these articles. Particularly interesting is that the ban on images is not absolute.

44. Ibid., 217.
    O'Meara makes the following observation: "The Calvinist creeds emphasize the Virgin Birth and Mary's conception and bearing of God's Son; they omit, in contrast to their Lutheran counterparts, reference to the perpetual virginity and Mary's sanctity. They reject any invocation of her" (136).

45. O'Meara, *Mary in Protestant and Catholic Theology*, 135.

46. Ibid., 167.

47. Ibid., 171.

48. Ibid., 170-171.

49. Ibid., 179.

50. Ibid., 178-179.

51. Ibid., 175.

52. B. A. Gerrish, *Reformers in Profile* (Philadelphia: Fortress Press, 1967), 133.

53. John T. McNeill, *The History and Character of Calvinism* (New York: Oxford University Press, 1954), 26.

54. Ibid., 84.

55. Here we are concerned with Anglicanism only, because other Reformation sects in England had, for all practical purposes, done away with Marian devotion altogether.

56. Wright, 172.

57. Ibid.

58. Ibid., 174.

59. Charles Miller, *Mary and the Eucharist: A Seventeenth-Century Anglican View* (Surrey, England: Ecumenical Society of the Blessed Virgin Mary, 1992), 2.

60. See Roger Greenacre, *I Sing of a Maiden* (Wallington, England: Ecumenical Society of the Blessed Virgin Mary, 1992).

61. Wright, 178.

62. Ibid., 161.

63. Ibid., 162.

64. O'Meara, *Mary in Protestant and Catholic Theology* 137.

65. Charles Hodge, *Systematic Theology* (Grand Rapids, Michigan: Eerdmans Publishing Co., 1973 [reprinted]) is still highly regarded by Fundamentalists and in use as a primary reference work in many Fundamentalist seminaries today (e.g., Reformed Theological Seminary in Jackson, Mississippi; Westminster Seminary in Philadelphia, the 1936 conservative offspring of Princeton Theological Seminary; Calvin Seminary in Grand Rapids, Michigan; Covenant Seminary in St. Louis). In a telephone conversation on April 14, 1992, the Reverend Kenneth Howell of Reformed Theological Seminary referred to Hodge as "*the* exemplar of nineteenth-century Calvinist orthodoxy at Princeton Theological Seminary." Similarly, it is listed as a classical reference work in R. C. Sproul's *Essential Truths of the Christian Faith* (Wheaton, Illinois: Tyndale House Publishers, 1992).

66. Hodge, 285.

67. Ibid.

68. Hodge, 286.

69. Particularly worthwhile in response to this kind of objection is the recent contribution of the Reverend Marcus Hodges, O.P., *Why Did St. Thomas Aquinas Reject the Doctrine of the Im-*

maculate Conception? (Wallington, England: Ecumenical Society of the Blessed Virgin Mary, 1992).

70. See Hodge, 288-290.

71. Ibid., 290.

72. Carl F. H. Henry, *Basic Christian Doctrines: Contemporary Evangelical Thought* (New York: Holt, Reinhart and Winston, 1962). Like Hodge's work, this is likewise an esteemed volume in contemporary Fundamentalist theological education.

73. Bruce, in Henry, 129.

74. James Barr, *Beyond Fundamentalism* (Philadelphia: Westminster Press, 1984), 166.

    Ignace de la Potterie, who wrote extensively on the personal role of Mary in our salvation (Daughter of Zion), sees the linkage between this doctrine and others. Thus he writes: "Three fundamental facts, historical facts, are inter-connected: the physical reality of the virginal conception, of the Incarnation; that of the miracles during public life; and that of the bodily resurrection of Christ. These are the pillars of the whole reality of the Word made Flesh. If doubt is cast on these facts, the ordinary faithful will find themselves confused, not knowing what they should believe" ("Exegesis: Awed and not Perplexed," *30 Days* [November 11, 1992]: 53).

75. It is interesting to note that even as current a work as that of Walter Martin's (*Essential Christianity: A Handbook of Basic Christian Doctrine* [Ventura, California: Regal Books, 1980]) deals with the matter in exactly the same manner.

76. H. Orton Wiley, *Introduction to Christian Theology* (Kansas City, Missouri: Beacon Hill Press, 1949), 145-146.

77. Ibid., 167.

78. Ibid., 103-104.

79. This work brings together the thought of many Evangelical theologians from various denominational affiliations but united in their Evangelical convictions, which seem to weigh in with greater depth and significance than their confessional adherence. Indeed, Wright asserts that "Bible-believing Evangelicals may have a distinctive contribution to make to Protestantism's

encounter with Catholic Christianity over Mary" (Wright, 9).
The Reverend John McHugh's review of *Chosen by God* says
that it "is a most serious book, severely critical of Catholic belief and practice, but never in a cheap, much less a polemic,
manner." That assessment makes him conclude that "this is the
book all Catholic members of the Society should read" (*Newsletter of the Ecumenical Society of the Blessed Virgin Mary*,
January 1991, 5).
80. Wright, 2.
81. Ibid., 8.
82. Ibid., 10.
83. Hans Urs Von Balthasar, *The Office of Peter and the Structure
    of the Church* (San Francisco: Ignatius Press, 1986), 197.
84. Wright, 11.
85. Ron Ferguson, *Chasing the Wild Goose: The Iona Community*
    (Glasgow: Collins, 1988), 193.
86. Wright, 12.
87. See Raymond E. Brown, et al., *Mary in the New Testament* (New
    York: Paulist Press, 1978).
88. Wright, 19.
89. Several Evangelical authors seem compelled to advert to this
    encyclical, perhaps because its more overt "biblicism" has placed
    them on the defensive. Paul Schrotenboer originally wrote his
    balanced and intelligent *Roman Catholicism: A Contemporary
    Evangelical Perspective* (Grand Rapids, Michigan: Baker Book
    House, 1992) in 1987; in the subsequent edition, he felt the
    need to devote an entire appendix to *Redemptoris Mater*, albeit
    assigning a negative judgment to its Mariology.
90. Wright, 25.
91. Ibid., 29.
92. Ibid., 35.
93. Ibid., 51.
94. Ibid., 57.
95. Ibid., 52.
96. Raymond E. Brown, *The Birth of the Messiah* (Garden City,
    New York: Doubleday and Co., Inc., 1977), 528.

97. Wright, 61-62.

98. See Section 2, below.

99. Wright, 24.

100. Ibid., 31.

101. David Crump, "The Virgin Birth in New Testament Theology,"
     in *Chosen by God: Mary in Evangelical Perspective*, ed. David
     F. Wright (London: Marshall Pickering, 1989), 84.
     Crump is associate pastor of a Christian Reformed church in
     Salt Lake City and teaches the New Testament at the Utah Insti-
     tute for Biblical Studies.

102. Ibid.

103. Tony Lane, "The Rationale and Significance of the Virgin Birth,"
     in *Chosen by God: Mary in Evangelical Perspective*, ed. David
     F. Wright (London: Marshall Pickering, 1989), 95.

104. Ibid., 106.

105. Ibid., 107.

106. Ibid., 110.

107. Ibid.

108. Ibid., 111.

109. Ibid., 117.

110. Wright, 120.

111. See those discussed in the following section.

112. Ibid., 121.

113. Ibid., 122.

114. Ibid., 131.

115. Cantalamessa, 56.

116. Karl Barth, *Church Dogmatics* I, 2 (Edinburgh: T. & T. Clark,
     1963), 138.

117. Wright, 131.

118. Wright, 130.

119. Ibid., 135-136.

120. Ibid., 136.

121. Ibid., 137.

122. E. L. Mascall, ed. *Mother of God* (London: Dacre Press, 1949),
     43.

123. Wright, 137.

An excellent and penetrating Lutheran treatment of the Mary-Church relationship is offered by the Reverend Mark E. Chapman in a paper he presented to the Ecumenical Society of the Blessed Virgin Mary in Washington, D.C., on October 2, 1993, entitled, "Sancta Maria, Sancta Ecclesia: A Lutheran Possibility for a Marian Ecclesiology."

124. Irenaeus, *Adversus Haereses* V, 2, 3.

125. Richard Bauckham, "The Origins and Growth of Western Mariology," in *Chosen by God: Mary in Evangelical Perspective*, ed. David F. Wright (London: Marshall Pickering, 1989), 143.

Bauckham is a Reader in the History of Christian Thought at the University of Manchester.

126. Ibid., 144.

127. Ibid., 145.

128. Ibid., 146. Note the erroneous reference to Jesus as a "human being," or human person. Orthodox Christology as defined by the ecumenical Councils of Nicaea, Ephesus, and Chalcedon professes Jesus Christ as a single divine *Person* (the Word, the second Person of the Trinity) possessing (from the moment of His Incarnation) two *natures*, human and divine. In philosophy, "nature" (also "essence" and "substance") refers to *what* something or someone is, whereas "person" refers to *who* someone is. The heterodoxy of much Fundamentalist discourse on the Person of Christ (see also n. 200, below) stems from Protestantism's general mistrust of philosophy.

129. Ibid.

130. Ibid.

131. Ibid., 147.

132. Ibid.

133. Ibid., 148.

134. Ibid., 149.

135. Ibid., 151.

136. Greenacre, 1.

137. Ibid., 156.

138. Ibid., 159.

139. Julian Charley, "Mary in Recent Catholic Theology," in *Chosen by God: Mary in Evangelical Perspective*, ed. David F. Wright (London: Marshall Pickering, 1989), 207.

140. Ibid., 213.

141. Ibid., 214.

142. Peter Toon, "Appreciating Mary Today," in *Chosen by God: Mary in Evangelical Perspective*, ed. David F. Wright (London: Marshall Pickering, 1989), 224.

143. Ibid., 225.

144. Ibid.

145. Ibid., 226.

146. C.E.B. Cranfield, "Some Reflections on the Subject of the Virgin Birth," *Scottish Journal of Theology* 41 (1988): 189.

147. Elliot Miller, "The Mary of Roman Catholicism," *Christian Research Journal* (Summer 1990): 9-15; (Fall 1990): 27-33.

148. Ibid., 9.

149. Ibid., 10.

150. Ibid.

151. Ibid.

152. *Unitatis Redintegratio*, n. 11, in Austin Flannery, *Vatican Council II: The Conciliar and Post-Conciliar Documents, rev. ed.* (Northport, New York: Costello Publishing Co, 1988), 462.

153. Miller, 11.

154. Ibid., 11-12.

155. Boniface Ramsey, "Matrimony: The Early Church," *The Catholic Answer*, September/October 1993, 42-43.

156. Nor does he do so with regard to the definition of the dogma of the Assumption by Pope Pius XII.

157. Miller, 15.

158. Ibid.

159. Ibid., 29.

160. Ibid., 30.

161. Ibid.

162. See n. 102.

163. Miller, 31.

164. Ibid., 33.

165. Ibid.
166. Ibid.
167. Subsequently published as a pamphlet: Father Mateo, *Refuting the Attack on Mary* (San Diego: Catholic Answers, 1993).
168. Elliot Miller and Kenneth Samples, *The Cult of the Virgin: Catholic Mariology and Apparitions* (Grand Rapids, Michigan: Baker Book House, 1992).
169. Ibid., 11.
170. Ibid., 12.
171. Ibid., 13.
172. Ibid.
173. Ibid., 24.
174. Ibid., 67.
175. Ibid., 70.
176. Ibid.
177. John de Satgé, "The Evangelical Mary," in *Mary's Place in Christian Dialogue*, ed. Alberic Stacpoole (Slough, England: St. Paul Publications, 1982), 25-33.
    While theologically Evangelical, De Satgé is not a Fundamentalist — a distinction already made at the outset of this study.
178. Ibid., 27.
179. See n. 141.
180. Ibid., 28.
181. Ibid.
182. Ibid., 31.
183. Ibid., 33.
184. Ibid.
185. Gottfried Maron, "Mary in Protestant Theology," in *Mary in the Churches*, eds. Hans Küng and Jurgen Moltmann (New York: Seabury Press, 1983), 40-47.
186. Ibid., 44.
187. Ibid., 46.
188. J. A. Ross Mackenzie, "Mary as an Ecumenical Problem," in *Mary's Place in Christian Dialogue*, ed. Alberic Stacpoole (Slough, England: St. Paul Publications, 1982), 34-41.
189. Ibid., 37.

190. Jimmy Swaggart, *Catholicism and Christianity* (Baton Rouge: Jimmy Swaggart Ministries, 1986), 114.

191. Patrick Madrid (in "Any Friend of God's Is a Friend of Mine," *This Rock* [September 1992], 12) evaluates his work thus: "While Boettner's pseudo-scholarly brand of anti-Catholicism is an embarrassment to better-educated Evangelicals, *Roman Catholicism* is widely used as a source for anti-Catholic arguments. His arguments must be reckoned with."

Significantly, Kenneth Samples and Dan Kistler, in their *Catholicism Bibliography* (San Juan Capistrano, California: Christian Research Institute, 1989), have this to say about Boettner, essentially giving credibility to Madrid's comments: "While this volume contains some valuable insights, overall it is biased and fails to accurately represent Catholicism."

It is worth observing that the CRI, open less than twenty years, has achieved a reputation as a voice of moderation and some theological sophistication within the Fundamentalist ambit.

192. Loraine Boettner, *Roman Catholicism* (Philadelphia: Presbyterian & Reformed Publishing Co., 1974), 149.

193. Swaggart, 96.

Samples and Kistler (see n. 190) say that Swaggart "lacks theological depth and accuracy."

194. Boettner, 156.

195. Swaggart, 108.

196. Boettner, 165.

197. Ibid.

198. Ibid.

199. Swaggart, 97.

200. M. L. Cozens, in *A Handbook of Heresies* (London: Sheed and Ward, 1974), makes the point thus: "Protestants, if asked to declare their belief in the Incarnation, nearly always define it in terms which prove their underlying Nestorianism. Even when they are willing to say that Jesus Christ is God, they shrink from the Catholic statement, that God was born of Mary; that God shed His blood for us on Calvary; that God died. Today as in the fifth century, in London as at Ephesus, the honor of Mary is the safe-

guard, the outpost of the adoration of her Son. To acknowledge the *Theotokos* is to believe in God the Son made man" (45).

For the same basic point, albeit made with more finesse and ecumenical sensitivity, see Yves Congar, *Christ, Our Lady and the Church* (Westminster, Maryland: Newman Press, 1957).

201. See nn. 71 and 100.

202. Swaggart, 101.

203. This becomes even more interesting when coupled with Swaggart's earlier references to Jesus as a "human being."

204. See nn. 65 and 111.

205. Swaggart, 102.

206. See n. 120.

207. Boettner, 134.

208. Kathleen C. Boone, *The Bible Tells Them So: The Discourse of Protestant Fundamentalism* (Albany, New York: State University of New York Press, 1989), 28.

209. Swaggart, 107.

210. Ibid., 111.

211. Ibid.

212. See Boettner, 137. Boettner also asserts that this doctrine places Mary "on a plane of absolute equality" with Christ (161).

213. Swaggart, 112.

214. Boettner, 146.

215. Ibid., 133.

216. Ibid., 140.

217. Ibid., 142.

218. The philosopher Peter Kreeft's explanation may be helpful: "We *think* of eternity as negative, as *excluding* time (for 'e-ternal' means, after all, '*not*-temporal'); but, in objective fact, God's eternity is positive and *includes* all times, for it can lack nothing actual, positive, and perfect that time contains. A remote parallel: the mind of an author contains, at once, all his characters and the events of his plot" (*A Summa of the* Summa: *The Essential Philosophical Passages of St. Thomas Aquinas'* Summa Theologica *Edited and Explained for Beginners* [San Francisco: Ignatius Press, 1990], 108, n. 71).

219. Boettner, 146.

220. Ibid., 149.

221. Ibid., 154.

222. Swaggart, 98.

223. Boettner, 155.

224. Joseph Zacchello, *Secrets of Romanism* (Neptune, New Jersey: Loizeaux Brothers, n.d.), 130.

   Interestingly, the same statistic is cited by Ralph Woodrow in *Babylon Mystery Religion* (Riverside, California: Ralph Woodrow Evangelistic Association, Inc., 1981), 24.

225. Ibid., 132.

226. Swaggart, 103-104.

227. Boettner, 136.

228. Woodrow, 17.

229. Ibid.

230. Ibid., 19.

231. One must regrettably observe that Woodrow's style and content are not unique to him and are, in fact, the norm in the anti-Catholic and anti-Marian proselytism of most Fundamentalists, as will be seen in Chapter 5.

232. Barth, 143.

   Put in a more popular mode, the staff members of the Christian Research Institute warn, in the context of a discussion of the pagan origins of Easter, against what they term "the genetic fallacy — i.e., the view that just because a belief or practice is of unfavorable origin it should automatically be discarded or condemned today." See *Should Christians Practice the Celebration of Easter?* (San Juan Capistrano, California: Christian Research Institute, 1993).

CHAPTER 4

The Psychology and Methods of Proselytism

Proselytism is not a new phenomenon in religion; but it certainly is raising concerns in the Catholic Church at every level from the local parish to regional groupings of bishops to entire episcopal conferences and the Holy See itself. *Webster's New Collegiate Dictionary* defines the verb "proselytize" as: "to induce someone to convert to one's faith; to recruit someone to join one's party, institution, or cause." Needless to say, the word always bears a negative connotation because it implies "sheep-stealing" and less-than-full knowledge and/or freedom on the part of the recipient of the campaign.[1]

The methods used in "proselytiz[ing] aggressively" include personal contact, house-to-house visitations, distribution of literature, preaching in public places, and massive recruitment campaigns.[2] Proselytism involves dishonest techniques and the luring away of persons from one creed to another. It is not sufficient, however, for the Catholic Church to decry the action as "poaching in a field to which it has perpetual and exclusive rights."[3] Rather, the Church must look at the religious, psychological, and sociopolitical factors involved. For example, many sociologists of religion question the strong influx of immigrants into sectarian groups. British research on this development has revealed that "the degree of felt deprivation increases sect membership."[4] In the same vein, Hans Mol has indicated "no surprise that foreign-born individuals are often over-represented in sects" like the Seventh Day Adventists, Church of God, or Jehovah's Witnesses. Why? Because "sects provide cohesive shelters" against meaninglessness and isolation.[5] The Catholic bishops of Guatemala

125

have pointed out that, while proselytism is directed at all levels of Latin American society, it aims primarily at the poorest and most marginalized.[6] In other words, we may often be witnessing something akin to a "rice-bowl Christian" commitment, instead of a genuine conversion experience,[7] especially among those on society's margins.

At the same time, one must admit that spiritual elements are surely operative in many instances, particularly among those who express "dissatisfaction with the Catholic Church or its teachings."[8] A reason common to both young and older dropouts was inadequate emphasis placed on the study and reading of the Bible. The Most Reverend Ricardo Ramírez, C.S.B., of Las Cruces (New Mexico) identified part of the reason Catholics are susceptible to Fundamentalist advances, saying that Catholic "people are sacramentalized, but not evangelized."[9] In many instances now it is not possible to presume even a basic catechetical foundation that supports and explains Catholic teaching.[10]

The failure of the Church, however, to impart her own teachings unambiguously cannot be blamed on the Fundamentalists, a point stressed by Pope John Paul II in his 1992 opening address to the bishops of Latin America. While not hesitating to refer to the proselytizers as "rapacious wolves," the Holy Father very bluntly locates the burden of responsibility on the shoulders of those who should exercise a shepherd's care: "As many of you have pointed out, the advance of the sects highlights a pastoral vacuum, often caused by a lack of formation, that leads to the undermining of Christian identity. A further effect is that large masses of Catholics who are without adequate religious attention — among other reasons because of a shortage of priests — are at the mercy of very active sectarian proselytizing campaigns. It may also happen, however, that the faithful do not find in pastoral agents that strong sense of God that such agents should be transmitting in their lives."[11]

José Valderrey has studied the question of proselytism from a Central American vantage point, but several of his conclusions apply equally to North America. He cites the following weaknesses in Roman Catholicism:

◆ Priestly and religious vocations have declined.

◆ The laity have scarcely been given any role to play in pastoral work.

◆ Clergy and religious are exposed to "abstract" training.

◆ It is due to "widespread popular piety that Protestant sects proliferate successfully."

◆ "Attention to sensitivity or emotion" is not sufficient.

◆ "Deep splits within the Catholic Church" have surfaced, especially in the wake of Vatican II.[12]

The Reverend Juan Diaz Vilar summarizes the state of the question:

> Proselytism is offensive for these reasons:
>
> Proselytism impedes the road to ecumenism and unity and makes it difficult to achieve these goals.
>
> Proselytism attempts to divide and further fragment Christian unity. Furthermore, proselytism not only separates but rejects: Those who do not belong to the sect are considered to be evil, and only the members of the sect can attain salvation.
>
> Proselytism wants to impose itself, not to engage in constructive dialogue. It does not respect members but instead puts pressure on them. It is aggressive, generally criticizing rather than preaching.
>
> Therefore, in the final analysis, the practice of proselytism is in complete opposition to the wish of Jesus for unity. . . .[13]

Is Proselytism Successful?

The success of proselytizing efforts is made evident by the urgent tone of the Latin American bishops, who in 1979 counted the "invasion of sects" among the most urgent problems of the day, together with the displacement of population, offenses against human rights and dignity, and society's relapse into paganism.[14]

The problem has also hit Africa where, we are told, "everywhere on the continent the proliferation of sects is of great concern."[15] This is also a growing problem in the countries of the former Soviet Union.

During his 1993 pastoral visit to Lithuania, Pope John Paul II "took particular exception to Evangelical Protestant movements that the Vatican calls sects luring young people away from the Catholic Church." He went on to argue that those who do become involved with sects "leave themselves open to great disillusionment."[16]

A 1988 Gallup study estimated that there are fifteen million inactive Catholics in the United States, with Catholic defections "50% higher than that of Protestant denominations."[17] This lack of practice makes these individuals more likely to defect to a Fundamentalist sect. The success of proselytism can be seen in the growing number of Fundamentalist churches and the size of their congregations. The Willow Creek Church claims as members 12,000 former Catholics of a total membership of 25,000[18]; similarly, the Calvary Church of Santa Ana estimates that 30 to 50 percent of its members between the ages of 18 and 35 are former Catholics.[19] The emphasis on "What do I get out of this church?" when choosing among competing sects is important for Evangelicals,[20] which causes an attraction for disenfranchised Catholics who see the Catholic Church as irrelevant in daily life. The success is closely linked to a portion of the strategy that emphasizes heavy doses of popular, emotionally satisfying religious experiences, as Pope John Paul II noted in his 1990 message for World Migration Day.[21]

Where do former Catholics go when they leave the Church in the United States? "Thirty-nine percent say they have now no religious affiliation"; 23 percent are now "moderate Protestant," with 9 percent belonging to "liberal Protestant" communities, another 9 percent having joined "conservative Protestant" denominations, and a full 17 percent belonging "to groups described as 'other.' "[22] But this is not unique to this country, although the hemorrhaging of Hispanic Catholics is especially severe and well-known,[23] as at least a fifth of the Catholic population of Latin America is supposed to have switched to some kind of Protestantism in the past generation, with as many as one million Catholics in the Philippines doing the same.[24] David Stoll reports: "In Brazil, as long ago as 1973 the newspaper *Estado São Paolo* argued that there were more 'real' Protestants in the country (ten million) than 'real' Catholics. The thirteen thousand Catholic priests in Brazil were said to be outnumbered by seventeen thousand ordained Protestant pastors and thirteen thousand non-ordained ones."[25]

Several "traditionally Catholic countries" in the Caribbean are also experiencing significant growth in Evangelical adherents: "the Dominican Republic (in the 2 to 7 percent range), Haiti (15 to 20 percent), and Puerto Rico (7 to 30 percent)."[26]

Particularly vulnerable targets, however, are immigrants, as already noted. Hence, Finke and Stark assert that "sects arise to satisfy the needs of those less fortunate in pursuit of the world's goods."[27] Trabold, in an unpublished master's thesis, observes that a special difficulty for Caribbean immigrants lay in the fact that great numbers of them arrived without their clergy, as "sheep without a shepherd," frequently ready to accept spiritual nourishment from almost any source.[28] Because of the necessity of an ordained ministry in Catholicism (preceded by extensive schooling),[29] this has been a recurring problem for Catholic immigrants throughout the ages when they have not been accompanied by their priests; this was a major cause of heavy losses among certain ethnic groups in the last century or among the pioneers who trekked westward and remained cut off from the Church's sacramental life over a prolonged period of time. One can easily be a Baptist without a minister; being a Catholic without a priest is an altogether different predicament.[30]

The Southern Baptists, who have no real tradition for ethnically oriented work, have come to see that their converts "do not have to be 'Americanized' to become Christians."[31] This insight assuredly contributes to the fact that "today Southern Baptists are probably five to ten years ahead of most other denominations in perceiving the true spiritual needs of Americans who are unmelted."[32] Conversely, in American Catholicism since Vatican Council II, one often finds that "our parishes are more interested in *Americanization* . . . than *evangelization*. There also exists a very strong 'anti-national parish' . . . phobia. This phobia affects the majority of our priests, I believe. It is only beginning to change as we see the majority of our non-English-speaking peoples joining the various non-Catholic churches."[33]

Wagner maintains that "new church-planting is the single most

effective evangelistic methodology known under heaven."[34] Procedures are carefully planned: "A high profile without putting up sectarian barriers was the ideal in these ventures, at least at the start. In
an Assemblies of God text on how to plant churches, evangelist David
Godwin stressed the importance of keeping the crusade as open as
possible to newcomers. For example, a good way to start out was by
reciting core doctrines shared with the Catholic Church; campaign-
ing against the Catholic clergy was to be avoided at all costs. The
model evangelist, according to Godwin, even tried to avoid prema-
ture classification as a new religious group. Construction of a church
building was to be put off as long as possible, for up to several years,
to avoid erecting walls that would discourage people from wandering
into the festive meetings."[35]

Ironically enough, not infrequently one encounters resistance to
this notion of "church-planting" among the very Catholics most ide-
ally situated to perform works of charity and evangelization in tan-
dem:

> I find your interest in the pastoral care of our new immi-
> grants most encouraging. Our Protestant brothers and sisters do
> all that they possibly can to encourage refugees to become mem-
> bers of their churches. This interest begins right in the camps in
> Thailand, the Philippines, Indonesia, etc. Anyone who shows an
> interest in the Seventh Day Adventist church would be directed
> to a community of Seventh Day Adventist people. Our Catholic
> agencies are more interested in social services than in evangeli-
> zation. In fact, many offices of the USCC [United States Catho-
> lic Conference] would bend over backwards to make certain new
> immigrants are not connected with churches in a pastoral sense.
> Perhaps the idea is always to appear "professional" and not re-
> peat the mistakes of *some*, and only some, of our separated brothers
> and sisters in Christ.[36]

Pope John Paul II seems to concur: "The new religious movements base their recruiting efforts on two weak points: precarious-
ness and uncertainty. That is what they use in their strategy for mak-

ing overtures. By offering [migrants] care and a number of indispensable services, they seek to make the migrant abandon the faith which he or she professes and join a new religious group. Presenting themselves as the only ones who possess the truth, they assert that the religion which the migrants belong to is false and demand that the migrant make a sharp and immediate change of course. No one is blind to the fact that this constitutes real and true moral aggression, which is difficult to shake off in a polite fashion, since their ardor and insistence are harassing."

Yet again, he says: "The Catholic migrant, whatever his or her destination, is an integral part of the local Church. He or she is an effective member of that Church, with all the consequent rights and duties. The welcome which the local Church accords these people is a witness and a proof of her catholicity. In the Church there are no strangers. . . . The community must lay claim to them as members, not so much in order to assert its rights but rather to offer a service to the humble."[37]

Fundamentalist sects also succeed because they offer "an attractive coherent package." Furthermore, they "have considerable financial resources at their disposal, including radio and television programs. . . . [Some] have built enormous places of worship capable of holding 25,000 people."[38]

The question of finances requires a bit more attention. Where do the sects get their money? Although most of these denominations subscribe to some sort of tithing policy, there may be more than meets the eye. Stoll asserts that "much of the money, planning, and organization behind their growth came from the behemoth from the north," that is, the United States, leading him to say that "inevitably, the question arose of whether North American missionaries were serving their country rather than Christ."[39] Just what is his point? It has been alleged, with varying degrees of assuredness, that much of the Fundamentalist effort in Latin America was coordinated by American government agents to counterpoise some of the more extreme, Marxist-inspired elements of Catholic liberation theology.[40] Indeed, "the Brazilian bishops sent the Vatican a report suggesting that behind sectarian infiltration in Latin America stood the Central Intelligence Agency."[41] How much of that can be proven remains to be seen.

Yet another group to consider consists of those Catholics who have been "approached by alternative [i.e., non-Catholic] groups for proselytism." Some of the principal findings of the then-Reverend Roberto Gonzalez and Michael LaValle include:

♦ [Fully] 78.8% of the sample population have, in fact, been approached.

♦ English-speakers, females and those in upper-income brackets were approached more frequently than Spanish-speakers, males and those in lower-income [groups].

♦ Among those who had joined a sect at one time, Hondurans, Guatemalans, Peruvians and Puerto Ricans were more likely to have been members than Cubans, Mexicans, Ecuadorans and Spaniards. English-speakers more than Spanish-speakers; males more than females; and highest- and lowest-income people more than those from the middle seem to have dallied with such associations.

♦ The divorced and widowed were also more likely to have been involved with the sects than those married in the Church.

♦ About 37% of the survey participants have a favorable attitude toward the proselytizers, especially among those born in Ecuador and Puerto Rico.[42]

These data are important, of course, because they provide information about the persons who are of most interest to the proselytizers and who are the most willing subjects, and thus most in need of pastoral care to guard against such efforts.

What is the "holding power" of these groups? The situation is too recent to have hard data available in most cases. Some information exists on the results of Mormon missionary activity. Roy Rivenburg says: "The most explosive gains are abroad — in Africa and South America. Almost half of the church's 8 million followers live outside North America. Many drop out, however, within five years. Sociologists report that about 40 percent of members are inactive."[43] Do these people return to their former religious homes, or do they remain permanently unaffiliated? Once again, only speculation is possible at this stage of the development.[44]

What Are the Strategies of the Proselytizers?

The methods of proselytism are many: preaching in public places; distribution of literature on the streets; house-to-house canvassing with literature and an invitation to attend services; visitation of the sick, including praying with and for them; and crusades at the local, regional, and national levels.[45] Interestingly, most of these approaches are not unknown to Catholicism and have been used with varying degrees of success in our history.[46] Just as important as the method, however, is the content, which emphasizes:

◆ the vision of a lost world without Christ, bolstered by ample, memorized biblical texts;

◆ the imminent Second Coming and need for preparation, entailing conversion and acceptance of Jesus as one's personal Savior;

◆ an invitation to the audience to accept Jesus, along with the solicitation of names and addresses of participants, and immediate follow-up;

◆ personal witness talks given in simple, concrete language in a style which is warm, welcoming, and emotional.[47]

Beneath the surface, one finds elements that are less attractive:

◆ biblical fundamentalism and literalism;

◆ Manichean dualism (sharp opposition of matter and spirit);

◆ apocalyptic pre-millennialism;

◆ individualistic morality;

◆ an almost exclusively "other-worldly" spirituality;

◆ social non-involvement.[48]

The last characteristic might be found in Latin American Fundamentalism, but would surely not be so in the United States. It is important to expose these disagreeable aspects of Fundamentalism in a manner that is clear, convincing, concrete, and charitable, as do the Guatemalan bishops: "They offer room for active participation of their members; they employ all the technical means of communication; they manipulate biblical texts; they utilize group dynamics and psychological techniques of brainwashing."[49]

One biblical scholar has remarked that Fundamentalism employs a "static, non-developmental, non-contextual approach to life and Scriptures. It puts the Word before life." However, he goes so far as to declare that there are "no ultimate answers,"[50] the very hook used with such consistent positive results by the Fundamentalist sects who believe and proudly assert that there *are* absolutes, and they are more than willing to impart them.

As can be readily imagined, massive Evangelistic endeavors must be well orchestrated and demand the involvement of many — and not only in an isolated cultic or liturgical framework. Once the sects obtain their converts, they give them something to do. Wagner has suggested that "denominations that require college and seminary for ordination will not be able to move ahead rapidly in planting churches in most ethnic groups."[51]

This need not be so if personnel are utilized in such a way as to realize the Vatican II principle of "a diversity of members and functions."[52] Where a revival is taking place in Latin America, for instance, it is happening because Catholics — and youth, in particular — have been turned "outward to the world."[53] They have been made conscious of their Christian obligations and have accepted them. Is it hard to envision not a few of these apostolically-minded youth committing themselves as clergy and religious? Over the long haul, this style of evangelization and catechesis should prove far longer-lasting. In all likelihood, this is what Pope John Paul II has in mind when he writes: "Other reasons which can lead to an acceptance of the tenets of these new religious movements are the poor consistency with which many of the baptized live out their Christian commitment and also their desire for a more intense religious life which they hope to experience within a certain sect. This arises when the community which they attend is inactive."[54]

A key quality essential for one engaged in proselytism is confidence. Stoll recounts a conversation he had with one such person:

> "Latin America is a Catholic region," church-growth planner Jim Montgomery of O.C. (for Overseas Crusades) Ministries conceded, "but there's no reason to assume that this need always be so. It could become an Evangelical region at some point in time. I believe that if . . . Guatemala becomes the first predominantly Evangelical nation in Latin America, it will have a domino effect.
>
> "Of course, our emphasis is not political or to destroy the Catholic Church," Montgomery continued, "but we have succeeded in gaining their attention. Many negative things are being written, and the Evangelicals are accused of trying to take over the country. Unfortunately, the battle lines are drawn, although it's not our objective to be at war with the Catholic Church." Montgomery was the author of *Discipling a Whole Nation* (DAWN or *Amanecer* in Spanish), a church-growth scheme tested in the Philippines before being taken to Central America.[55]

An interesting irony in all this is that ecumenism can be seen as at least partially responsible for Fundamentalist incursions, particularly in Latin America. Stoll explains it this way: "Loyal Catholics who had never felt free to associate with Evangelicals were now visiting their services and finding out what they believed; some became converts. The Catholic Church wished to interpret ecumenism like a 'comity' agreement between two missions, in which each confines itself to a certain sphere to avoid trespassing on the work of the others. In exchange for being tolerated, Evangelicals were to refrain from further poaching."[56]

Obviously, that did not happen. Beyond that, the process of proselytism often gets ugly, as Bishop Ramírez describes it:

> It is unfortunate that recruiting approaches by Protestant groups to our people often include attacks on elements of our Faith and traditions. Bishops are concerned that even mainline Protestant groups are actively recruiting members to their churches

from among Hispanic Catholics. Neither the proselytism that is going on nor the attitude of some of our bishops creates a healthy climate for dialogue nor for united efforts and collaboration in issues of common concern. . . .

One bishop explained to me that perhaps there are different ways of looking at ecumenism. For us Catholics, he explained, ecumenism means dialogue; for some of our Protestant brothers and sisters, it means permission to recruit from among Hispanics.[57]

The bishops of Latin America have also taken cognizance of considerations related to ecumenism and religious pluralism. "A false interpretation of religious pluralism has permitted the propagation of erroneous doctrines" concerning faith and morals, causing much confusion among the People of God.[58]

Sects will prosper to the extent that their adherents are prepared "to listen, to repeat, but not to think." They are "very accessible upon coming into them, but it is very difficult to leave them."[59] This is certainly a harsh evaluation, but unfortunately accurate. Richard Yao, the founder of Fundamentalists Anonymous, alleges that "involvement in Fundamentalist churches is a threat to mental health."[60] Although this may be true in some or even many cases, Catholics ought not be too quick in getting on to what is often a secularistic bandwagon of critics who might be just as negative in their estimation of Catholicism, especially as that is filtered through the lenses of fallen-away Catholics or former clergy and religious.

The Holy See's document on proselytism summarizes the attraction of the sects in their venturing forth into these areas:

◆ providing a sense of community;
◆ giving theoretical and practical answers;
◆ forming cultural identity;
◆ recognizing individuals and opportunities for participation and involvement;
◆ stressing transcendence;

◆ rendering spiritual guidance and strong leadership;
◆ conveying a clear vision.[61]

Not unrelated were the findings of Dean Kelley: "It is ironic that religious groups which persist in such 'unreasonable' and 'unsociable' behavior should be flourishing, while more 'reasonable' and 'sociable' bodies are not. It is not only ironic, but it suggests that our understanding of what causes a religious group to flourish is inadequate. Some dynamic seems to be at work which contradicts prevailing expectations."[62]

He spells out the dynamic in three simple propositions: "Strong organizations are strict . . . . the stricter, the stronger."[63] Further, "a strong organization that loses its strictness will also lose its strength."[64] Finally, "strictness tends to deteriorate into leniency, which results in social weakness in place of strength. . . . Traits of strictness are harder to maintain in an organization than traits of leniency."[65]

The more recent research of Finke and Stark confirms Kelley's assertions: "Religious organizations are stronger to the degree that they impose significant costs in terms of sacrifice and even stigma upon their members."[66] Directly echoing Kelley, they say: "People tend to value religion according to how much it costs — and because 'reasonable' and 'sociable' religion costs little, it is not valued greatly. It seems appropriate here to explore this thesis in greater depth, invoking recent work on the micro-economies of religious commitment."[67]

Finally, "the demanding sects speak of 'conversions,' 'being born again,' and 'submitting their lives to the Lord.' The less demanding churches refer to affiliations that are seldom life-altering events. Sectarian members are either in or out; they must follow the demands of the group or withdraw. The 'seductive middle-ground' is lost."[68]

In short, the winning combination for conversions to sects is: basic human needs for community and social exchange; heavy doses of popular, emotionally satisfying religious experiences[69]; religious ignorance[70]; and skilled proselytism.[71] The formula is quite simple and presents the Catholic community with a ready-made program of action, both in anticipation and in response.[72]

Distinguishing Evangelization from Proselytism

"Jesus Christ, the Good News of God, was the very first and the greatest evangelizer," wrote Pope Paul VI.[73] "The Church exists in order to evangelize," says the same Pontiff,[74] merely reflecting the self-understanding of the Church down the ages and underscored by Vatican II's *Ad Gentes*: "The Church on earth is by its very nature missionary."[75] But what is involved in the process of evangelization? Perhaps a good beginning would note what is not involved, namely, coercion. Pope John Paul II has stressed the need to safeguard freedom of conscience and immunity from all pressure, respecting the dignity and freedom of all to whom the offer of salvation is made.[76]

In a more positive vein, the bishops of Texas teased out some of the significance of evangelization thus:

> Evangelization implies outreach to those who do not yet know and love Jesus Christ or realize how much He knows and loves them. It implies enthusiasm and apostolic zeal in the proclamation of the Gospel, a passionate desire to help people fall in love with Jesus and commit themselves to Him forever.
>
> More than a program, evangelization is an attitude. It is a mentality of sharing, of inviting, of welcoming people into the joy of communion with Jesus Christ.[77]

Who should be a part of the Church's work of evangelization? The obvious answer is: "everyone," but certain individuals and techniques suggest themselves in a particular manner. The family, writes Pope Paul VI, should be "the evangelizer of many other families, and of the neighborhood of which it forms a part."[78] He also envisioned a special place for small ecclesial communities "which come together within the Church in order to unite themselves to the Church and to cause the Church to grow."[79] The peer-dimension and personalism of these two avenues have been tapped with great success by the proselytizers. And what should such "evangelization teams" do? "[Their] main responsibility will be to reach out to the unchurched, to welcome newcomers, to invite back to the Church those who, for whatever reason, have become alienated from it, and to promote the growth and exten-

sion of Church into the homes and neighborhoods of the parish. Such
teams, in cooperation with pastors and parish pastoral councils, will
also help those already Catholic to develop a love relationship with
Jesus Christ through retreats and conferences on mission-conscious-
ness. These parish evangelization teams will engage in home visitation
and will regularly bring Catholic neighbors together to build community among one another and to pray for one another."[80]

An unspoken but valid assumption in all this, of course, is that if
Catholics are evangelizers they will not fall into the ranks of the proselytized.

The reader will likewise see that the primary emphasis is on
dealing with those who are already members of the Church. Why so?
The Reverend Avery Dulles reminds: "A second evangelization, or
re-evangelization, is required in areas where large groups of Christians have lost a living sense of the Faith and no longer consider
themselves members of the Church."[81] The Most Reverend Karl
Lehmann, as both a theologian and a pastor of souls, offers the following observations:

> The clearly necessary second evangelization must rekindle
> the original freshness and timeless novelty of the Christian Faith.
> How can this be accomplished in a world both hardened and
> quickly given to prejudice? In a situation such as this, it will no
> longer suffice merely to administer existing structures and tradi-
> tional value, as if we owned them. Neither will it be a matter of
> expanding the institutional dimensions of the Church; rather, all
> the structures must be evaluated in accordance with their ability
> to enable the faithful to witness their faith. Every plan, every
> investment must be designed to serve the principal cause, that is,
> to prepare people to bear witness to the world. This does not call
> for an increase in the number of specialists and experts; rather,
> the goal of new evangelization is to promote the infectious testi-
> mony of every individual Christian. This can never be accom-
> plished solely with the help of institutions or professionals. More-
> over, parish council members must determine for themselves
> where their attention is most urgently needed: Must not empha-

sis be placed on the ever-increasing living witness to faith, hope, and love within the congregation?[82]

It is obvious that Bishop Lehmann is proposing something much more radical than "institutional maintenance" and that he sees reevangelization most especially as falling within the ambit of the apostolate of the laity.

Similarly, Pope John Paul II has stressed the importance of the involvement of the laity in combatting the indifference that fails to recognize that the Faith is the only valid response to the problems of the present world. In *Christifideles Laici* he exhorted the laity to narrow the gap between faith and culture,[83] and went on in *Redemptoris Missio* to note that "the witness of a Christian life is the first and irreplaceable form of mission."[84] Words are not sufficient for evangelization, just as they are never used in isolation in proselytizing. "Missionary dynamism," according to the Pope, "is not born of the will of those who decide to become propagators of their faith. It is born of the Spirit, Who moves the Church to expand, and it progresses through faith in God's love."[85] This is the key difference between evangelization and proselytism.

While the "new evangelization" generally seeks to "bring back" those who have strayed from the Catholic flock or have grown indifferent to their Catholic identity, and evangelization in general is concerned with preaching the Gospel in new climes, one potential audience for Catholic outreach is frequently forgotten or ignored: the Fundamentalist proselytizers themselves. John Mark Reynolds presents some interesting ideas in this regard. He believes that Catholics should rally to the defense of the Fundamentalist whenever possible because he "is the Protestant who doctrinally comes closest to the confessions of the historic Church." "One can criticize the Fundamentalist," he says, "for the way he fought the battle, or for failing to be Catholic, but in splitting with Modernism, the Fundamentalist was right."[86] He continues: "The Church should, perhaps, defend the weaker brethren where she can without supporting the error which distorts the truth the Fundamentalists hold." And then in exploring an interesting angle, he writes: "In reaching out to theological liberals, the Church often alienates the religiously conservative, whose numbers are growing. The Catholic Church, with her overwhelming resources, is appealing to the wrong audience. While the Church tries to woo vanishing liberal Protestants, who question every command of pope and Scripture, millions of Americans accept every word of the creed, but perish for lack of a shepherd."[87]

Taking account of some fascinating changes within Catholicism and Fundamentalism, Reynolds asserts: "Liberal Catholics decry the Church's stand on birth control while more and more Fundamentalists come to accept the Church's position. Persons who used to view the Church as the 'whore of Babylon' now march in her vanguard at pro-life demonstrations."[88]

While taking a somewhat excessively irenic view of Fundamentalism, Reynolds's points are well taken. But how should Fundamentalists be approached? They "can be convinced by thoughtful argument that is not accompanied by derision." What else can be done? "The answer is to be more Catholic, to reaffirm the full-throated faith of Pius XII and not just the softer voice of John XXIII. Fundamentalists love to hear the great truths of the Faith." He likewise encourages Catholics to defend Fundamentalists who are unjustly pilloried in the secular media.[89] Finally, he asks if the Church "wish[es] to gain highly motivated converts." To do so, "she need only affirm orthodoxy, keep the historic Faith, and act with charity toward the Fundamentalists."[90]

In the final analysis, in order to have the Christian Faith, a full-bodied catechesis is necessary, which is both cognitive and affective in scope. The process is most fruitful in the individual who has encountered Christ. As Dulles expresses it: "Too many Catholics of our day seem never to have encountered Christ. They know a certain amount about him from the teaching of the Church, but they lack personal familiarity. The hearing of the gospel, personal prayer, and especially the reception of the sacraments should establish and deepen that saving relationship. When Catholics regard religious worship as a mere matter of duty or routine, they become an easy prey for sectarian preachers who, notwithstanding their incomplete and distorted understanding of the Christian message, give witness to a joyful encounter with the Lord."[91]

The outcome of study and prayer should be a desire to communicate the saving truth revealed in and by Our Lord to others. Such an exposition must always respect the freedom of the one hearing the message and should not seek to use cultural and sociological problems to exploit that individual. Without realizing that evangelization is primarily the work of Christ — and one that we are invited to share — it can slip very easily into a negative campaign that does not have the Truth at its core. The Church must respond to the spiritual needs of the day by reevangelizing with the message of hope and not through proselytizing — a point that many other Christian groups need to take to heart. Proselytism, then, "should not be confused with evangelization or conversion, which is carried out with respect, with dialogue, by sharing, not by imposing, by helping, not by conquering."[92]

Finally, it is legitimate to ask what the relationship is between the work of evangelization and dialogue of an ecumenical or interreligious nature. In *Redemptoris Missio*, Pope John Paul II contends that there is no opposition between these two realities. Dialogue among Christians is necessary, he holds, because "the division among Christians damages the holy work of preaching the Gospel and is a barrier for many in their approach to the Faith" (n. 50). Furthermore, he reminds all of the communion — albeit imperfect — which already exists among all the baptized and then calls on all disciples of Christ to work toward the full unity to which the Master beckons us (see n. 50).

With regard to non-Christians, the Pope declares that the Church sees no conflict between proclaiming Christ and engaging in interreligious dialogue; in fact, he considers them to be but two sides of the same coin (see n. 55). He stresses the need for all involved in dialogue to be faithful to their own proper religious convictions and to seek to discover the "seeds of the Word," a "ray of that truth which enlightens all people; these are found in individuals and in the religious traditions of humanity" (n. 56).

The *Catechism of the Catholic Church* deals with ecumenical dialogue and interreligious relations in much the same way as *Redemptoris Missio*. Thus, in regard to other Christians, we read: "The Church's mission stimulates efforts *towards Christian unity*. Indeed, 'divisions among Christians prevent the Church from realizing in practice the fullness of catholicity proper to her in those of her sons who, though joined to her by Baptism, are yet separated from full communion with her. Furthermore, the Church herself finds it more difficult to express in actual life her full catholicity in all its aspects.' "[93]

Similarly, for non-Christians, we find: "The missionary task implies a *respectful dialogue* with those who do not yet accept the Gospel. Believers can profit from this dialogue by learning to appreciate better 'those elements of truth and grace which are found among peoples, and which are, as it were, a secret presence of God.' They proclaim the Good News to those who do not know it, in order to consolidate, complete, and raise up the truth and the goodness that God has distributed among men and nations, and to purify them from error and evil 'for the glory of God, the confusion of the demon, and the happiness of man.' "[94]

Ecclesiastical Responses

That proselytism is being taken as a threat to authentic pastoral ministry is witnessed by the number of studies and articles treating the subject at various levels. Pope John Paul II laid the necessary groundwork for the response in issuing the encyclical *Redemptoris Missio*. There it is affirmed that the Kingdom of God as we know it from revelation cannot be detached either from Christ or from the Church,[95] and that the Spirit, "Who was at work in the world before Christ was glorified . . . is the same Spirit Who was at work in the Incarnation and in the life, death and resurrection of Jesus and Who is at work in the Church."[96] The Holy Father also addressed the topic in the extraordinary consistory of the College of Cardinals, April 4-7, 1991. The communiqué from that body observed that the Church "is faced not only with the urgent task of reaching those who have never known the Gospel, but also with the phenomenon which leads numerous Catholics to get involved in religious communities which are alien to their tradition and contrary to their membership in the Church."[97] The nature of the Church's missionary activity has been restated in *Redemptoris Missio* and provides the foundation for authentic evangelization. Francis Cardinal Arinze, of the Holy See's Council for Interreligious Dialogue reiterates, however, that "it is not enough to supply people with intellectual information. Christianity is neither a set of doctrines nor an ethical system. It is life in Christ which can be lived at ever deeper levels."[98]

The bishops of Texas have picked up on this, too: "In fact, the biggest task may very well be that of inspiring active Catholics to fall in love with Jesus, to be converted to Him, to make Him central in their lives, to imitate Him, and to share their experience of Him with others. After all, our greatest resource is our own Catholic people, and so much of evangelization is encouraging one another to appreciate the breadth and length, the height and depth of the Catholic experience of Jesus Christ."[99]

Nowhere is the seepage from Catholicism probably greater than in Latin America, and David Stoll has documented the process most accurately. The first response of the bishops there seems to have been silence, a "non-response": "For some fifteen years after Vatican II, nonetheless, Catholic authorities usually refrained from complaining about Evangelicals in public. The informal gag rule seems to have originated in Rome, anxious to avoid further accusations of religious persecution. Local clergy trying to defend parishes against sectarian intruders resented their superiors' cool, distant attitude. But by the early 1980s, alarm over Protestant growth was once again respectable in the Catholic hierarchy. Besides the obvious gains Evangelicals were making, another reason was their frank and hopeful talk about making the entire continent-and-a-half Protestant."[100]

Becoming more specific, he recalls one conversation, which he treats as typical: "In Costa Rica, Evangelical missionaries told me that charismaticism [sic] had become a major source of defection [from Catholicism] to their own churches. Following a charismatic movement, they claimed, the Costa Rican hierarchy had suddenly clamped down at the end of the 1970s. 'Whole groups of charismatics suddenly saw the contradiction between mystical experience, Bible reading for themselves, and the [Catholic] hierarchy,' the Latin America Mission's Paul Pretiz told me. 'They went over to Protestantism en masse. So now the hierarchy always places a popular priest in charge, who is careful to include prayers to the Virgin and reinforce Mother Church.' "[101]

Stoll spends a good deal of time outlining the personal attempts of Pope John Paul II to return Latin America to the Church. Stoll says that "when asked to specify who [sic] he was denouncing as 'false prophets' on a Latin American trip, John Paul II referred to the Seventh Day Adventists, Mormons, and Jehovah's Witnesses, not to more orthodox Protestants." He continues: "Evangelicals were not convinced, however. Accusations against such groups, they pointed out, were usually followed by indiscriminate blasts against 'sects,' which included their own churches."[102]

And what has been the reaction to such papal efforts? "The messianic fervor greeting the Pope on his 1983 Central American visit, William Taylor of Central American Mission claimed, was producing a wave of old-fashioned Catholic polemicism. Evangelicals were afraid that the Pope's campaign to bring together the various factions in the Catholic Church was at their expense, by making them the enemy to be rallied against. Like it or not, opposition to their inroads was a way to bring the different tendencies in the Catholic Church back together."[103]

From this less-than-objective and understandably concerned source, it appears that the Pope may be having a positive effect in restoring "our sense of mission."[104]

But what concrete things has the Pope done? Stoll again shares anecdotal information: "One way the Pope tried to restore centralized authority, Dayton Roberts of the Latin America Mission pointed out, was by encouraging traditional Catholic piety, such as the cults of the Virgin Mary and the saints. The Pope also stressed the role of the priest as essential intermediary between God and the faithful. To Protestants and Catholics who saw themselves in a personal, direct relationship with Jesus Christ, these were ominous steps backward. Since the Reformation in Europe, Protestants had regarded saint cults as idolatry. Reviving communal Catholic rituals, older Evangelicals in Latin America feared, would revive the persecution they had suffered for refusing to join in."[105]

Aside from the somewhat paranoid evaluation at the end, one should notice the Holy Father's intuition that devotion to the Blessed Mother is integral to holding fast to the Catholic Faith and in keeping

the faithful within the one flock of Christ, the very point to be considered in the next chapter.

Realizing the importance of the Church, especially for immigrants, one must view the present activity of the hierarchy of the United
States in its historical context: "The loving concern of the Church for
immigrants and refugees is a thread that ties together more than three
centuries of its history in the U.S. The growth and crises, the achievements and occasional failures of the Church are linked to its struggle
to include in one community of faith peoples from a hundred diverse
cultures and then lead this new People of God toward a creative service in a pluralistic society."[106]

The American Catholic Church in the early-twentieth century
dealt with a diversity of groups speaking twenty-eight different languages. "The dialectical process between unity and cultural pluralism became the trademark of Catholicism in the United States and it
continues to the present."[107] All ethnic groups arrived with their own
devotional life and old-country traditions, which provided a stable
identity while looking for a niche in the structure of American society.[108] Historian Jay Dolan observes:

> One institution that remained in the neighborhood and
> helped to give it a special identity was the immigrant parish. Most
> often founded by the people, the church was the most enduring
> and important cultural institution in the neighborhood. As a so-
> cial organization that brought people together through a network
> of societies and clubs, it helped to establish a sense of commu-
> nity. As an educational organization, it taught both young and
> old the meaning of America, its language as well as its culture; as
> a religious organization, it brought the presence of God to the
> neighborhood, nurturing and sustaining the presence of the holy
> through worship, devotional services, and neighborhood proces-
> sions. Important as this religious dimension was, the immigrant
> parish was more than just a religious institution in which people
> could satisfy their spiritual needs and desires. This was the mani-
> fest purpose of the parish, but it also was a key social institution.
> Indeed in most Catholic neighborhoods it was the cement that

bound the people together, enabling them to establish some sem-
blance of a community life. Families were indeed the building
blocks of every immigrant community, but the church was the
mortar that sought to bind them together.[109]

This experience with the European immigrants teaches that in the
long run the pastoral institutional structures developed separately became successful strategies for including these ethnically diverse individuals in the overall Catholic community.

Immigrants today are faced with the same old difficulties. Diversity of regional traditions, varying compositions of diocesan populations, availability of clergy and other personnel within the local
Church, personal ideologies — all of these things continue to make
the response of the hierarchy appear as concrete and bearing any fruit
only on the local level. This concern is not new, of course. In the
1954 apostolic constitution of Pope Pius XII, *Exsul Familia*, a citation of Lateran IV is given for this thrust: "We find in most countries,
cities, and dioceses people of diverse languages who, though bound
by one Faith, have varied rites and customs. Therefore, we strictly
enjoin that the bishops of those cities or dioceses provide the proper
men, who will celebrate the liturgical functions according to their
rites and languages. They will administer the sacraments of the Church
and instruct their people by word and deed."[110]

Exsul Familia goes on to comment that "the Church has followed this instruction scrupulously even down to our own days."[111]
In our own time, Vatican II's *Christus Dominus* put the weight of an
ecumenical council behind such endeavors: "Special concern should
be shown for those members of the faithful who, on account of their
way of life are not adequately catered for by the ordinary pastoral
ministry of the parochial clergy or are entirely deprived of it. These
include the many migrants, exiles and refugees, sailors and airmen,
itinerants and others of this kind."[112]

The bishops have given extended study to the issue, realizing it
to be more than a sociological problem. The problems have led to a
new sense of urgency, underscoring the necessity of evangelization.
As the then-Reverend Silvano Tomasi puts it: "The Church does not

build unity on culture, but on Christ and the Eucharist. All cultures are respected, but faith cannot be identified with any. Popular religiosity, multiculturalism, inculturation have now moved from the limited area of migration documents to the whole Church's concern with evangelization."[113]

Local responses to the challenge have been varied. The former apostolic pro-nuncio to the United States stated the case starkly: "The annual loss of Spanish-speaking Catholics to non-Catholic sects is significantly — I would say, disturbingly — high."[114] This realization is evidenced by the fact that in the Archdiocese of Los Angeles the Church is not playing dead while Fundamentalists campaign for Hispanic converts. As early as 1970, the Most Reverend Donald Montrose, then-auxiliary bishop, began working to make the parish presence felt in the community-at-large. Julie Sly explains: "Parishioners were organized to make home visits to parish families, lead prayer groups, the Rosary and Marian devotions in individuals' homes and to invite neighbors who weren't coming to Church to these activities."[115]

This outreach took advantage of everyday moments and also "times of crisis, such as the death of a relative in the community. Parishioners would visit the home and offer to aid the grieving family with the *novenario de difuntos* (devotion to Mary through a variety of novenas following the death of a family member) and the *velorio* (wake), which often included using the Rosary and other prayers complementary to mourning."[116] She offers the following practical conclusion: "Pastors working with Hispanics should use any means they can for calling on homes and inviting people back again to Church."[117] Of course, common sense indicates that what has been outlined above has application beyond the Hispanic community.

"If the Hispanics are visibly changing the face of America, we can assume that their impact on the Catholic community will be even more dramatic,"[118] says Tomasi. Furthermore, the growing ethnic communities of today include the Haitians, Filipinos, Indochinese, Chinese, Koreans, and Europeans from Poland and Portugal. Clearly, the involvement of the Church with immigrants is not something limited to the early part of this century. Instead, these new immigrant groups will give rise to a new chapter in Catholicism in the United States. "Latino, Caribbean, and Oriental Catholics are now, in different political styles, knocking at the door for full participation as new constituencies of the Church."[119]

When these immigrants feel out of place in the average middle-class American parish, "many of them stay home or switch to Protestant churches."[120] Pope John Paul II has highlighted the connection between a feeling of social uprootedness and ecclesial alienation: "For this very reason, the Church has to engage in more intense activity, increase her vigilance, put in motion intelligently and intuitively all the proper initiatives to counteract that tendency and avoid the risks which are its consequences. It is the Church's constant task to contribute towards tearing down all the barriers that human selfishness places in the way of the weakest."[121]

According to the Most Reverend Plácido Rodríguez, former auxiliary bishop of Chicago, "although Mass attendance is the major U.S. yardstick of what it means to be a Catholic, Hispanics have a different cultural and religious perspective — one more rooted in the very structure of society, faith and life. . . ."[122] The present pastoral policies have met with varying degrees of success. There is no uniform answer, even though there has been a more coordinated effort, given the role of episcopal conferences since Vatican II.

A positive response has been given to the Vietnamese refugees, estimated at over 150,000 since 1975. "In a decade, the Vietnamese developed an articulate network of successful Catholic communities, movements, publications and associations because of the committed leadership of their religious personnel."[123] This clearly indicates the advantage of having clergy among the immigrants. "Over 130 Vietnamese Catholic communities and Catholic Vietnamese Unions are actively functioning in 28 dioceses throughout the United States. Among these, ten ethnic and personal parishes have been decreed and established by the bishops in various states from Virginia to Nebraska."[124] This organization among the Vietnamese Catholics has not only prevented successful proselytizing by Fundamentalists among the members, but serves as an outreach, inviting non-Christian Vietnamese to join the Church.

Unfortunately, the situation with Haitian refugees has not encountered this kind of success. Although the vast majority of the Haitians are baptized Catholics, without the assistance of their own clergy and other support structures, many have either changed religion or are now indifferent to it. "The Southern Baptist Convention had 80 Haitian churches affiliated in 1985."[125] The problem of defection and indifference in a community that numbers nearly 800,000 must be a source of concern.

The Church in the United States has dealt with large numbers of immigrants in the past, and present trends give no indication to the contrary for the future. To all of the difficulties to which these immigrants are exposed, the Church must be prepared to respond at the national, regional, and local levels, clearly articulating the mission entrusted to every baptized Catholic by the Holy Father in his call for a new evangelization.

One area of concern, common to both native-born populations and immigrants, is that of ecclesial unity. Valderrey, cited earlier, alluded to the difficulties of conflicting messages being given to the Catholic faithful, due to theological dissent,[126] and the Holy See's document mentioned one special attraction of the sects as their "clear vision."[127] Until that phenomenon is addressed in a definitive manner, it seems that we shall fail to keep many of our own, let alone bring others into the Church. Gabriel Fackre reflects on the dilemma in this way: "Where the trumpet has given an uncertain sound in our own ranks, we can expect a response to a call from other quarters. And can we not honor those intentions to maintain continuity with the Tradition when the conventional wisdom appears to speak only of discontinuity? Especially so when Fundamentalist fervor is able to reach constituencies of the poor, the disinherited and the defeated that our blander counsels seem unable to touch?"[128]

A facet of the problem hardly touched upon by most commentators is the need for a revival of Catholic apologetics. This lacuna is specifically cited in the Working Paper for the 1994 African Synod.[129] While admitting that "dialogue with these sects is often difficult because of an unyielding Fundamentalism or aggressive proselytizing,"[130] the document also wisely observes that "since the Bible is sometimes the only tool for dialogue, the Catholic Church would do well to promote the deeper biblical formation of its faithful."[131]

Another question to be answered is the one raised by David Schindler: "How do we reverse the drift into secularism, and overcome the loss of Christian identity that makes Catholics vulnerable to the evangelizing efforts of the various sects?"[132] Angel Cardinal Suquia touches on a crucial element of such a response: "The Church must cease to be afraid of her own truth; she must be brave enough to recover the consciousness of her identity and to dare to be simply and transparently herself."[133] He spells it out further: "What the Catholic communities must give is a concrete testimony in everyday life that will demonstrate existentially the validity for life of the experience of the Church in relation to those questions that the man of today cannot evade without destroying himself, and without destroying some of his most precious possessions."[134]

Engaging in a healthy dose of soul-searching, the Guatemalan bishops cite the need for a thorough evaluation of Catholic approaches in all spheres of Church life, from catechetical methods to pastoral care to organization. "Without falling into an easy irenicism," they see the need for dialogue on "the essential elements of the Gospel" and "the sacramental practice of the Catholic people, with a view to forming authentic Christian communities through the adequate use of the means of social communication."[135]

Stransky offers a similar exercise for American Catholics: "If [Fundamentalists] are faulted because they believe that other Christians, including Catholics, have lost passion for God's truth, then at least we Catholics can examine our consciences. Has that passion dwindled?"[136] And Pope John Paul II sees the laity having a specific role in staving off "the spread of sects."[137] The King study revealed that "in nearly half (47%) of these respondents, interest in the new church was sparked by an invitation to attend a service; most of these invitations were extended personally (41%). . . ." Astutely, the report goes on: "This finding has implications for Catholic evangelization: The single most important reason these people joined another church or denomination is that they were invited to attend."[138]

Understanding the relationship between faith and culture is also vital. And it is precisely in this sphere that many proselytizers fail as they try to impose theological categories at odds with the lived experience of the people for whom theological notions have been subsumed into a general consciousness.[139] Pope John Paul II presented this theme in one of his talks during his fourth pastoral visit to Spain in this fashion:

> Your devotion to the Blessed Virgin represents a *key experience in popular piety* and, at the same time, constitutes a complex socio-cultural and religious phenomenon. It combines the values of historical tradition and folklore, and natural and man-made beauty, with the rich human sentiments of shared friendship, equality of treatment and respect for all the beauty that life contains in the common joy of a celebration. However, in the deep roots of this religious and cultural phenomenon we can see the *authentic spiritual values of faith in God* and the acknowledgement of Christ as the Son of God and the Saviour of mankind, of love and of devotion to the Blessed Virgin and of Christian fellowship, which is born of the knowledge that we are children of the same heavenly Father [emphasis in original].[140]

In that same talk, the Holy Father even spoke about "a *faith which becomes culture*" (emphasis in original).[141]

It should be clear by now that the Pope thinks that the answer to proselytism is to be found in evangelization.

Endnotes

1. For the necessary distinction between evangelization and proselytism, see the definition of terms in Chapter 1; for a more detailed discussion, see pp. 138-143 of this chapter.
2. Catholic Bishops of Texas, *Mission: Texas* (Lubbock, Texas: 1989), 9.
3. Jaime R. Vidal, "Proselytism of Hispanic Migrants: A Challenge to the American Church," *Migration World* (1991/2): 13.

4. Hans Mol, "Theory and Data on the Religious Behavior of Migrants," *Social Compass* (1979/1): 36.

5. Ibid.

6. Guatemalan Bishops' Conference (Office of Laity), *Elementos para una Reflexión Pastoral en Preparación de la IV Conferencia General del Episcopado Latinoamericano* [*Items for a Pastoral Reflection in Preparation for the IV General Conference of the Latin American Episcopate*] (Bogotá, 1990), 99.

7. See Jack Cheevers, "Mormon Recruiting Stirs Up Refugees," *The Tribune*, July 27, 1986, A-17.

David Stoll describes the process in Latin America as follows: "Whether they like it or not, these groups are engaged in what can be called disaster evangelism. Drawn to wars and natural catastrophes, evangelists hand out food, set up medical clinics, help re-build communities, and train leaders to start churches. The first occasion on which the modus operandi came to wide attention was the 1976 earthquake in Guatemala. When the earthquake tumbled the seemingly secure adobe walls of Mayan Indian towns, it took tens of thousands of lives and also shook the confidence of survivors in their old ways. Helping them pick their way out of the rubble was the now familiar legion of evangelists" (*Is Latin America Turning Protestant? The Politics of Evangelical Growth* [Berkeley: University of California Press, 1990], 11).

8. Dean Hoge, *Converts, Dropouts, Returnees: A Study of Religious Change among Catholics* (Washington: United States Catholic Conference, 1981), 93.

Earlier, Hoge cites these reasons in some detail: "Most common was a dissatisfaction with doctrine or practices, usually with the perceived inadequate Bible study and the lack of relevance of religion for daily life. Some were unhappy with the excessive emphasis on money, and some found the Mass and the sermons boring." Continuing, he states: "Seventeen percent stated that an important reason for dropping out was that they had found spiritual help or religious truth in other religious groups, 16% said that personal conversion experiences had led them out of the Catholic Church, 14% had experienced a sense of need or void in their feelings about life that had influenced them to drop out, 13% told of conflict or tension with priests or nuns, and 13% were influenced by other people (mostly friends, parents, and siblings)" (3).

9. Interview with Bishop Ricardo Ramírez, National Catholic News Service, April 29, 1986.

10. In this connection, Pope John Paul II sees catechesis as part of "the whole process of evangelization" (*Catechesi Tradendae*, n. 20.)

11. Pope John Paul II, "Opening Address to the Fourth General Conference of the Latin American Episcopate," *Origins* (October 22, 1992): 326.

12. José Valderrey, "Sects in Central America," *Pro Mundi Vita* (1985/Bulletin 100): 26.
    These complex problems are addressed in the final section of this chapter.

13. Juan Diaz Vilar, *Religious Sects* (New York: Catholic Book Publishing Co., 1992), 18.
    The Guatemalan bishops stress the final point, when they observe that enumerating the various sects is practically impossible, given the rate at which these groups fragment and multiply (99).

14. Latin American Episcopal Conference, *La Evangelización en el Presente y en el Futuro de América Latina* [*Evangelization in the Present and in the Future of Latin America*] (Caracas: Puebla, 1979), 114.

15. "Working Paper for the 1994 Special Synod for Africa: Evangelizing Mission of the Church in Africa," *Origins* (March 11, 1993), 659.

16. Alan Cowell, "In Baltics, Pope's Message Is for the Eastern Orthodox," *New York Times*, September 7, 1993, A-4.

17. Robert J. McClory, "Why Did the Catholic Cross the Road?" *U.S. Catholic* (January 1991): 7.

18. Ibid.

19. Jim Graves, "Evangelical Movement Offers Challenges to Catholics," *Diocese of Orange Bulletin*, August 1992, 12.

20. Ibid., 7.

21. Pope John Paul II, "Proselytizing of Migrants by Sects Is a Challenge the Church Must Meet," *L'Osservatore Romano*, August 6, 1990, 1.

22. Liz O'Connor, "Research Shows Where Catholics Go," *Long Island Catholic*, March 4, 1992, 5.

   Studying older dropouts from Catholicism, Hoge found that "nineteen percent . . . are now participating in other religious groups. Most are in Pentecostal, Assemblies of God, Baptist, or non-denominational churches, and a disproportionate number of these live in the West or Southwest. Only four out of twenty-three are now in mainline Protestant denominations, such as the United Methodist, Lutheran, Presbyterian, or Episcopalian" (Hoge, 93).

23. The Reverend Andrew Greeley indicates that each year sixty thousand Hispanic-American Catholics join sects, mostly Baptist and Fundamentalist. (See *The Catholic Myth: The Behavior and Beliefs of American Catholics* [New York: Scribner, 1990], 120.)

   This position is seconded by Robert Suro in a front-page story in the *New York Times*: "From storefront churches in urban slums to gleaming temples along suburban freeways, perhaps more than four million of the roughly 20 million Hispanic Americans now practice some form of Protestant Christianity, according to several demographic studies. And the movement away from Catholicism, which traditionally claimed virtually the entire Hispanic population, has accelerated in the 1980's" ("Hispanic Shift of Allegiance Changes Face of U.S. Religion," *New York Times*, May 14, 1989, 1).

24. Thomas O'Mahoney, "Suicide of the Missions," *Religious Life* (February 1992): 10.

25. Stoll, 6.

   See also the charts the author provides (333-338); particularly disturbing is Appendix 3: Estimate of Evangelical Growth Factors in Latin America from 1960 to 1985, with Extrapolation to 2010.

26. Ibid., 8.

27. Roger Finke and Rodney Stark, *The Churching of America, 1776-1990* (New Brunswick, New Jersey: Rutgers University Press, 1992), 43.

28. Robert Trabold, "Building an Immigrant Community" (master's thesis, Long Island University, 1982).

29. Pablo A. Deiras notes: "Most of the best-known Fundamentalist Latin American ministers and evangelists have no formal education and have never been in a seminary."
   "Protestant Fundamentalism in Latin America," in *Fundamentalisms Observed*, eds. Martin E. Marty and R. Scott Appleby (Chicago: University of Chicago Press, 1991), 193.

30. In response to this point, people often refer to the maintenance of the Catholic Faith in Japan for centuries after the clergy had been martyred or expelled. Stephen Turnbull, however, documents a less-than-felicitous situation that emerged: confused doctrines, syncretism, and the lack of a true ecclesial sense. (See *Devotion to Mary among the Hidden Christians of Japan* [Surrey, England: Ecumenical Society of the Blessed Virgin Mary, 1993].)

31. James Lee Young, "Hispanic Southern Baptists," *Historical Commission News of the Southern Baptist Convention*, April 27, 1983.
   Just how interested Fundamentalists have become in Hispanics can be seen from the availability of materials in Spanish for this target group. In this connection, for example, one finds an article in the November/December 1993 Newsletter of the Christian Research Institute, entitled: "CRI Serving Hispanic Believers with Spanish-Language Resources."
   Some, however, would dispute this self-declared "open-mindedness." The Guatemalan bishops, for instance, observed that foremost in the minds of the "evangelists" is the de-Catholicizing of Latin America. (See Guatemalan Bishops' Conference, 9.)

32. Young, op. cit.

33. Private communication to the Office for the Pastoral Care of Migrants and Refugees of the National Conference of Catholic Bishops, May 8, 1986.

34. C. Peter Wagner, "A Vision for Evangelizing the Real America," *International Bulletin of Missionary Outreach* 10, no. 2: 63.

35. Stoll, 128.

36. See n. 33.

37. John Paul II, "Proselytizing," 1.

38. "A 'United States of Latin America'?" *Catholic World Report* (November 1992): 7.

39. Stoll, 14.

40. Certainly, one of the biggest problems, especially in Latin America, is that "the teaching of [Catholic] Church doctrine is often marked by ideology, while the Protestant churches and sects often rely on a simple presentation of the Bible" (n. 37).

41. Stoll, 32.

    The interest of the Brazilian hierarchy is hardly peripheral, since they "acknowledged in 1990 that about 600,000 of their members had joined Protestant religious movements" ("Protestant Growth," *One World* [March 1993], 21-22).

    Similarly, Stoll maintains that politics had much to do with Fundamentalist conversions in Guatemala as "conservative Evangelicals ended up supporting a right-wing equivalent of what they rejected in left-wing Christianity and a more violent regime than the one they condemned" (261); this was also the case in El Salvador where the Evangelical communities increased rapidly because "they served as a haven from government violence" (167).

42. Roberto O. Gonzalez and Michael LaValle, *The Hispanic Catholic in the United States: A Socio-Cultural and Religious Profile* (New York: Northeast Catholic Pastoral Center for Hispanics, 1985), 147-152.

    See also Eleace King, *Proselytism and Evangelization: An Exploratory Study* (Washington: Center for Applied Research in the Apostolate, 1991), in which the researcher discovered that "when asked to describe their experience of the Catholic Church, about a fourth [26%] make an accusation. These respondents characterize the Catholic Church as hypocritical, idolatrous or boring. . . . Others tell of feeling ostracized and unwelcome because they're immigrants; several of these people say that although the Catholic Church celebrates Mass in their language, it doesn't accept their culture" (41).

43. Roy Rivenburg, "Odysseys of Faith," *Sunday Star-Ledger*, October 4, 1992, 39.
44. An interesting piece of anecdotal evidence, however, is the following cited by Thomas Quigley: "A poll after a 1992 [evangelistic] campaign in Costa Rica found that 80 percent of the 5,000 people who said they had changed religions as a result of the campaign were back in the Catholic Church five months later." He goes on to comment: "The revolving-door phenomenon is a commonplace with movements of enthusiasm, especially where 'conversion' occurs in the white heat of an intense emotional experience, not one easily sustained over time" ("Overview: Myths about Latin America's Church," *Origins* [October 28, 1993]: 366-367).
45. Valderrey, 28.
46. Jay P. Dolan holds that even revivalism (in the form of parish missions) was used to good effect in American Catholicism: "Historians have always considered revivalism as a major force in American religious history. Yet, they have consistently limited their vision to the Protestant phase of this phenomenon, believing that Roman Catholics were not so evangelically oriented. . . . The religion of revivalism not only found a home among Catholics, but indeed was a major force in forming their piety and building up the Church" (*Catholic Revivalism* [Notre Dame, Indiana: University of Notre Dame Press, 1978]: xix).
47. Ibid., 28-29.
48. Ibid., 32.

The bishops of Guatemala concur in this judgment: "The content of their message, while quite varied and diverse in each group, reduces and simplifies traditional Christian truths concerning Jesus Christ, the Church and mankind. These are expressed with a pseudo-spiritualism of exaggerated mystical and emotive emphases . . ." (Guatemalan Bishops Conference, 100).

49. Guatemalan Bishops Conference, 100.
50. Lois Spear, "Fundamentalism 'Interferes' in Church Life, Priest Says," National Catholic News Service, May 7, 1986.
51. Wagner, 63.
    Finke and Stark also mention another aspect of this question: "It may be that secularization ensues whenever religion is placed within a formal academic setting, for scholars seem unable to resist attempting to clear up all logical ambiguities. Rather than celebrate mysteries, religious scholars often seek to create a belief system that is internally consistent. Finding that things do not fit exactly, they begin to prune and revise and redefine" (45).
    Although apparently true for many religious bodies, that never seemed to be a problem for Catholicism until recently, because of the creative tension maintained between the mystical and the academic/theological.
52. Vatican Council II, *Christus Dominus,* ed. Austin Flannery, O.P. (Northport, New York: Costello Publishing Co., 1980), n. 7.
53. Allan Figueroa Deck and Joseph A. Nuñez, "Religious Enthusiasm and Hispanic Youths," *America* (October 23, 1982): 233.
54. John Paul II, "Proselytizing of Migrants," 14.
55. Stoll, 32.
56. Ibid., 31.
57. Bishop Ricardo Ramírez, "Bringing Ecumenism to Hispanic Christians," *Origins* (May 28, 1992): 42.
58. Latin American Episcopal Council, 55.
59. Juan Diaz Vilar, *Las Sectas: Un Desafio a la Pastoral* (New York: Northeast Catholic Pastoral Center for Hispanics, 1985), 103.
60. Interview with Richard Yao, *National Catholic Reporter*, June 21, 1985, 3.
61. See "Vatican Report on Sects, Cults and New Religious Movements," *Origins* (May 22, 1986), 4-6.

The Guatemalan bishops pick up several of the above themes, implicitly acknowledging particular failures of the recent past, especially the secularizing trends in the Church. The "vertical" and "horizontal" aspects of theology are held in balance by setting legitimate concern for temporal well-being against the broader background of spiritual salvation: the solution of temporal problems is not the Church's ultimate mission, but rather "the proclamation of the Gospel of transcendent salvation in Jesus Christ, the Son of God" (160).

62. Dean Kelley, *Why Conservative Churches Are Growing* (New York: Harper and Row, 1972), 26.
63. Ibid., 95.
64. Ibid., 96.
65. Ibid.
66. Finke and Stark, 238.
67. Ibid., 250.
68. Ibid., 254.
69. The Guatemalan bishops point out the need to appreciate the place of popular religiosity in the work of evangelization (130).
70. CELAM highlights this difficulty, noting that popular Latin American religion suffers from the divorce between the elite and the common people, signifying a lack of education and catechesis (121).
71. Renato Poblete, *Movimiento Pentecostal y Iglesia Católica* [*Pentecostal Movement and Catholic Church*] (Santiago, Chile: Centro Bellarmino, 1984), 125.
72. It must be stressed that although much of the research demonstrates a concerted Fundamentalist outreach to immigrants in general and Hispanics in particular, the King study also documents organized Fundamentalist efforts to attract blacks and Native Americans. (See King, 6.)
73. Pope Paul VI, *Evangelii Nuntiandi* (Washington, D.C.: United States Catholic Conference, 1976), n. 7.
74. Ibid., n. 14.
75. Vatican Council II, *Ad Gentes,* ed. Austin Flannery, O.P. (Northport, New York: Costello Publishing Co., 1980), n. 7.

76. See *Redemptoris Missio*, nn. 8 and 39.

77. Bishops of Texas, 3.

78. *Evangelii Nuntiandi*, n. 71.

79. Ibid., n. 58.

80. Bishops of Texas, 14.

81. Avery Dulles, "John Paul II and the New Evangelization," *America* (February 1, 1992): 52.

    Pope John Paul first coined the expression "new evangelization" on March 9, 1983, as he called for "a new evangelization: new in ardor, methods and expression" ("The Task of the Latin American Bishops," *Origins* [March 24, 1983], 661).

82. Lehmann, 545-546.

83. See *Christifideles Laici*, nn. 34 and 44.

    The Guatemalan bishops, too, discuss the essential bond between faith and culture, and how the Fundamentalist character of these proselytizing movements impinges upon this bond (see n. 37).

84. *Redemptoris Missio*, n. 42.

85. Pope John Paul II, "Address of February 12, 1988, to Italian Bishops on Liturgical Course," *L'Osservatore Romano*, March 14, 1988, 5.

86. John Mark Reynolds, "Are Fundamentalists Really So Bad?" *New Oxford Review* (October 1992): 6.

87. Ibid.

88. Ibid., 7.

89. Ibid.

90. Ibid., 9.

    What is Reynolds advocating here? "In the face of dechristianization, many pastoral theologians and religious educators in Western Europe became convinced that the best remedy was a confident proclamation of the basic message of salvation through Jesus Christ" (Dulles, "John Paul II and the New Evangelization," 53).

91. Ibid.

92. Vilar, *Religious Sects*, 18.

93. *Catechism of the Catholic Church* (San Francisco: Ignatius Press-Libreria Editrice Vaticana, 1994), n. 855.

94. Ibid., n. 856.

95. See Pope John Paul II, *Redemptoris Missio* (Vatican City: Libreria Editrice Vaticana, 1990), n. 18.

96. Ibid., n. 29.

97. Vatican Press Office, "Communiqué: College of Cardinals Meeting," *Origins* (April 25, 1991): 747.

98. Francis Cardinal Arinze, "The Challenge of New Religious Movements," *Origins* (April 25, 1991): 748.
    The Cardinal's statement merely echoes *Redemptoris Missio*, n. 33.

99. Catholic Bishops of Texas, 10.

100. Stoll, 31-32.

101. Ibid., 37.

102. Ibid., 40.

103. Ibid.

104. Karl Lehmann, "The Meaning of a New Evangelization of Europe," *Communio* (Winter 1992): 548.

105. Stoll, 40.

106. NCCB Administrative Committee, "Together, A New People: Pastoral Statement on Migrants and Refugees" (Washington, D.C.: United States Catholic Conference, 1980), 1.

107. Silvano M. Tomasi, *A Lesson from History: The Integration of Immigrants in the Pastoral Practice of the Church in the United States* (New York: Center for Migration Studies, 1987), 4.
    The author continues: "In the November 1986 General Meeting of the National Conference of Catholic Bishops, the 'National Pastoral Plan for Hispanic Ministry' was presented. It states: 'The plan has its origins in our Pastoral Letter. . . . It takes into account the socio-cultural reality of our Hispanic people and suggests a style of pastoral ministry and model of Church in harmony with their faith and culture. For this reason it requires an affirmation of the concept of cultural pluralism in our Church within a fundamental unity of doctrine as expressed so many times by our Magisterium.' "

108. James S. Olson emphasizes this: "For millions of Roman Catholic immigrants, the nationality parish played a key role in eas-

ing the adjustment to urban society in the United States. . . , with the assistance of a priest who spoke their language and shared their past. . . . [It] became a mainstay of Roman Catholic survival in the United States, the single most important institution in deflecting the proselytizing campaigns of evangelical Protestants. . ." (*Catholic Immigrants in America* [Chicago: Nelson Hall, 1987], 125).

109. Jay P. Dolan, *The American Catholic Experience* (Garden City, New York: Doubleday, 1985), 204.

110. Giulivio Tessarolo, ed., *'Exsul Familia': The Church's Magna Charta for Migrants* (New York: St. Charles Seminary, 1962), 13.

111. Ibid.

112. *Christus Dominus,* n. 18.

113. Silvano M. Tomasi, *The Pastoral Challenges of the New Immigration* (New York: Center for Migration Studies, 1990), 4.

114. Archbishop Pio Laghi, "Stemming the Outflow of Hispanic Catholics," *Origins* (November 24, 1988): 387.

115. Lois Spear, "The Church Fights Back to Stop Defections," *Our Sunday Visitor*, February 10, 1985, 8.

116. Ibid.

117. Ibid.

In this context, it is a hopeful sign that the Northeast Catholic Pastoral Center for Hispanics has produced a bilingual video alerting Catholics to the danger of proselytism and what they can do about it. In commenting on "The Family of God: Hispanic Catholics and the Sects," the Most Reverend Sean O'Malley, O.F.M. Cap., observes that "the presentation in English, even if dealing with Hispanics, can be of great interest to other components of the parish community which are not spared the threat."

118. Silvano M. Tomasi, *The Response of the Catholic Church in the United States to Immigrants and Refugees* (New York: Center for Migration Studies, 1984), 3.

119. Ibid., 3.

120. Tomasi, *A Lesson from History*, 11.

Tomasi also pinpoints another possible scenario, with an ironic twist. When immigrants experience derision in "regular" or "normal" American parishes, they "may risk to move out of their devotional religiosity, their popular religion and to leave behind the symbols and the worldviews they provided, and embrace a lifestyle that middle-class parishes exhibit and which is itself in need of evangelization" (*Pastoral Challenges*, 6).

This intuition of Tomasi is borne out by the observations of Richard Rodriguez, the son of Mexican immigrants and now a professor at Stanford University, in his book *Hunger of Memory: The Education of Richard Rodriguez* (New York: Bantam Books, 1988, pp. 85-86):

"Above all mediators there was Mary, *Santa María*, the Mother. Whereas at school the primary mediator was Christ, at home that role was assumed by the Mexican Virgin, *Nuestra Señora de Guadalupe*, the focus of devotion and pride for Mexican Catholics. The Mexican Mary 'honored our people,' my mother would say. 'She could have appeared to anyone in the whole world, but she appeared to a Mexican.' Someone like us. And she appeared, I could see from her picture, as a young Indian maiden — dark just like me.

"On her feastday in early December my family would go to the Mexican church for a predawn High Mass. The celebration would begin in the cold dark with a blare of trumpets imitating the cries of a cock. The Virgin's wavering statue on the shoulders of men would lead a procession into the warm yellow church. . . . Invariably, my attention settled on old women — mysterious supplicants in black — bent deep, their hands clasped tight to hold steady the attention of the Mexican Virgin, who was pictured high over the altar, astride a black moon.

"The *gringo* Catholic church, a block from our house, was a very different place. In the *gringo* church Mary's statue was relegated to a side altar, imaged there as a serene white lady who matter-of-factly squashed the Genesis serpent with her bare feet. (Very early I knew that I was supposed to believe that the shy Mexican Mary was the same as this European Mary trium-

phant.) In the *gringo* church the floors were not made of squeaky wood but of marble. And there was not the devotional clutter of so many pictures and statues and candle racks. 'It doesn't feel like a church,' my mother complained. But as it became our regular church, I grew to love its elegant simplicity."
121. Pope John Paul II, "Proselytizing of Migrants," 1.
Also see Stoll for an examination of the same issue (13).
122. "Hispanic Catholics: How Culture Shock Can Charge Up a Parish. The Editors Interview Bishop Placido Rodriguez, CMF," *U.S. Catholic* (December 1986): 33-39.
123. Tomasi, *A Lesson from History*, 12.
124. NCCB Committee on Migration, Office of Pastoral Care of Migrants and Refugees, "Pastoral Care of Vietnamese Catholics in the United States: A Preliminary Report," unpublished (Washington, D.C., 1985).
125. John Dart, "Immigrants called 'Ripe Harvest Field' for Churches," *Los Angeles Times*, Part II, April 20, 1985, 6.
126. See n. 12.
127. See n. 59.
128. Gabriel Fackre, "Positive Values and Honorable Intentions: A Critique of Fundamentalism," *New Theology Review* (May 1988): 69.
129. "Working Paper for African Synod," 663.
130. Ibid., 671.
131. Ibid., 670.
132. David L. Schindler, "Towards a Eucharistic Evangelization," *Communio* (Winter 1992), 551.
133. Angel Cardinal Suquia, "The New Evangelization: Some Tasks and Risks of the Present," *Communio* (Winter 1992), 528.
134. Ibid., 533.
135. Guatemalan Bishops Conference, 33.
136. Thomas F. Stransky, "A Catholic Looks at American Fundamentalists," *New Catholic World* (January/February 1985): 11.
137. Pope John Paul II, *Christifideles Laici* (Vatican City: Libreria Editrice Vaticana, 1988), n. 34.
138. King, 41.

139. An example may be helpful here. Fundamentalists shrink from human mediation, since they see it as an obstacle between the believer and Christ. Theologically, Dulles explains the Catholic mentality in this way: "As mediator, she [the Church] participates in the extremes which she unites. She does not present herself as a third party, interposing herself between the faithful and their Lord, but as a bridge or meeting ground, sharing in the functions of the Redeemer and the redeemed" (Avery Dulles, *Revelation and the Quest for Unity* [Washington, D.C.: Corpus Books, 1968], 114).

Hispanic Catholics, for instance, have internalized that theological concept, so that "the Evangelical penchant for reducing the mediation between God and humanity to the Scriptures is antithetical to the Hispanic tendency to multiply mediations. Not only the Church but the saints, angels and especially the Virgin Mary are viewed as mediators in addition to Jesus Christ Himself." On the other hand, "the more democratic, egalitarian ethos of Evangelicalism is somehow foreign to the hierarchical configuration of both the Hispanic family and society" (Allan Figueroa Deck, *The Challenge of Evangelical/Pentecostal Christianity to Hispanic Catholicism in the United States* [Notre Dame, Indiana: Cushwa Center for the Study of American Catholicism, 1992], 14).

Needless to say, capitalizing (in the best sense of the word) on this cultural-theological fact of life would work mightily to keep proselytizers at bay but also assist in fruitful evangelization of those who had left the Catholic fold or who had never been a part of it.

140. Pope John Paul II, "Hail the Blessed Mother of God!" *L'Osservatore Romano*, June 30, 1993, 3.

141. Ibid.

It is not surprising, therefore, that several bishops at the Santo Domingo meeting of CELAM felt compelled to highlight this aspect of the question. The Brazilian Raymundo Damasceno Assis noted that "what is needed is that the Gospel goes to the root of the culture. . . ." At the same time, Karl Josef Romer, auxiliary bishop of Rio de Janeiro, spoke of "a very strong Catholic culture in Latin America" (Stefania Falasca, "Santo Domingo: Fall of the Walls of Old," *30 Days* [November 11, 1992]: 18-19).

A wonderful example of how this has "worked" in real life comes across in the autobiography of a Stanford University professor: "After dinner we all went to the front room where the priest took a small book from his jacket to recite some prayers, consecrating our house and our family. He left a large picture of a sad-eyed Christ, exposing His punctured Heart. . . . That picture survives. Hanging prominently over the radio or, later, the television set in the front room, it has retained a position of prominence in all the houses my parents have lived in since. It has been one of the few permanent fixtures in the environment of my life. Visitors to our house doubtlessly noticed it when they entered the door — saw it immediately as the sign we were Catholics. But I saw the picture too often to pay it much heed.

"I saw a picture of the Sacred Heart in the grammar school classroom I entered two years after the priest's visit. The picture drew an important continuity between home and the classroom. When all else was different for me . . . between the two worlds of my life, the Church provided an essential link. During my first months in school, I remember being struck by the fact that — although they worshipped in English — the nuns and my classmates shared my family's religion. The *gringos* were, in some way, like me, *católicos*. Gradually, however, with my assimilation in the schoolroom, I began to think of myself and my family as Catholics. The distinction blurred. At home and in class I heard about sin and Christ and Satan and the consoling presence of Mary the Virgin. It became one Catholic Faith for me" (Richard Rodriguez, 82-83).

CHAPTER 5

Mary Among the Proselytizers

As the present research has already abundantly demonstrated, Fundamentalism is a growing religious phenomenon that, for at least the past two decades, by its own admission, relies largely on disenchanted or uncatechized Catholics to increase its membership. What is relatively recent in the Fundamentalist outreach to Catholics, however, is a specifically Marian dimension used to attract and keep Catholics who would otherwise refuse to be part of their communities.

This has come into focus only gradually. Less than a decade ago pastoral workers, especially among Hispanic Catholics in the United States, began to relate isolated stories of independent or "store-front" churches that were relying on some kind of Marian imagery in their outreach. What was perceived as idiosyncratic and isolated has come to be acknowledged by the Church across the board as a phenomenon to be reckoned with. This can be seen from the array of statements from local Church leaders, bishops, episcopal conferences, and the Holy See itself — all cited in the Bibliography.

The Marian approach must be fully appreciated as the significant development it is, both theologically and pastorally: theologically, for Fundamentalism, because the methodology violates the absolute refusal in classical Fundamentalism to accord to Mary any role of intercession or mediation; and pastorally, for Catholicism, because the faithful will be less guarded with the proselytizers, since the line of demarcation is now less clear.

Fundamentalist involvement with Marian devotion falls into two broad classifications, moving on parallel tracks and depending on the proselytizing agent. In the first, Catholics are invited to consider the "unbiblical" nature of an attachment to Mary, or else to attend in the future a lecture or sermon on the topic. In the second (the novel approach for Fundamentalism), Marian images, prayers, hymns, and devotions are regarded as either neutral or positive. An examination of both procedures is in order.

A word of caution is also in order, a caveat issued already in Chapter 2 but important to reiterate here. Fundamentalism is not a unitary system of theology or practice. Therefore, it is not possible to posit theological or pastoral stances, as though Fundamentalism shared in the Catholic approach to decision-making. Since there are no synods or ecumenical councils or popes for Fundamentalism (the absence of all of which causes Fundamentalists to rejoice), one cannot expect any kind of unified system of thought or worship. Admittedly, this makes research of the present kind more difficult, but this is precisely the nature of the phenomenon. Luis Leon says this regarding Pentecostalism: "Since its inception, Pentecostalism has developed into a wide variety of forms and practices; there is very little theological or practical uniformity about Pentecostalism. It is perhaps best, then, to speak of not a single Pentecostal experience, but of many Pentecostalisms with their regional, class, ethnic, gender and denominational adaptations and expressions."[1]

This applies to the entire sphere of Fundamentalism, not merely to its Pentecostalist manifestations. Therefore, what is found in studies and research in one particular community can be taken as no more than one indicator; numerous incidents of the same can suggest a trend, but little more can be said with any degree of certitude. Of course, in the present context, twenty years ago one would have been hard-pressed to find even a single example of what is apparently emerging as a definite trend, if not a development that — at some future moment — may be seen to have decisive consequences for Fundamentalism.

Mary in the Traditional Fundamentalist Mode

Even the Protestant theologian Karl Barth, by no means a Fundamentalist, could declare: "We reject Mariology, (1) because it is an arbitrary innovation in the face of Scripture and the Early Church, and (2) because this innovation consists essentially in a falsification of Christian truth. . . . It means that Marian dogma is neither more nor less than the critical, central dogma of the Roman Catholic Church, the dogma from the standpoint of which all their important positions are to be regarded and by which they stand or fall. . . . In the doctrine and worship of Mary, there is disclosed the one heresy of the Roman Catholic Church which explains all the rest."[2]

How much less nuanced and sophisticated becomes the denunciation on the lips of Fundamentalists in general and their proselytizers in particular.[3] Reacting to Fundamentalist incursions in the Philippines, the Catholic bishops of that nation observed in a pastoral letter that the "literal interpretation of biblical passages taken out of their context is then used to aggressively attack Catholic teachings and practices like our teaching on the Blessed Virgin Mary and our veneration of sacred images."[4]

Some of the worst examples of this come from tracts emanating from Chick Publications.[5] *Why Is Mary Crying?* teaches that "Mary is embarrassed, because the [Catholic] people are bowing down to statues of her. . . . Mary sheds tears because men call her 'The Mother of God.' . . . Mary weeps because men teach she was really sinless. . . . Mary is crying for the deceived multitudes who look to her as a mediatrix . . . and pray to her."[6] The pamphlet goes on to assert that Marian devotion is a fabrication of Satan, who "devised a wicked plan to confuse the people into putting their trust in a counterfeit virgin . . . named Semiramis . . . and he used her to put untold millions into hell." How will this play out finally?

> In these last days, the key to pulling all the religions together is the worship of the satanic mother goddess. Almost a billion Moslems will join because the Virgin Mary was carefully placed in their holy book, the Koran. Even the "New Agers" refer to a Mother/Father god.
>
> Satanic powers will impersonate Mary in future apparitions of the "Virgin" worldwide, including Communist countries, to bring the world under Satan's antichrist.
>
> The devil knows his time is running out. Jesus is coming soon, and Satan is desperate.[7]

As ludicrous as this might sound, it is important to realize that millions of Catholics have been influenced by this type of literature.[8] In another Chick publication, *Are Roman Catholics Christians?*, readers are instructed once more about the pagan origins of Marian devotion, linked to Semiramis and Venus, too. Quoting from the Legion of Mary handbook that Christ's Blood was drawn from the veins of His Mother Mary, Chick declares this a "total blasphemy against the precious blood of Christ." Continuing, he says, "this 'Mary' was deliberately exalted to get the eyes of Roman Catholics off Jesus. They made her the co-redeemer and the queen of heaven." Answering the title question of the work, he writes: "I'm sorry. But the answer is 'no'! [Catholics] are very religious and very lost. Because the system they trusted has betrayed them." Finally, the point is made thus: "Many Roman Catholics are doing their best to serve God and to please Him. That is why this false religious system is so evil. Those trapped within it may be sincerely seeking God, but if you are not serving God according to His Word, you are sincerely *wrong*" (emphasis in original).[9]

A less rabid but no less forthright denunciation of Catholicism's Marian beliefs and devotions occurs in a pamphlet by William R. Kimball. In the section on Mariology (generally citing St. Alphonsus Liguori's *Glories of Mary* as an authority for the Catholic position advanced), one finds the following statements:

◆ In spite of the great emphasis upon Mary in Roman Catholicism, the Bible says very little about her.

◆ Rome claims that Mary acts as a mediator between sinners and God and teaches that sinners receive pardon through Mary. This is refuted by the Scriptures.

◆ "The Holy Church commands a worship peculiar to Mary," but the Bible rejects this demand on the grounds that it is idolatry.

◆ But the Bible rejects Rome's claim that Mary is an intercessor or advocate who intercedes to [sic] God on our behalf in order to obtain grace for the sinner.

◆ The Bible rejects Rome's claim that "Mary is the peacemaker between sinners and God."

◆ The Bible rejects Catholic claims that Mary is "the gate of heaven because no one can enter that blessed kingdom without passing through her."

◆ The Bible gives absolutely no support to the many exalted titles which the Roman Catholic Church has bestowed upon Mary. . . . These titles represent Rome's attempts to elevate Mary to a glorified position which is not taught in the Scriptures.

◆ The doctrine of the Immaculate Conception . . . is contrary to the Scriptures.

◆ The Roman Catholic doctrine of the Assumption of Mary . . . is a teaching which can't find the slightest support in the Bible and was not made an official doctrine in the Catholic Church until 1950.

◆ Roman Catholicism's emphasis on Mary's perpetual virginity is clearly refuted in the Bible. . . .[10]

To those insufficiently formed in their Catholic Faith, the above litany of "Roman" teachings and the concomitant biblical rejection of each presents an impressive case that at least raises doubts if not an immediate movement outside Catholicism.

Another approach used by Fundamentalist proselytizers is the so-called "witness literature," that is, personal testimonies of former Catholics, preferably priests or nuns, who once subscribed to Catholic Mariology and even taught it, but who subsequently have abandoned it all in favor of "biblical truth." One of the most famous contributors to this genre is the ex-priest from Canada, Charles Chiniquy, who lived in the nineteenth century and titillated anti-Catholics with his *The Secrets of the Confessional*.[11] Less well known is his short tract, *The Gift*, which purports to document his gradual enlightenment on the proper place of Mary in the life of the Church. Most effective, from a proselytizing angle, is his use of an alleged conversation with his bishop whom he confronted with the "biblical truth" about Mary, only to find the bishop totally devastated and unable to respond: "Then the poor bishop was as a man who is condemned to death. He trembled before me, and as he could not answer me, he pleaded business and left me. His 'business' was that he could not answer me."[12] He also recounts his own departure from the Catholic Church and his final address to his people in which he proclaimed: "It is time for me to go away from you, my friends. I have left the Roman Catholic Church forever. I have taken the gift of Christ, but I respect you too much to impose myself on you; if you think it is better for you to follow the Pope than to follow Christ, and to invoke the name of Mary than the name of Jesus, in order to be saved, tell it to me by rising up."[13]

He concludes by noting that not one parishioner stood in defense of Rome. All remained his disciples, with four thousand converts made within six months and twenty-five thousand by the time of the first edition of the tract. Hyperbole aside, Chiniquy was a man to be reckoned with, and Mariology was a frequent theme he employed in his efforts to lure Catholics from the Church.[14]

Equally colorful material is produced by Bartholomew F. Brewer, who claims to be an ex-priest, too. In fact, he is the founder of "Mission to Catholics International," an organization whose sole function is to lead Catholics into his own brand of Fundamentalism.[15] Brewer serves up to his readers people like Anthony Pezzotta, Charles Berry, Eileen Doran, and Amy Bentley — all of whom declare themselves to be ex-religious in their autobiographical tracts, and all of whom discuss the liberation that came to them when they gave up the cult of the Virgin for the worship of Jesus Christ. Brewer's own personal odyssey, *The Conversion of a Catholic Priest*, makes the very same points,[16] as does his full-length autobiography.[17]

Tony Coffey's combination of autobiography and theology is rather similar, albeit in a much more irenic mode. For instance, he expresses the following concerns at the outset: "First, [this book] might be used in a manner never intended. *Once a Catholic* has not been written to fuel the fires of sectarianism or to provide ammunition for overzealous persons who delight in scoring cheap points at the expense of the beliefs of others. I want to distance myself from those who engage in such unholy warfare. Second, I fear that some people will see this book only in a negative light, as being out of touch with the ecumenical climate of the day. The idea of refuting the beliefs of another person is seen as belonging to the distant past."[18]

The author, described on the dust jacket of the book as "ministering to a community of Christians in Dublin," devotes a full chapter to Marian doctrine, tackling the usual questions of Our Lady's perpetual virginity, Immaculate Conception, Assumption, intercessory role and apparitions. He presents the Catholic Church's doctrines on each of these, seeking to refute them from Scripture, even though he does begin by agreeing that "Mary displayed a spirit that is worthy of imitation by every Christian."[19]

Not surprisingly, then, in the King study, it was found that "nearly three out of five (58%) of the respondents have heard someone from another church say something [negative] about the Catholic Church. . . . The Catholic tradition of praying to Mary and the saints has been criticized to these respondents more frequently than any other aspect of Catholicism (23%)." Furthermore, the respondents to the same survey "report hearing comments such as, 'Catholics are idol worshippers,' 'Mary is not a virgin,' and 'Catholics worship statues.' "[20]

With good reason, then, did the Hispanic bishops of California warn that: "To accept the teaching of the sects is to reject Mary and what she stands for in God's wonderful plan of redemption. To join these sects is to betray the Marian tradition of our *ancestros*, who saw so clearly the terrible contradiction involved in accepting and loving Christ while rejecting or ignoring His Mother."[21]

And although it is impossible at the present time to know how many Catholics have actually left the Church as a direct result of the use of Mariology by proselytizers,[22] we do know that a full six percent of the unchurched in a nationwide survey gave Marian devotion as the primary reason for their refusal to affiliate with the Catholic Church.[23] It is significant that another ten percent cite the use of rosaries, statues, medals, and the like as raising difficulties of a theological and/or personal nature. When the two groups are put together, those categories are then exceeded only by topics related to human sexuality, which garnered about twenty-one percent for most aspects of the question.

New Approaches to the Marian Dimension

Open, virulent hostility to Catholic Marian belief and devotion has held sway from Fundamentalism's beginnings. It was only as recently as the late 1980s that the first hints of a change of attitude and practice in some Fundamentalist quarters begin to appear.[24] It might actually be more precise to say that Catholics had just begun to look for such phenomena and thus began to see what may well have been present at an earlier moment.

Since then, slowly but surely, data have been surfacing to indicate a novelty in some segments of Fundamentalism, namely: the use of Marian symbols. Their use in some Fundamentalist communities aims at making would-be converts to "true Christianity" feel more "at home," with a view gradually to weaning the newly-proselytized from Mary. In other Fundamentalist communities, however, Marian symbols have become permanent fixtures. On both coasts of the United States, as well as in the southeast and southwest, one discovers Fundamentalist communities scheduling novenas and rosary services, singing Marian hymns, using statues and pictures of Mary, even naming churches in her honor, especially under Hispanic titles.[25]

Mary and the Proselytizers in Perspective

"About 44% of the diocesan ethnic ministers told Sister [Eleace] King about non-Catholic churches using Catholic devotions to attract members."[26] Interestingly enough, this has happened before. The first example of the use of this kind of subterfuge appears in Japanese Catholic history. After the martyrdom or exile of the Jesuit missionaries and their adherents, efforts were made to reattract those who had accepted Christianity. Stephen Turnbull discusses the specifically Marian outreach of one such shrine, with a somewhat amusing twist: "One of the most remarkable examples is to be found in Hondo, on the Amakusa Islands. Here a Buddhist temple, the Meitoku-ji, was founded in 1645 as a deliberate attempt to win back the allegiance of the former Christians. The contemporary statue in its grounds is supposed to be Kannon, but a local tradition identifies it as a Maria-Kannon, and the sculptor as a Hidden Christian, who thereby got the last laugh!"[27]

Evidence exists that a similar event also occurred at least once before in American Catholic history, as Gerald Shaughnessy observes in regard to the Italian immigrants in the early part of the twentieth century: "Statues, altars, candles and similar appurtenances are used by certain sects, in their 'Italian missions,' to entrap the unwary and the ignorant."[28] This type of approach is all the more problematic, since "many of the signs and symbols non-Catholic churches are using to attract Catholics are the very things that have been disappearing from our Catholic churches."[29] Antonio Lopez y Guzman puts an even finer point on it: "Traditional Catholic devotion to Our Lady and saints is downgraded in many places — a downgrading taken advantage of by the *santeros*"[30]; but this is true beyond its connection to *santería* (a syncretistic mixture of Catholicism and voodoo), as highlighted by the Most Reverend Robert Sanchez, former Archbishop of Santa Fe (New Mexico), in a paper presented to the Pontifical Commission for the Spiritual Care of Migrants and Itinerants. Archbishop Sanchez said that, among "the effective methods most often used by proselytizers" was "the use of traditional Catholic devotions or symbols (e.g., statues or banners of Our Lady of Guadalupe) to confuse newcomers and to attract them to their church."[31] The change of policy among such Fundamentalists is reflected upon by the Reverend Juan Diaz Vilar: "In the past, the heart of the message of the various sects was the Bible, along with criticism of devotion to statues or images and to the Virgin. Such pious practices are popular among Hispanic Catholics. Today, some sects play down their attacks on Catholics' devotion to Mary and saints' statues. They now try, rather, to respect the popular religiosity of the Hispanic, to the point where some sects now are quite ready to accept devotion to the Virgin of Guadalupe and even to endorse statues of Mary, the rosary and pilgrimages to Marian shrines. If a plan works, they use it."[32]

Father Vilar's analysis is confirmed by narrative evidence, such as the following: "Thus far, eighteen members of Maria and Victor's extended family have transferred to the large Baptist church, where a Mexican-born minister preaches every Sunday. The place is packed with Hispanics who warmly support each other's decision to depart from the Catholic Faith. 'I don't feel bad about this at all. I think I have more faith than ever before,' says Maria; she adds, a bit self-consciously, that her only relic from the past is a small figurine of Our Lady of Guadalupe that she keeps in her room."[33]

Gilbert Padilla sees an interesting angle, which is rarely noticed, let alone used to pastoral advantage:

> But if they [fallen-away Hispanic Catholics] can be brought back to the veneration of the Mother of God through the Evangelicals, then it is a source of joy and hope for all of us! The way I look at it is that the tender loving devotion to the Blessed Virgin Mary will do more than anything else to counteract the hostile argumentative attitude that is so characteristic of the Fundamentalists, who appear to be angry about religion. Their religion does not bring them peace. That is what happens when you take the mother and the feminine out of religion. A certain hardness sets in. And it seems that their conversion from the Catholic Faith brings them to the point of attacking the Blessed Virgin. If the Evangelicals reintroduce the devotion to the Blessed Mother, then there is renewed hope! . . . This might be a most important factor for the future.[34]

In their "National Pastoral Plan for Hispanic Ministry," the American bishops raise some of the same points: "The Hispanic people find God in the arms of the Virgin Mary. That is why Mary, the Mother of God, as goodness, compassion, protection, inspiration, example . . . is at the heart of Hispanic spirituality."[35] Quite realistically, however, they also acknowledge that "at various times through the centuries these devotions have gone astray or have been impoverished due to the lack of a clear and enriching catechesis. This pastoral plan . . . can be a source of evangelization for these popular devotions and an encouragement for enriching liturgical celebrations with cultural expressions of faith."[36]

The Bibliography of this research project is replete with pastoral plans of the Church at every level, all designed to deal with the problem of proselytism. They come from various dicasteries of the Holy See, from episcopal conferences, and from individual bishops.[37]

They all provide analyses of the situation; they all seek to offer ways of combatting the onslaught through a stronger outreach (e.g., liturgy and catechesis) and through greater sensitivity toward the groups and individuals targeted. Only a handful — most notably the statements of Archbishop Sanchez, the Latin American and Filipino episcopates, the Hispanic bishops of California, and the NCCB's Plan for Hispanic Ministry — note the threat posed to Marian devotion by the sects. Archbishop Sanchez alone, however, has taken cognizance of the proselytizers' novel use of Marian symbols, rather than their attack on such things.

What does this mean concretely? Nearly all of the institutional pronouncements on this topic predate the work of Sister Eleace King and myself. Following, then, are data that are critically important from a pastoral point of view, since Church leaders will have to take into account this new method of proselytism and adequately prepare both pastoral workers and the faithful to confront it effectively.

Two Major Studies

The findings of the 1987 Stravinskas study caused the NCCB's Office for the Pastoral Care of Migrants and Refugees and the Secretariat for Hispanic Affairs to seek out more detailed information on the impact of proselytism. An Ad Hoc Committee for a Pastoral Response to the Challenge of Proselytism was formed, and it commissioned a pilot study on attitudes of ethnic ministers toward proselytism. The survey instrument was developed by the Center for Applied Research in the Apostolate (CARA), with Sister Eleace King, IHM, as the survey director. A random sample of five hundred pastoral workers in ethnic apostolates was taken from a field of five thousand such persons in the NCCB network; a thirty-percent return rate was realized.

King and Gillespie cited the following as salient in terms of the identity of the participants and the results:

Who were the personnel considered?

◆ These respondents represent 87 dioceses and two nationwide ethnic apostolates, located in 35 states, the District of Columbia.

◆ Three-fourths of the respondents are designated diocesan officers to ethnic minorities.

◆ More than three-fourths of the respondents are ordained clergy and/or professed religious.

What findings were deemed critical?

◆ The three groups most frequently mentioned as proselytizing ethnic minorities are Jehovah's Witnesses, Mormons and Pentecostals.

◆ These respondents perceive the three most successful methods of proselytizing to be: offering a personal invitation to join a church, house-to-house canvassing, and ministering in the idiom of the people.[38]

They also felt compelled to highlight four other points on which a most significant degree of consensus emerged:

◆ Respondents are aware of churches or groups proselytizing in the diocese (96%).

◆ Proselytizing by non-Catholic groups is a serious problem in the diocese (90%).

◆ In welcoming new ethnic minorities to the Catholic Church, it is important to have a pastor who speaks the language of the ethnic minority (98%).

◆ Liturgical celebration of the patronal feasts of ethnic minorities is important in welcoming new immigrants to the Catholic Church (94%).[39]

They conclude their reflections by referring to "the pervasiveness of the phenomenon" of proselytism.[40]

In dealing with the specific thrust of this chapter, the study found that "nearly half (47%) agree that the Catholic Church's neglect in promoting popular devotions has hampered the Church's outreach to ethnic minorities."[41] Furthermore, the project directors received documented evidence for the first time regarding "the use of Catholic statues and icons in non-Catholic churches. Several respondents stated that statues of Our Lady of Guadalupe were being placed in non-

Catholic churches and were attracting many converts from Catholicism."[42]

The King and Gillespie study thus set the stage for a full-blown
analysis of the problem. The same episcopal Ad Hoc Committee once
again contacted Sister Eleace King of CARA to produce "an exploratory study of proselytism of new immigrants, refugees and ethnic
groups,"[43] which would follow up and make more specific the findings of the pilot project. King explains how the selections were made:
"According to the *Statistical Yearbook of the Immigration and Natu-
ralization Services*, three-fourths of all immigrants in 1986 (the last
year for which statistics were available) resided in six states. It was
decided that at least one arch/diocese from each of these states be
included in this study. In order to include arch/dioceses from various
geographical areas and small as well as large arch/dioceses, eight
arch/dioceses were selected. The arch/dioceses of Brooklyn, Chicago,
Galveston-Houston, Los Angeles, Miami, Providence, New Orleans
and Yakima participated in the study."[44]

She goes on to note that "the study consisted of three separate
components: a review of the literature, a content analysis of national
and arch/diocesan evangelization plans, and a series of individual
and group interviews."[45] Staking out the turf for the study, King put it
as follows: "The current study was undertaken to investigate the phenomena of proselytism and evangelization of new immigrants, refugees and persons of various ethnic groups. It was hypothesized that
all ethnic groups would be targets of proselytizing efforts of non-
Catholic churches and denominations, but that some ethnic groups
would be more aggressively sought than others. Further, it was hypothesized that some conversions from Catholicism would be due to
a lack of effective Catholic evangelization, rather than the result of
proselytism by other religious groups."[46]

"Ethnic ministers" (i.e., pastoral agents working in ethnic
apostolates) in the target dioceses were interviewed by King or her
research assistant; they, in turn, were charged with disseminating interview schedules to 545 parishioners; seventy-eight percent were
returned and validated. A further 215 interview schedules were distributed to former Catholics, with a forty-two-percent return rate. Sixty

Catholic pastors were also interviewed. The researchers spent twelve days in each diocese, observing the overall situation and meeting pastoral workers, ordinary Catholics, former Catholics, and even non-Catholic ministers.

Some of the more interesting findings included:

◆ More than half of the Catholic parishioners have been invited to join another church or denomination, and most of these people have received more than one invitation.

◆ Less than half of all the Catholic parishioners interviewed have experienced some form of overt proselytism.[47]

◆ Catholic parishioners are more apt to have heard criticism of Catholic devotion to Mary and the saints than any other criticism.

◆ Virtually all the diocesan ethnic ministers and pastors of multi-cultural parishes that were interviewed are aware of proselytism among the people they serve.[48]

Forty-four percent of the so-called "ethnic ministers" are "aware of non-Catholic churches or denominations in their arch/dioceses that use Catholic devotions to attract Catholics to join their churches." They go on to observe that "Marian devotions and statues of both the Blessed Virgin and saints account for nearly a fifth (18%) of the Catholic symbols these respondents know are being used by other churches." Interestingly, "some respondents have seen pictures of the Pope in non-Catholic churches, and others are aware of Protestant denominations that celebrate Catholic rituals and feastdays such as *quinceañeras* and Our Lady of Guadalupe. . . . Some denominations appear to attract Catholic parishioners by including a title of Our Lady in the title of the parish, such as the First Baptist Church of Our Lady of Guadalupe."[49] The project director herself attests to the fact that "images of Our Lady, especially Our Lady of Guadalupe, Our Mother of Perpetual Help and El Caridad del Cobre, are enshrined in some Protestant and non-denominational churches. . . ."[50]

A display is offered below as Table 10 (so designated in the King Report), concerned with "Catholic symbols used in non-Catholic worship" and is reproduced below in full. Groups cited include: Spiritual, Shaker, Santería, Banal Na Pag-aaral, Non-denominational, "Protestant" (a generic term in the survey). The report mentions that "a quick glance at Table 10 reveals that the Blessed Virgin Mary, the saints and candles have been adopted by every group." With a note of irony, the report continues that "the symbols that these groups have kept (i.e., statues, crucifixes, vigil lights) are the very symbols that have been de-emphasized in the decor of Roman Catholic churches in the post-Vatican II era." In point of fact, says King, "in some arch/ dioceses these symbols were more readily seen in non-Catholic than in Catholic churches."[51]

Table 10: Catholic symbols used in non-Catholic worship

Catholic Symbol	(BA) Spir	(AI) Shak	(Cub) Sant	(Fil) BNP	(His) Non-D	(His) Prot
Mary	Yes	Yes	Yes	Yes	Yes	Yes
Saints	Yes	Yes	Yes	Yes	Yes	Yes
Sacred Heart	No	Yes	Yes	No	Yes	?
Crucifix	Yes	Yes	?	Yes	Yes	Yes
Sign of the Cross	Yes	Yes	?	?	Yes	Yes
Candles	Yes	Yes	Yes	Yes	Yes	Yes
Healing	Yes	Yes	Yes	?	Yes	Yes
Eucharist	No	No	?	Yes	Yes	Yes

? = uncertainty about the presence of a particular symbol.
The ethnic abbreviations are as follows: **BA** = Black Americans; **AI** = American Indians; **Cub** = Cubans; **Fil** = Filipinos; **His** = Hispanics.

The 1991 King study and conversations with King led me to consider this matter in greater depth by reflecting on the place of Mariology in what may be termed "classical Fundamentalism" (statistically the most numerous and aggressive proselytizers of Catholics), as well as the whole question of proselytism. Specific attention would then be directed to determine, by broadening the geographical scope of the King studies, how widespread the proselytism problem was, with particular care given to discover the Marian link already documented by King. Regrettably, it was not possible to go back directly to participants in either the King/Gillespie or King studies for clarifications and elucidations of the Marian dimension, since CARA guarantees anonymity and also since all raw data are destroyed within six months of survey publication.[52]

The Present Study

David Blackbourn, in the introduction to his monumental study on the apparitions at Marpingen in the nineteenth century, indicated the traps of which he was aware and which we sought to avoid; he likewise felt compelled to reveal his own mindset from the start. His reflections are worth quoting in some detail, since they relate to the present project as well:

> It should be clear already what sort of approach I take to the events described in this book. To take them seriously is in itself a declaration of sorts. Even twenty years ago a mainstream historian — of modern Europe, at least — would hardly have done so. Marian apparitions occupied a kind of historical limbo along with other manifestations of superstition and delusion. If the role of religion in modern Europe was generally neglected, popular religious phenomena were truly the lost souls of historiography. They were usually passed over, and what attention they did receive was slighting. They were, at best, a sign of how slowly modernization spread its benefits, at worst the symptom of a worrying irrationalism. Writers might be urbane, sorrowful or chiding, according to individual taste; they seldom paid such matters the compliment of viewing them levelly. . . .
>
> There are obvious gains to be had from a sympathetic study of popular religious mentalities and movements. I hope that this study demonstrates some of them. There are potential pitfalls too. One of them is to abdicate the properly critical stance of the historian by confusing it with improper presumption, throwing out the "cold abstraction" of theory along with the arrogance of mod-

ern certainties. We are well rid of the second, but need to hang on
to the first. . . . A related pitfall is the sentimentality that sometimes attends studies based on a small community. . . .[53]

All things being equal, the application is pertinent to the present
study and the process that guided it.

At the outset, telephone interviews with pastoral workers in Texas
confirmed the use of Marian symbols in that area.[54] The Reverends
Benjamin Rodriguez of St. Philomena's in Peoria and Richard
Soseman of St. Mary's in Moline, Illinois, likewise attested to the
same lure being employed in their areas; Father Soseman also spoke
of similar developments in Chicago.[55] The Reverend John West of
the Office of Religious Education in the Archdiocese of Detroit indicated that, although unaware of this methodology in Detroit, he had
experienced it personally in Mexico; this was the first time anyone
alluded to this practice outside the United States.[56]

It was possible to discuss this phenomenon with several bishops
during the NCCB's Fall 1992 meeting. The Most Reverend Raymond
Peña of El Paso knew of Fundamentalist use of Marian images and
certain other dimensions of Marian devotion. He believes that in his
area, whatever is initially used is permanently maintained, even after
the conversions are made.[57] The Most Reverend Plácido Rodríguez,
then-auxiliary bishop of Chicago and current diocesan bishop of Lubbock, Texas, indicated that Hispanic Fundamentalists in metropolitan Chicago brought Catholics into their communities through Marian
images, hymns, and other devotions; as time went on, however, the
former Catholics were weaned off these things.[58]

Reflecting on the situation from the reports of Diaspora Cubans,
the Most Reverend Agustín Román of Miami divided Fundamentalist proselytizers into two groups: orthodox and liberal. The "orthodox" Fundamentalists, he said, never dabble in Mariology of any kind.
"Liberals," on the other hand, do use Marian images, devotions, and
processions. He finds theirs to be a two-tiered approach. At first, they
neither encourage nor discourage any Marian "baggage" brought with
the former Catholics, merely following the lead of the proselytized to
some degree. Later on, however, when the hold is more firmly estab-

lished, they attack Marian symbols as unbiblical and eventually eliminate them from the spiritual diet of the converts.[59]

The problem in southern Florida is so great in this regard that the Chancellor of the Archdiocese of Miami has even issued an official communiqué to warn unsuspecting Catholics of this. Robert O'Steen reports:

> The Archdiocese of Miami is concerned that some Catholics in South Florida are going to churches that are not actually true Roman Catholic churches — and the people may not even be aware of it.
>
> There are currently about nine churches in Dade and Broward Counties with typical Catholic or Catholic-sounding names, which are not authentic Catholic churches in union with the Pope and the Church's bishops. And many of these congregations are being led by someone who is either not an ordained Catholic priest or who no longer has faculties in the Roman Church.[60]

Of interest to the present study is that at least three of the churches cited above have Marian titles, causing the chancellor of the archdiocese, the Reverend Tomás Marin, to declare that "it's very confusing" to many Catholics.[61]

The Most Reverend Silvano Tomasi, former secretary of the Pontifical Commission for the Spiritual Care of Migrants and Itinerants in Rome, recalls that on a pastoral visitation of American parishes in his capacity as provincial superior of the Scalabrinian Fathers several years ago, he was stunned to find a statue of the Blessed Virgin set up in front of a Fundamentalist church in Immokale, Florida. This was his first direct experience of the apparent willingness of Fundamentalists to modify their traditional intransigence on two issues at once: the use of "graven images," and devotion to the Blessed Mother.[62]

An extensive meeting with the Reverend Juan Diaz Vilar revealed that in his experience, largely in Orange County, California, Fundamentalists (Pentecostals and Baptists, but not Jehovah's Witnesses) used the Guadalupe image, but no prayers or other such devotions. Father Vilar thought it accurate to say that Catholics who have joined these groups did not go precisely for any Marian dimension and would have gone over to them even without that element. He thinks the use of Marian imagery is perceived most as a symbol of the willingness of the sects to adapt to Spanish culture. He also stressed the need to offer a rationale for Catholic devotions, demonstrating the biblical, liturgical, and doctrinal bases.[63]

Finally, Paul Bail has found that "some priests feel that the numbers lost to the Church would be much greater if not for the tenacious hold of popular Catholic devotions upon Latin Americans."[64] In some instances, "local Catholic pastors say that Latino Protestant converts find it hard to resist their heritage. Some who attend Protestant churches return to the parish to celebrate the feast of Our Lady of Guadalupe. . . ."[65] But even this rather tenuous connection to Catholicism is obviously undermined when the Fundamentalists themselves resort to Marian devotion. The problem is exacerbated, however, because the Church in the United States "must deal with the polarization of religious and devotional practice, especially when some see certain elements of popular piety, devotion and religiosity as retrograde in a post-Vatican II Church."[66] It should be underscored that this is not a new tension on the Catholic landscape of the United States. Robert A. Orsi describes a similar attitude over a century ago:

> Besides being an embarrassment both to American Catholicism and to the Italian-American clergy, who at times longed for their people to behave in ways more acceptable to the American Church within which they had to function too, *feste* challenged the authority of official Catholicism over the religious lives of the immigrants. . . .
> . . . [The clergy's] criticism of the street life of the devotion — the parties, food, games, noise and dancing that are an inseparable part of the religious meaning of *feste* — intensified at Mount Carmel as the church became more of an American parish in the 1940s and 1950s.[67]

While the anecdotal evidence was interesting and supportive of the intuitions of this study, it was deemed worthwhile to engage in a more formal study of the question of proselytism (see below for the survey instrument, adapted from the CARA study, so as to maintain continuity of response possibilities)[68] in thirty-three representative archdioceses and dioceses of the United States.[69] The survey was conducted through telephone interviews. The first office in each diocese sought for input was the department of evangelization; where such an office did not exist, referrals were usually made to the office for ethnic concerns or occasionally to the chancellor or other official. Dioceses were selected to reflect geographical diversity, as well as various other demographic concerns (e.g., ethnic groups, rural versus urban, etc.), also taking into account the dioceses covered by the King study.

The data may be summarized as follows. Every diocese noted that proselytism is a current problem, generally naming various Fundamentalist sects as the primary agents, quite often mentioning Mormons and Jehovah's Witnesses as well. The overwhelming majority of respondents indicated that Hispanics were the most proselytized group within their local churches; significant, however, was also the frequent citing of African-Americans, Haitians, Native Americans, and Vietnamese, with one diocesan official indicating that important efforts were made by proselytizers right at the port of entry, thus providing the first genuine human contact in the new land. Personal connection through home visitations seems to be the most common method of a first contact; many noted that one of the "drawing cards" is the meeting of immediate material needs (e.g., housing, food, jobs).[70]

Respondents were about evenly divided in terms of their perception that their respective dioceses were "doing an effective job of evangelizing minorities," but all agreed that much more had to be done. Two refused to answer this question at all. A full two-thirds considered that "proselytizing by non-Catholic groups is a serious problem in my diocese."

On the specifically Marian component of this survey, the following data surfaced. Thirty-six percent of the diocesan officials were clearly aware of the use of Marian symbols and imagery in the proselytizing campaigns[71]; thirty percent, however, were simply not sure about this dimension (although several had heard rumblings about

such). Most interesting of all, however, was the fact that certain respondents, apparently charged with the pastoral care of the Catholics
under siege from proselytizers, did not answer this question affirmatively — even though priests or bishops interviewed in other phases
of this project cited clear and certain examples of the use of Marian
symbolism in attempts at conversion of Catholics to Fundamentalist
sects within those same jurisdictions. This highlights a significant
problem for the Church, namely, that either data "from the field" are
not getting into central headquarters, or that office personnel are
woefully out of touch with reality. In either instance, corrective measures are needed or at least further detailed exploration.[72]

Eighty-seven percent of the respondents believed that "the
Church's neglect in promoting popular devotions [processions, Marian
devotions, novenas] has hampered the Church's outreach to ethnic
minorities." At the same time, several did say that while true in general, such a judgment did not apply in their own dioceses where serious efforts were made to maintain or revitalize such manifestations
of popular religiosity.[73]

A final fleshing out of the Marian element was attempted by
returning to all who responded affirmatively to that question in any
phase of this project, so as to learn just what types of Marian devotion were being practiced by the proselytizers. More than two years
after the original contact, Sister Angela of the Diocese of Dallas reported that the procedure was still being used and had actually spread.
An almost wholesale use of Marian symbols was in evidence: medals, statues, hymns, banners, and holy cards, with an emphasis on Our
Lady of Guadalupe. One anecdote was of special interest. She noted
that a Catholic woman in conversation with a fallen-away Catholic-
turned-Fundamentalist had expressed shock at the mention that her
former Catholic friend had gone on a pilgrimage to the shrine of Our
Lady of Guadalupe while home in Mexico, to which the retort came:
"I may be a Baptist, but I am also a Mexican!"[74] Deacon Manuel
Facio of the Archdiocese of Santa Fe spoke only of image use, especially but not exclusively tied to Our Lady of Guadalupe.[75] Marsha
Whelan of the Archdiocese of Miami knew only of Marian statues
being used.[76] The Reverend Matthew McGuinness of the Wichita

Diocese similarly could identify only the use of Guadalupe statues.[77]

One of the respondents suggested contacting Sister Rosa Icaza, CCVI, a professor at the Mexican-American Cultural Center in San Antonio. She was most aware of the phenomenon and cited the placement of Marian logos on Fundamentalist tracts as allurements for unsuspecting individuals. She also referred to the use of the rosary, Marian hymns, and processions in honor of Our Lady as "widespread." In her experience, however, these devotions are used only as "bait" and then discontinued once the relationship between proselytizer and proselytized is secure.[78]

The Reverend Juan Alfaro of San Antonio could speak with certitude only on the use of the Guadalupe image — although he had heard of many other Marian symbols being employed.[79] Similarly, the Most Reverend Raymond Peña (formerly of El Paso) noted that the Guadalupe image was surely used, and probably Marian hymns and processions for her feast.[80] The Reverend Charles O'Connor, former director of the Hispanic Apostolate for the Metuchen (New Jersey) Diocese, saw the Marian dimension as an epidemic.[81] The Reverend Michael Scott, pastor of St. Mary's in Perth Amboy in that same diocese, said that within his parish boundaries one could find "Mount Carmel Pentecostal Church," which had the statue of Our Lady of Mount Carmel, enrolled their members in the Brown Scapular, and prayed the Rosary![82] The Reverend Raymond Jarbo, pastor of Blessed Sacrament in Ontario, Oregon, indicated that Marian imagery had been operative in his area, but the ecumenical clergy association pressured the Fundamentalists to end the practice, since they deemed it dishonest; interestingly enough, they complied.[83]

Perhaps the most extensive information, both qualitatively and quantitatively, came from Benny Espaillat of the Boston Archdiocese. His information claims that Fundamentalists sing Marian hymns and have begun to present Mary as a role model for girls in Sunday school, especially as an example of humble obedience. Marian images are found in their churches, but with little signs beneath them saying things like, "In memory of Mary. . . ." These statues or pictures are frequently depictions of the Mother and Child or Our Lady of Guadalupe but never the triumphant Woman of the twelfth chapter of the Book of Revelation. He has learned of churches where Bible studies are devoted to Marian passages. In reading aloud the Annunciation pericope, for example, the men take the part of the angel, while the women assume the role of Mary. In regard to the Rosary, many Hispanic converts to Fundamentalism are being instructed not to throw away their grandmothers' rosaries but to cherish them; however, they are urged not to use them, since they are "not for today." He has also observed that Fundamentalist radio shows are actually speaking positively of Mary, and most are now shying away from discussing "the brothers and sisters" of Jesus, since they apparently get a very negative reaction from their would-be converts on that topic. Espaillat refers to the movement of Hispanics into Fundamentalism as "an exodus." He sees the proselytizers as "much less anti-Catholic" than in the past, but finds their use of Catholic symbols — and especially Marian ones — as presenting major pastoral problems, since uncatechized Hispanics often cannot distinguish between "the real thing" and the counterfeit.[84]

An unexpected piece of information surfaced in the context of a conversation with Patrick Madrid of *This Rock* on a completely unrelated issue. He mentioned that when staff members of his apologetics apostolate were in Denver for the 1993 papal visit, they were told of proselytizing tracts being distributed to the youth "by the thousands."[85] He sent me a copy of the brochure that has a picture of Our Lady on the cover and the words "Blessed Art Thou Among Women" below it. Madrid remarks in the cover letter, "As you can see, it is designed to fool an unsuspecting Catholic into thinking it's a pro-Mary leaflet. Notice that his [Bill Jackson's] organization's name (Christians Evangelizing Catholics) was abbreviated to 'C.E.C.' to further conceal the anti-Catholic nature of the tract." The deceit continues on the back cover, which refers to the item as "Special Commemorative Issue — Visit of Pope John Paul II — Denver, Colorado — August 13-15, 1993." The anti-Marian thrust is low-key and subtle. After rehearsing in almost tender fashion Mary's association with Our Lord at every significant juncture of His life and ministry, it then talks of the need of everyone for a Savior: "In her response to the angel, Mary spoke of God as her Savior. Mary knew she needed salvation, and if

Mary needed a Savior, I certainly do." It then moves off the Marian question and continues in an ecclesiological mode: [Jesus] never instructed anyone to have faith in a church. . . . No angel or saint is able to take your sins away. No church is able to take your sins away. Jesus paid your complete debt to God for you."

Reflecting on the present study in context, then, one can see points of comparison and points of contrast with the work of Sister Eleace King. Like her 1991 report, this project sought data from the field on the issue of proselytism. Likewise, it solicited information on how the proselytizers function. Yet again, as noted earlier, similar questions were used for the sake of continuity. Several important differences also exist, however. First, in this study immigrants were not the only people considered as potential targets of proselytism (although, in fact, they still appear to be the audience of choice). Second, the 1991 King study dealt with eight arch/dioceses, selected on the basis of immigrant arrival in such states; the current effort broadened that base to thirty-three sees, chosen to reflect geographical and demographic diversity and representing urban, suburban, and rural America. Furthermore, once a determination was made that Marian imagery had been employed, follow-up questions were given to tease out some of the specifics of the phenomenon.

In a desire for professional collaboration and peer review, I sent this data and report to King. She responded by asserting that it both "strengthens and expands" her work and also "sets the stage" for further development, thus providing a "significant" link in the chain of research on this question.[86] Dr. Philip Kayal, chairman of the sociology and anthropology department of Seton Hall University, wrote that "I believe you can draw the conclusions that you have from the data that you collected. The evidence you have garnered in support of your research design and proposal is empirical and methodologically valid." He continues, "given the difficulty of comparing data over time with previous studies and changing samples, your use of interviews, phone conversations, evidence from the literature, etc., is appropriate for the case at hand."[87] Finally, Dr. George Gallup, Jr., chairman of the George H. Gallup International Institute, concluded that "you have drawn upon valid sources to build a case." He sums up his overall reaction thus: "I found [the study] to be most interesting and helpful."[88]

Conclusions

All in all, the present study reinforces the findings of the King Report, as well as the anecdotal evidence shared above. The obvious conclusion is that proselytism is indeed a major pastoral problem, and that the Marian dimension bears closer monitoring. Finally, it seems that offering the Marian element within parishes and dioceses would be one way to forestall this mode of Fundamentalist outreach.

A pastoral response from the Catholic Church is certainly required at the levels of adult education and communal worship, including sound liturgical preaching and giving appropriate play to popular religion in parochial life. One anonymous pastor, who describes himself as a theological liberal, has noted with great irony and some degree of bitterness, that he spent the last decade in a suburban parish eliminating the last vestiges of Marian devotion, only to find himself now in a Hispanic situation in which he is "reduced" to rescheduling the very same events unless he wants to face even greater attrition to the sects than has already occurred. Clearly, this is the very mentality alluded to by Stoll: "Such presumptions often become apparent in collisions with popular religion, the folk Catholic traditions that clergy left, right, and middle have often tried to suppress or reform."[89] Just how critical this matter is, particularly within the Hispanic community, can be seen from the finding that "almost eight out of ten [respondents] consider Mary to be very important in their own lives, and only 1.1 percent say that Mary is not important at all."[90] The disjunction between various "elites" (whether clerical or cultural) and popular piety was scored by Pope John Paul II in speaking to the media: "I also think that representatives of 'Atlantic civilization,' and especially Europeans, must be very careful about applying their own criteria of judgment to South American piety."[91] Obviously, it is possible and even necessary to extend the Holy Father's evaluation beyond a uniquely Latin American context.

The picture portrayed in this chapter has a largely Hispanic hue to it and is also highly anecdotal in nature. Therefore, some observa-

tions are in order. First, just because data do not exist in any significant body at present about the Fundamentalist use of Marian imagery
beyond the Hispanic community (or some other immigrant populations) does not necessarily mean that it is not being done or is not
being contemplated.[92] Some late-developing data indicates that
Melkite Catholics are being proselytized in some areas by those who
continue to employ Marian devotion with those being sought and
attracted.[93]

In point of fact, the only serious study of Fundamentalist incursions into Catholicism has been done in regard to immigrant Catholics. Furthermore, it could well be true that the immigrant segment of
the Catholic community is being tested by Fundamentalist proselytizers and, if the technique is successful with them, its use will be
expanded to others. Second, the reliance upon personal accounts (especially of pastoral workers but also of the proselytized themselves)
provides certainly valid data, even if not the most usual form. This
type of source is essential at a stage in the process when this particular method of proselytism is just beginning; hence, written reports
are scarce, and analyses are even scarcer. This exploratory research
has used a qualitative methodology, in an attempt to provide a holis-
tic view through interviews, review of the literature, and observation
to determine the perceptions of either the proselytized themselves or
those charged with their pastoral care within the Catholic Church.
The data of this chapter, then, are on the cutting-edge of a significant
development in theology and pastoral practice, which development
will require much closer surveillance as time goes on.

Endnotes

1. Luis D. G. Leon, "*Somos Un Cuerpo en Cristo:* Notes on Power
   and the Body in an East Los Angeles Chicano/Mexicano Pentecostal Community," *Latino Studies Journal* (September 1994):
   71.
2. Karl Barth, *Church Dogmatics*, Volume I, Part 2 (Edinburgh: T.
   & T. Clark, 1963), 143.
3. The literature cited here originates in the United States, unless
   otherwise noted; its application and impact, however, extend

beyond these borders, as can be seen from Chick's listing of outreach centers in Australia, Canada, England, New Zealand, and
even Germany.

4. "Philippine Bishops' Statement on Biblical Fundamentalism,"
   Origins (February 23, 1989): 627.

5. Samples and Kistler, in their *Catholicism Bibliography*, caution
   their Fundamentalist readers thus: "We do *not* recommend any
   materials published on Catholicism by such ministries as Chick
   Publications, Antichrist Information Center (Alberto Rivera), and
   the Alamo Christian Foundation. The materials published by these
   organizations are unscholarly, often inaccurate, and decidedly
   sensationalistic in their approach [emphasis in original]" (San
   Juan Capistrano, California: Christian Research Institute, 1989),
   unpaginated. It should be noted that all three organizations cited
   by Samples and Kistler have produced Marian tracts.

6. The approach used is not to attack Mary personally but to present
   her as a victim of her devotees and to portray her as unsettled by
   the "unbiblical" and unwarranted attention given to her by them.

7. Jack T. Chick, *Why Is Mary Crying?* Chino, California: Chick
   Publications, undated and unpaginated. A rough estimate of publication would be possible, insofar as the present researcher has
   seen it in circulation at least since 1985.

8. At least if the proselytizers themselves are to be believed. See,
   for example, nn. 11-13 below. Perhaps it would be more accurate to say that "millions" of copies have been distributed, and
   thus have potentially touched large numbers, but nothing beyond
   that can be said with any degree of certainty.

9. Jack T. Chick, *Are Roman Catholics Christians?* Chino, California: Chick Publications, undated and unpaginated.
   In contradistinction to the previous pamphlet, in this one Catholic laity replace Mary as the victim of the Roman Catholic institution.
   The present researcher recalls working weekends in a northern
   New Jersey parish in 1985 in which parishioners constantly found
   these tracts stuffed into novena booklets and missalettes in the
   pews of the church, always accompanied by an invitation to leave

the church building at that very instant, abandon pagan practices, and come to Christ.

10. William R. Kimball, *The Bible and Roman Catholicism* (South
Lake Tahoe, California: Christian Equippers International, 1985):
13-17.
Significantly, proof is offered for none of these apodictic statements, except for an isolated Scripture text, but surely nothing of
a substantive — let alone sustained — theological engagement
of the propositions attacked.

11. Charles Chiniquy, *The Secrets of the Confessional* (Chino, California: Chick Publications, 1983). It should be noted that although
originally published in the last century, this work has been re-
printed recently — an indication of the perduring nature of the
problem and the methodology alike.

12. Charles Chiniquy, *The Gift* (Philadelphia: Continental Press, n.d.):
10.

13. Ibid., 15.

14. In point of fact, in the sparse fifteen pages of *The Gift*, Chiniquy
manages to have Our Lady or some aspect of the Marian question feature prominently on at least nine pages!

15. In his autobiographical tract, *Pilgrimage from Rome* (Greenville,
South Carolina: Bob Jones University Press, 1982, pp.119-121),
Brewer gives the background for the establishment of his organization:
"I prayerfully and deliberately decided to return to San Diego,
where I once served as a parish priest. Aware that Vatican II had
brought many Roman Catholics confusion and disillusionment, I
felt led to begin a ministry to help them in the transition from the
Catholic denomination. Before long, the Lord opened doors to
speak. People wanted to know the name of the ministry. Our
answer was that it was like a mission to Catholics. . . .
"Mission to Catholics International was incorporated and granted
non-profit status. Since that time it has distributed millions of
tracts, books, and tapes exposing the contradictions between
Roman Catholicism and the bible and presenting biblical salvation. A monthly newsletter is available to any contributor re-

questing it. The Lord has allowed us a bit of radio and television exposure, and we are pleased that my autobiography, *Pilgrimage from Rome*, has been published and is receiving an excellent acceptance in both English and Spanish. We have held meetings and taken literature into many foreign countries, and mail orders are sent out five days a week from our home office in San Diego. Meetings keep us busy often for as much as thirteen weeks traveling throughout both the U.S.A. and other countries. A School of Roman Catholic Evangelism provides a week or more of intense training for pastors and key workers who desire to establish ministries for effectively reaching the Roman Catholic community through their churchs [sic]. Missionaries and ex-Catholics are also encouraged to attend (especially ex-priests and ex-nuns, so that they may be prepared to minister within Biblical Fundamentalism)."

Interestingly enough, Brewer's establishment of his "Mission to Catholics" was in some measure responsible for the establishment of Karl Keating's apologetics apostolate, "Catholic Answers," and its publication, *This Rock*, according to staff member Patrick Madrid (telephone conversation, April 24, 1994).

The autobiography alluded to by Brewer contains the following about "Mission to Catholics": "In 1973, my wife and I founded the Mission to Catholics in San Diego, so that we could be more effective instruments in reaching Catholic friends and winning them to Christ through ministering in churches, by radio, and through literature. We love them and understand their condition and the frustration in their hearts."

Offering a kind of *apologia* for his actions, Brewer continues:

"Many times I have been asked why I did not remain in the Roman Catholic Church and work for reforms from within. We are often criticized because we are not more benign in our attitude toward the Catholic Church. We are asked to be 'more constructive.'

"But we cannot and dare not. Can the incredibly rich empire that replaced that of the Roman Caesars be reformed? Martin Luther initially tried to end the corrupt practice of selling indulgences, but he failed to win Catholic reformation, even though he used nothing other than Scripture to uphold his teachings, and even today he is labeled a heretic, an enemy of God! The Catholic Church never hesitates to place its condemnation on anyone who points out its false teachings or who exposes the wrongs of its leaders. Thus it tries to frighten into submission any who would reveal its deceptions. . . .

"We have found this new ministry a joyous work, for we are kept by the power of God through faith. I have been reviled and physically assaulted. Nor have my wife and son been spared persecution. We have received bitter denunciations with packages of ashes containing letters of hate saying, 'This will be your fate.' "

16. See Anthony Pezzotta, *I Found Everything When I Found Christ*; Charles Berry, *The Conversion of a Catholic Priest*; Eileen Doran, *The Conversion of a Catholic Nun*; Amy Bentley, *The Conversion of a Catholic Nun (My Return to Christ)*. All of these are undated but published by Brewer's Mission to Catholics International in San Diego; internal evidence also calls for a post-Vatican II date.

Bentley's style and content should be viewed as paradigmatic and typical: "[Christ] has satisfied my soul — something that twenty-four years in the convent, vows, sacrifices, Masses, rosaries, 'offering it up,' processions, saints, trifle traditions (from pagan-adopted practices), mixed up theological debates, and a controlled religious system could never begin to do."

17. Therein we read statements like the following:

He alleges to have been taught during his novitiate that "the Church had a great repository of merit available through the pope. And, then, the Virgin could help; and in the last analysis even Jesus might be of some help. Today I can hardly help laughing at such ridiculous pretenses. But it is far more sad than humorous" (28).

Describing the profession ceremony, he explains that "we had made our vows to God and Blessed Mary. In the ceremony I had besought her, for I had been taught that without her help I would not be able to save one soul, not even my own" (29).

To demonstrate Catholic confusion on merit, he cites St. Anselm as having said that "at times we are saved more quickly by invoking Mary's name than by invoking the name of Jesus." He also explains the supposed pagan origins of "worshipping" Mary as the Queen of Heaven (40). He denies her intercessory role on the following page.

When realizing that he was going through a crisis of faith, he says: "I besought the help of Mary, the mother of Jesus, calling her my intercessor, coequal with Christ, and I believed that the saints can and do protect Catholics who venerate them and ask them to appeal our cases in heaven" (117). He was disabused of all this when he began to understand the Word of God: "Then I knew that I needed no intercessor between God and me, neither Mary nor any saint" (118).

Listed in the category of "what the Church doesn't want you to know," he includes: "Many new doctrines were added to the Bible: belief in purgatory, adoration of Mary and the saints, confession to a priest . . ." (126).

In an appendix to the work, under the heading of "Roman Catholic False Doctrine," he considers "veneration" and comes up with the following analysis, worth quoting in full:

"My questioning of the veneration of images led me to question the veneration of the Virgin Mary, also called 'the Mother of God,' 'the Queen of Heaven,' 'the Door to Paradise,' and 'the Sorrowful Mother.'

"Assuredly, the Virgin Mary was a special woman, chosen of God. When she was carrying Jesus in her womb, she sang, 'My soul doth magnify the Lord, and my spirit hath rejoiced in God my Savior. For He hath regarded the low estate of His handmaiden: for, behold, from henceforth all generations shall call me blessed' (Luke 1:46-48).

"Yes, she is 'blessed.' But there is not one verse in the Bible that elevates her to divinity as the Queen of Heaven or as an intercessor between Christ and the Christian. In fact, the Bible teaches quite the contrary. Mary, too, claimed God as her Savior (Luke 1:47); she, too, was a sinner. There was once a woman who said to Jesus, 'Blessed is the womb that bare thee, and the paps which thou hast sucked.' Jesus replied, 'Yea rather, blessed are they that hear the Word of God, and keep it' (Luke 11:27-28). Jesus once asked a rhetorical question of His followers: 'Who is my mother? And who are my brethren?' Then He answered His own question: 'Whosoever shall do the will of my Father which is in heaven, the same is my brother, and sister, and mother' (Matthew 12:48, 50).

"Is Mary an intercessor? No, our intercessor is Christ. 'We have an advocate with the Father, Jesus Christ the righteous: And He is the propitiation for our sins: and not for our's [sic] only, but also for the sins of the whole world' (1 John 2:1-2). 'There is one God, and one mediator between God and men, the man Christ Jesus' (1 Timothy 2:5)" (see *Pilgrimage From Rome* [Greenville, South Carolina: Bob Jones University Press, 1982], 133-134).

18. Tony Coffey, *Once a Catholic: What You Need to Know about Roman Catholicism* (Eugene, Oregon: Harvest House Publishers, 1993), 13-14.

    This is so, even if the preface to the work by a former priest from India is less than irenic.

19. Ibid., 113.

20. Eleace King, *Proselytism and Evangelization: An Exploratory Study* (Washington, D.C.: Center for Applied Research in the Apostolate, 1991), 26.

21. Hispanic Bishops of California, "Responding to Proselytism," *Origins* (June 23, 1988): 84.

22. In this context, it is also worth repeating that "nearly three out of five approached about joining another church heard criticism of the Catholic Church, particularly the traditions of praying to Mary and the saints," says Bill Dodds in "Strangers Need not Apply," *Our Sunday Visitor*, August 2, 1992, 10.

23. George Gallup and Jim Castelli, *The American Catholic People* (Garden City, New York: Doubleday and Co., 1987), 173.

24. See Peter M. J. Stravinskas, *Proselytism among Today's Immigrants: A Preliminary Report* (Washington, D.C.: United States Catholic Conference, 1987).

This seminal study of thirty pages surveyed the identity and methods of those proselytizing traditionally Catholic immigrant groups, as well as the historical response of the Church in this country to immigrants. It concluded with a series of recommendations, among which was one calling for a rediscovery of the value of so-called "popular religion" and its place in keeping Catholics "within the fold" and spiritually fulfilled.

25. Bill Dodds, "Strangers Need Not Apply," *Our Sunday Visitor*, August 2, 1992, 10.

26. Ibid.

27. Stephen Turnbull, *Devotion to Mary among the Hidden Christians of Japan* (Surrey, England: Ecumenical Society of the Blessed Virgin Mary, 1992), 10.

28. Gerald Shaughnessy, *Has the Immigrant Kept the Faith?* (New York: Macmillan Co., 1925), 221.

29. Dodds, 11.

30. Antonio Lopez y Guzman, "Mexican-Americans: A Vibrant Spirituality," *Catholic Twin Circle*, August 9, 1992, 5.
    Santeros here refer to the practitioners of *santería*, a syncretistic blend of Catholic and voodoo symbols and beliefs.

31. Robert Sanchez, "Responding Pastorally to Sect Activity among Immigrants," *Origins* (January 11, 1990): 528.

32. Juan Diaz Vilar, "The Success of the Sects among Hispanics in the United States," *America* (February 25, 1989): 175.

33. Robert J. McClory, "Why Did the Catholic Cross the Road?" *U.S. Catholic* (January 1991): 12.

34. Gilbert Padilla, "Proselytism, Conservatism, and the Hispanics," *Pastoral Life* (November 1989): 17.

35. National Conference of Catholic Bishops, "National Pastoral Plan for Hispanic Ministry," *Origins* (December 10, 1987): 461.

36. Ibid., 462.

37. See Section II of the Bibliography: Conferencia Episcopal de Guatemala; Conferencia General del Episcopado Latinoamericano; Consejo Episcopal Latinoamericano; Pope John Paul II; National Conference of Catholic Bishops; Philippine Bishops' Statement on Biblical Fundamentalism; Pontifical Commis-

sion for the Spiritual Care of Migrants and Itinerants; Pontificio
Consiglio della Pastorale per I Migranti e gli Itineranti; Catholic
Bishops of Texas; Jozef Cardinal Tomko; Vatican Press Office;
Vatican Report on Sects, Cults and New Religious Movements;
Working Paper for 1994 Special Synod for Africa.
38. Eleace King and Francis P. Gillespie, *Final Report on the Survey of
Attitudes towards Proselytism of Ethnic Minorities* (Washington,
D.C.: Center for Applied Research in the Apostolate, 1988), 4.
Section III of the study dealt directly with "the phenomenon of
proselytism." Questions of particular interest in the present con-
text would be the following:

115. Are you aware of any churches or groups proselytizing in
your diocese?
116. In your diocese, which ethnic minorities seem to be the most
vulnerable to proselytizing?
117. What would you say are the principal means used by non-
Catholics to proselytize in your diocese?

Then were listed fourteen options to be graded on how successful the participant considered that strategy "in attracting converts from Catholicism." These included choices like televangelism, house-to-house canvassing, promises of employment.
"Proselytizing in their idiom" was rated as "most successful" in
its outcome by sixty-nine percent, with sixteen percent according it a judgment of "somewhat successful"; many respondents
indicated that the use of a Marian dimension was an aspect of
this type of openness and willingness to minister to the proely-
tized in familiar and comfortable categories. The last option offered was simply a blank to be filled in; this is generally where
responses on Marian imagery were registered (20-21).
39. King and Gillespie, 4-5.
40. Ibid., 6.
41. Ibid., 10.
The exact wording of the question was framed thus: "The
Church's neglect in promoting popular devotions (e.g., proces-

sions, Marian devotions, novenas) has hampered the Church's outreach to ethnic minorities." Responses came in this manner: Strongly agree (8%); Agree (39%); Disagree (22%); Strongly disagree (13%); Not sure (15%); Missing (4%) (22).

42. Ibid.

When asked to name the "*principal* means for proselytizing used by non-Catholics," only one percent cited "Catholic statues/icons in non-Catholic churches" (7).

When invited to list "methods of proselytism 'most successful' " in such activity, nine percent listed "ministry in minorities' idiom." It was here that many respondents explained in anecdotal remarks that use of Catholic imagery (especially Marian devotion) was included, in their minds (9). This latter point also came up in spots where free responses were possible (10).

43. King, 1.

44. Ibid.

45. King, 2.

46. Ibid.

47. "Overt" here refers to a kind of *quid pro quo* arrangement, whereby jobs, housing, or money are offered in exchange for becoming affiliated with the proselytizing denomination.

48. King, 6-7.

49. Ibid., 52.

It is significant that a generic question on the use of Catholic imagery yielded a very specific and strong Marian response.

50. Ibid.

The proselytizers' desire to relate to the culture of the proselytized becomes clear when we realize that their use of Our Lady is generally tied to that title that is most commonly regarded in the particular Hispanic group targeted (e.g., Our Lady of Guadalupe for Mexicans or El Caridad for Cubans), and not to a standard, interchangeable, or "transcultural" image of the Madonna.

51. King, 53.

52. Telephone interview by author with Sister Eleace King, April 27, 1994.

53. David Blackbourn, *Marpingen: Apparitions of the Virgin Mary in Nineteenth-Century Germany* (New York: Alfred A. Knopf, 1994), xxxiii-xxxiv.

54. The Reverend Msgr. Robert Rehkamper, then-Vicar General of the Diocese of Dallas, telephone interview by author, March 11, 1992; Sister Angela of the Dallas Diocesan Office for Evangelization, telephone interview by author, March 12, 1992; the Reverend Juan Alfaro in the Hispanic Ministry Department of the Archdiocese of San Antonio, telephone interview by author, March 12, 1992.

55. Telephone interviews by author with the Reverend Benjamin Rodriguez, October 5, 1992, and with the Reverend Richard Soseman, October 7, 1992.

56. Telephone interview with the Reverend John West, December 13, 1993.

This may well suggest that the proselytizers, having found this tactic successful in the States, are now exporting it "south of the border," which development would be fascinating to follow up in future studies.

57. The Most Reverend Raymond Peña, interview by author, November 11, 1992, Washington, D.C.

58. The Most Reverend Plácido Rodríguez, interview by author, November 17, 1992, Washington, D.C.

59. The Most Reverend Agustín Román, interview by author, November 16, 1992, Washington, D.C.

60. Robert O'Steen, "Some 'Catholic' Churches Really Aren't Catholic," *The Florida Catholic*, May 13, 1994, B3.

61. Ibid.

62. The Reverend Silvano Tomasi, interview by author, May 29, 1993, Rome.

63. The Reverend Juan Diaz Vilar, interview by author, October 27, 1992, Jersey City, New Jersey.

64. Paul Bail, "Latinos Remain Loyal to the Virgin," *National Catholic Register*, August 18, 1985, 7.

65. Ibid.

66. Dodds, 10.

67. Robert Anthony Orsi, *The Madonna of 115th Street: Faith and Community in Italian Harlem, 1880-1950* (New Haven: Yale University Press, 1985), 57-58.

68. The following is the questionnaire on proselytism:

> [Arch]Diocese: _____
>
> Source of Information: _____
>
> 1. Are you aware of any churches or groups proselytizing in your diocese? If so, specify which ones.
>
> 2. In your diocese, which ethnic minorities seem to be the most vulnerable to proselytizing?
>
> 3. What would you say are the principal means used by non-Catholics to proselytize in your diocese?
>
> Is Marian imagery used? [This is the only significant deviation from the CARA questions.]
>
> 4. What would you say is the most successful means used by others to proselytize in your diocese?

Calling for "Agree" or "Disagree" responses (with the possibility of qualifications) were the following items:

> 1. Proselytizing by non-Catholic groups is a serious problem in my diocese.
>
> 2. The Catholic Church in my diocese is doing an effective job of evangelizing ethnic minorities.
>
> 3. The Church's neglect in promoting popular devotions (processions, Marian devotions, novenas) has hampered the Church's outreach to ethnic minorities.

69. The survey included the following: archdioceses — Boston, Chicago, Dubuque, Los Angeles, Miami, New Orleans, Philadelphia, Portland in Oregon, St. Louis, St. Paul, Santa Fe, and Washington, D.C.; dioceses — Arlington, Baker, Birmingham, Bridgeport, Camden, Charleston, Columbus, Corpus Christi, Green Bay, Helena, Jackson, Kalamazoo, Lincoln, Lubbock, Memphis, Metuchen, Paterson, Peoria, Rapid City, Tulsa, and Wichita.

70. One diocesan official indicated that Hispanics are actually

paid $200 outright for registering in a local Fundamentalist church.

On the last point cited, once more we must realize that this is not a technique of recent vintage. Indeed, Orsi writes of how poor Italian Catholics found Protestant missionaries more than willing to tend to their physical needs: ". . . they try to buy the immigrants," he says, and he thus deems this all "an economically exploitative ministry" (Orsi, 159).

71. It is important to note that use of Marian imagery was found only among proselytizers whom this study has consistently identified as "Fundamentalists."

72. In point of fact, if the responses by diocesan officials are "corrected" by the information from those directly engaged in pastoral work, the 36% figure of those acknowledging Marian imagery being used by proselytizers rises to 48% and the "unsure" category falls from 30% to 18%.

73. The following are some of the survey results:

1. Is Marian imagery utilized in proselytizing of Catholics in your diocese?

Yes:	36% [12]
No:	33% [11]
Unsure/unaware:	31% [10]

2. Proselytism by non-Catholic groups is a serious problem in my diocese.

Agree:	73% [24]
Disagree:	27% [9]

3. The Catholic Church in my diocese is doing an effective job of evangelizing ethnic minorities.

Agree:	52% [16]
Disagree:	48% [15]
	[2 no response]

4. The Church's neglect in promoting popular devotions (processions, Marian devotions, novenas) has hampered the Church's outreach to ethnic minorities.

Agree:	87% [27]

Disagree: 13% [4]
                   [2 no response]

74. Sister Angela, telephone interview by author, April 27, 1994.

75. Manuel Facio, telephone interview by author, April 27, 1994.

76. Marsha Whelan, telephone interview by author, April 27, 1994.

77. Matthew McGuinness, telephone interview by author, April 27, 1994.

78. Sister Rosa Icaza, telephone interview by author, April 28, 1994.

79. Juan Alfaro, telephone interview by author, April 28, 1994.

80. The Most Reverend Raymond Peña, telephone interview by author, April 28, 1994.

81. Charles O'Connor, telephone interview by author, May 2, 1994.

82. Michael Scott, personal interview by author, April 28, 1994, Bayonne, New Jersey.

83. Raymond Jarbo, personal interview by author, April 24, 1994, Ontario, Oregon.

84. Benny Espaillat, telephone interview by author, April 27, 1994.

85. Patrick Madrid, telephone interview by author, April 26, 1994.

86. Telephone conversation with Sister Eleace King, January 31, 1994.

87. Letter to present researcher, December 5, 1994.

88. Letter to present researcher, October 31, 1994.

89. David Stoll, *Is Latin America Turning Protestant? The Politics of Evangelical Growth* (Berkeley: University of California Press, 1990), 313.

90. Roberto O. Gonzalez and Michael LaVelle, *The Hispanic Catholic in the United States: A Socio-Cultural and Religious Profile* (New York: Northeast Catholic Pastoral Center for Hispanics, 1985), 103.

91. Pope John Paul II, "The Church on Her Way," *L'Osservatore Romano*, August 25, 1980, 7.

92. At the same time, it should be stressed that this study does demonstrate that the tack is not being used exclusively within the Hispanic community, even if it is engaged there predominantly at the moment. A chancery official in one archdiocese, for example, said that she had "heard rumblings" that this approach

was also being employed lately by proselytizers of Black Catholics; this would not really be surprising, since many ministers of independent Black churches have used Catholic symbols for decades (e.g., clerical collars, vestments, candles).

93. In a personal conversation with Professor Philip Kayal of Seton Hall's sociology department discussing this project, the present researcher was apprised by Dr. Kayal of the same pattern of outreach with Marian imagery being used within his Greek-Melkite Catholic Diocese of Newton, Massachusetts. At his urging the Ordinary, the Most Reverend John Elya, was contacted to obtain further details; he indicated no awareness of any Marian dimension to the proselytism, but advised contact with the pastor who has complained about Fundamentalist incursions within his community.

The Reverend Archimandrite Charles Aboody and the Reverend James Babcock, in a telephone interview on December 6, 1994, spoke in great detail about the problem at Holy Cross Church in Fullerton, California, with specific attention given to the Marian aspect. Apparently, Arabic-speaking ministers have targeted recent immigrants from Jordan; their success resides in their ability to speak the language, whereas the number of priests who do so is minimal. Interestingly, they maintain Marian devotions of all kinds, even while eliminating the Eucharist!

CHAPTER 6

Summary, Conclusions, and Recommendations

Summary of Findings ✧ The principal findings of Chapter 2, dealing with Fundamentalism as a movement and a theology, may be summarized as follows:

◆ Fundamentalism sees itself as a theological movement with its roots in the Protestant Reformation, particularly grounded in Calvinism and committed to the opposition of whatever of a theological or cultural nature calls into question the historic Christian Faith. First emerging in the nineteenth century, it responded to the advances of Protestant liberalism.

◆ At a doctrinal level, Fundamentalism stands by the five "fundamentals" (inspiration and infallibility of Scripture; divinity of Christ; substitutionary atonement of His death; Christ's bodily resurrection from the dead; His literal return at the Second Coming), plus a heavy stress on dispensationalism or millennialism (although these are variously interpreted by the different sects within the movement). Unable to stave off the onslaught of liberal theology within their denominations of origin, the Fundamentalists have often formed their own ecclesial communities but have been plagued by sectarianism because of the reliance on *sola Scriptura* and the inadmissibility of any formal teaching authority. Particularly irksome to Fundamentalists is any suggestion of human mediation, whether that mediation be in the form of ministerial priesthood, sacraments, the Church's teaching office, or (especially) the intercession of Mary and other saints.

◆ From the outset, Fundamentalism has been strongly identified with revivalist and Pentecostalist tendencies. It is also known for its major thrust toward evangelization, using all the modern means of communication to propagate its message, gearing that in the direction of those they deem most "ripe" for it.

◆ Although rather "other-worldly" in the early years, Fundamentalism has taken on a decidedly political bent — pushed into it, some would say, by the increasing secularism of the general culture and the concomitant attack on traditional moral values (as evidenced in efforts to legalize abortion, a homosexual lifestyle, etc.). Another related development has been its establishment of a large private school system, to guarantee a hearing for Fundamentalist teachings among the young.

◆ While it would be correct to say that every Fundamentalist Christian is an Evangelical, the equation would not necessarily hold in reverse. "Fundamentalism" connotes not only doctrinal orthodoxy but also rigidity, excessive biblical literalism, and a more charismatic style of prayer and ecclesiastical governance.

◆ Unlike mainline Protestantism, Fundamentalism is the one "branch" that has experienced consistent growth during what has been an era of precipitous decline for the rest of Protestantism. That growth continues unabated (as witnessed by numbers of adherents, new congregations, schools, seminaries, etc.) and shows no signs of waning in the foreseeable future.

In Chapter 3, the following facts on the place of Mary in classical Fundamentalism came to the surface:

◆ Although Fundamentalism claims a historical link to the theology of the Protestant Reformers, its Marian doctrine is considerably different from that of Luther, Calvin, Zwingli, and the Anglican Reformers. This comes out most clearly in reference to the perpetual virginity of Mary, but also with regard to the Immaculate Conception and Assumption or in the observance of Marian feasts. Fundamentalists diverge with Luther most strikingly, but even at times with Calvin, to whom they declare a special allegiance.

◆ Until recently, the more theologically-minded Fundamentalists preferred not to discuss Mariology, except as a form of idolatry ("Mariolatry"). The one notable exception was the virgin birth, but

REV. PETER M. J. STRAVINSKAS

here the emphasis was on its Christological significance and on its miraculous nature, not on the person of Mary. Fundamentalists, and Protestants in general, seem to be unanimous in regarding the Blessed Virgin as too highly exalted in Catholicism. They find little if anything in the Bible to support such high veneration.

◆ Perhaps under the impulse of more open approaches to the study of the Scriptures or Church history, some Fundamentalist theologians are now willing to look at Mary's role in Christianity and to acknowledge that she should have some place, albeit Christologically based and without mediatorial significance. They still react nervously to titles such as "Mother of God."

◆ Popular Fundamentalist preachers and teachers are unwilling even to consider a place for Mary in "orthodox" Christianity. Perhaps they are motivated as much by anti-Catholicism as by a desire for biblical fidelity. Their methods and language tend to be extremely vitriolic toward Catholicism and Mary alike.

Chapter 4's consideration of proselytism's psychology and methods brought the following data to light:

◆ Proselytism is an aggressive means of bringing people into one's own religious community. It is generally done with psychological pressure, without regard for the dignity of the person and often enough in violation of normal canons of respectable discourse, let alone ecumenical sensitivity.

◆ Primary targets for proselytism are those who appear to be alienated or marginalized from society at large or from their current church community; hence the obvious outreach to immigrants (with a major effort being exerted among Hispanics), offering them a "shelter" and a sense of community. The proselytizers also seem to cater to people who have a need for clear-cut, absolute answers found in an authoritative, unchanging source (e.g., the Bible).

◆ Proselytizers are most successful with Catholics who are improperly or insufficiently catechized, or who find themselves adrift "at sea" in the wake of post-Vatican II changes (especially unauthorized changes).

◆ Those who have been successfully proselytized usually become, in turn, successful and enthusiastic proselytizers. Therefore, there are no indicators that the process will stop any time soon. On the contrary, everything points in the direction of even greater expenditure of time, talent, and financial resources to build on the successes already achieved.

◆ The Catholic Church has failed to prepare her members for the onslaught of the proselytizers, on the one hand, and has done little, on the other hand, to engage in active evangelization herself. This is a prime area of responsibility that can and should be accorded to the laity.

◆ A careful and necessary distinction must be made between proselytism and evangelization. With the former already defined, evangelization stands out as a necessary component of a lively Christian faith by the sharing of that faith in ways that respect human dignity and ecclesiastical unity.

◆ Pope John Paul II and other members of the hierarchy see the Blessed Virgin as playing a key role: first, in being considered as an essential and indispensable part of a full Christian life; and second, as a model for true evangelization.

Chapter 5 looked at the place occupied by Mary among the proselytizers and discovered the following:

◆ Traditional Fundamentalist proselytizers regard Marian doctrine and devotion as evils to be exposed and eradicated, because these allegedly are unbiblical and deny the all-sufficient mediation of Christ.

◆ Some contemporary proselytizers either do not discuss Mary at all, or speak of her in favorable ways (perhaps to the extent of tolerating displays of Marian devotion), in order to gain a hearing among those greatly attached to her. As time goes on, they seek to wean their new members from such teachings and practices.

◆ Other proselytizers have begun to give Mary a permanent place in their spirituality and theology, as evidenced by hymns, prayers, images, devotions, and even at times by the names given to their churches.

◆ The latter two approaches have been used most often among Hispanic Catholics. Their use is not well attested in other groups at present, although evidence exists that they were employed in other segments of the Catholic population in the past and, therefore, could be reactivated there in the future.

Conclusions ✧ What conclusions can be drawn from this body of research? Several points emerge, especially from a Catholic perspective:

◆ Fundamentalism is a phenomenon to be reckoned with, especially in its more aggressive and even hostile representations. In spite of the many obvious differences, there are also many possible areas of convergence between Fundamentalism and Catholicism (e.g., respect for a body of basic and nonnegotiable doctrine; concern for traditional moral values in secular society).

◆ By contrast with historic Reformation Protestantism, classical Fundamentalism admits no role for Mary. A few contemporary Fundamentalist theologians indicate a willingness to reflect on some possible position for the Mother of Jesus in Christian spirituality, within biblical limitations as they prescribe them.

◆ Proselytism is a serious problem for the Catholic Church, as thousands of the uncatechized become the prey of unscrupulous missionaries.

◆ Where basic human needs are not met by the Church or society, proselytizers move in, not only with their doctrine, but also with material assistance. This happens with regularity in traditionally Catholic immigrant communities; Hispanics stand out as the clearest example.

◆ Inasmuch as the Catholic Church has not been an active agent of evangelization over the past two decades, she has become an easy target of the proselytizers.

◆ Better catechesis and more effective use of persons would aid the Church in responding to proselytizing programs and also in the more positive work of evangelization.

◆ When proselytizers use Marian imagery superficially, without a corresponding Mariology, Catholics should be aware. Much more disarming is the practice of presenting Marian doctrine and devotion in a positive manner. Accordingly, the unsuspecting are led to assume that there will be no major differences between this group and Catholicism, if they even realize at all that they are being wooed into another community apart from the Church.

   Recommendations ✧ As a result of the findings and conclusions of this study, it is possible to offer the following recommendations for theological and pastoral activity:

   ◆ Catholics should be informed about the nature of Fundamentalism (basic doctrines, history, psychology), with due attention given to areas of agreement and disagreement in terms of the Catholic Faith.[1]

   ◆ Where common activity is possible with Fundamentalists, it should be encouraged, since this will help dispel myths about Catholics and Catholic theology within that movement.

   ◆ In formal theological dialogue, Fundamentalists should be brought to encounter the abyss which separates them from the leaders of the Protestant Reformation, on whom they rely for guidance and credibility today. Similarly, joint studies on the biblical witness to the place of Mary and human mediation in the Christian dispensation should be launched.

   ◆ When dialogue does occur (either formally between Church bodies or informally among friends), Catholics should be careful to use very precise language about the Blessed Mother, lest wrong impressions be given as to what the Church really believes, teaches, and practices.

   ◆ Catholics must be trained to see proselytism for the evil it is and to be adequately prepared to respond. Programs and materials of a biblical and doctrinal nature should be devised and made available, both for leaders and the grassroots population.[2] Central in all this are good catechesis and ongoing adult education in the Faith. Not only are defensive programs required, but also efforts to make Catholics comfortable in sharing their faith with others, seeking to bring others into the full communion of Christ's one Church.[3]

   ◆ Knowing what weaknesses the proselytizers capitalize on, the Church has a ready-made program of action to provide for legitimate human needs and true spiritual assistance. Thus, both the corporal and spiritual works of mercy must be practiced if Catholics are not to be lured into the grasp of the proselytizers. Special attention must be given to vulnerable immigrants.

◆ Marian devotion should be an integral aspect of Catholic life, lest some (ironically enough) find themselves going to Fundamentalist proselytizers for what should be readily available within the Catholic community. Or, as the King Report frankly puts it, it is essential "that the Church deal with the polarization of religious and devotional practice, especially when some would consider certain elements of popular piety, devotion and religiosity as being retrograde in a post-Vatican II Church."[4] Put in another way, Catholics should understand the relationship between their Catholic Faith and their particular culture, and the special place that Mary plays in all such Catholic cultures.[5]

◆ Catholics need to know precisely what the Church believes about Mary and why those teachings are true and necessary. Good scriptural, doctrinal, and liturgical undergirding should be given, so that they are not caught off-guard when approached by proselytizers who attack Mariology.[6] They should be possessed of what the Holy Father terms "a solid Marian piety."[7]

◆ At the same time, those most susceptible to being attracted to Fundamentalism by the unconventional use of Marian symbols should be advised of the dishonest nature of such ploys and made to see the whole interlocking network of Catholic Faith, which does not admit of piecemeal appropriations.

A Final Note

As should have been observed by now, Pope John Paul II insists on considering the question of proselytism from a Marian dimension. This is the case because of theological concerns but also due to the union of faith and culture, which he is fond of fostering. Stressing the roots of the contemporary situation, the Holy Father says: "There is no doubt that one of the most particular features of the evangelization of America was its strong Marian character. Indeed, the Gospel was proclaimed to the men and women of the American continent by 'presenting the Virgin Mary as its loftiest fulfillment' [Puebla, n. 282]. And the Marian faith of the Spanish missionaries was soon to crystallize in those lands so well that, as has been rightly said, the historic and cultural identity of the Hispano-American peoples 'is glowingly reflected on the mestizo countenance of Mary of Guadalupe who appeared at the start of the evangelization process' [Puebla, n. 446]."[8]

Bringing it up to the present, the Pope notes: "Just as Mary guided the evangelization of America, she must also be the guiding star of the New Evangelization to which the Church feels called on the threshold of the Third Christian Millennium. This is so because all evangelization follows and continues that process of faith which stems from Pentecost. Now 'at the beginning of this journey Mary is present. We see her in the midst of the Apostles in the Upper Room "prayerfully imploring the gift of the Spirit" ' " (*Redemptoris Mater*, n. 26; *Lumen Gentium*, n. 63).[9]

Making the Marian connection even more pointed, he concludes: "In circumstances such as the present, when the relentless advance of secularization is tending to suffocate the faith of Christians by endeavoring to confine it to the private sphere, the figure of Mary emerges as an example and stimulus for today's believers; it reminds them of the urgent need for their acceptance of the Gospel to be translated into concrete and practical actions in the most varied temporal and earthly situations, in the professional, social, economic, cultural and political worlds."[10]

Such a thrust shows the Pope to be part of a theological trajectory that links Mary and evangelization, explicitly since the Second Vatican Council but implicitly from the data of the New Testament itself (as seen in the Joyful Mysteries of the Rosary, especially in the Visitation). As T. F. Ossanna writes, Mary is "the force and the guide of evangelists."[11] John Paul's use of the title "star of the New Evangelization" likewise situates him within the school of Paul VI who, in *Evangelii Nuntiandi*, refers to Mary as "star of the evangelization" (n. 82).

The Reverend Bertetto Domenico reminds us that "Mary is the first missionary who has cooperated with Jesus in the procurement of salvation; She is the Mother of the first Missionary."[12] Beyond that, "Mary . . . continues from heaven her missionary work. She is mindful of the salvation of all praying and obtains for all the grace of eternal salvation." Quite appropriately, then, one should conclude that "Mary . . . continues to be Mother of the missionary Church (cf. LG 62)."[13]

Addressing the thirteenth national week of Marian studies in 1973 in Loreto, the Reverend Monsignor Armando Rolla gave to his talk a title that says it all: "The plan of salvation and evangelization includes Mary," with special attention given to the biblical data.[14] The Reverend Monsignor Brunero Gherardini demonstrates how "the Church experiences and manifests in worship the evangelizing presence of Mary."[15] He then underscores the intrinsic nature of the Marian dimension, saying that, for the Church, Mary is no stranger, and that the role she occupies is divinely accorded her . . . especially as that relates to her very personal and irrepeatable [sic] dignity as Mother of God. In the Church, Mary is the Mother of Christ and, in Him, of the Church herself."[16]

Several speakers at that same conference sought to particularize and concretize this missionary activity of Mary in terms of the parish, the family, the world of work and youth,[17] thus offering practical ways of applying these theological insights to the pastoral work of the Church.

In a most helpful manner, the Most Reverend Francesco Franzi stakes out normative principles for our concerns:

> 1. An evangelization that does not include Mary within the Christian mystery is incomplete and impoverished in its efficacy.
>
> 2. Mary must always be presented within the mystery of Christ and of the Church.
>
> 3. If the whole Church is bound to the work of evangelization — for which she exists . . . — she must show her vital rapport with Mary; better still, she needs to show her trust in Mary.
>
> 4. If the whole Church is bound to the work of evangelization, a particular competence pertains to those who in the Church are "promoters" of this activity, or through a singular consecration to the "ministry of the Church," like priests, or through an ecclesial choice made with freedom and responsibility, like catechists, religious and committed Christians. . . .
>
> 5. The great force of evangelization is the Holy Spirit; therefore, it is important to recognize and to respect the presence of Mary.

6. If Mary is recognized as the great efficacious evangelist, then it is equally important to recognize the singular place which she should hold in the devotional life of the faithful.[18]

From these principles, Bishop Franzi draws pastoral conclusions. Interestingly, from the perspective of this study, he concludes by citing some reflections of St. Louis de Montfort about the role of Mary in that aspect of evangelization concerned with attracting or bringing back people to the Catholic Church.[19]

The participants in the Loreto conference offered the following resolutions as summaries of their deliberations:

1. Awareness of Mary's presence in the work of evangelization should deepen, by study and prayer, the understanding of her mission in the plan of salvation and thus in the life of the Church.

2. It is necessary to give due emphasis to Mary in the program of evangelization, going beyond idle reticence in discussing Mary, a suspicion of practices of Marian piety, and the reductionist tendency in the presentation of her mission, but also avoiding exaggerations in doctrine and piety.[20]

It is significant and interesting to note that the International Congress on Mariology would assemble in Loreto twenty-two years later, this time as an ecumenical gathering of Catholic, Orthodox, and Protestant theologians, "meet[ing] to discuss the Mother of the Lord. Their goal: greater Church unity,"[21] according to the Reverend Fathers Stefano DeFiores and Ugo Vanni, interviewed for the article. Not surprisingly, one finds a conviction expressed fifteen years earlier by DeFiores that Mary ought to be reflected upon as "Mother of reconciliation."[22]

Hence, within this overall context of viewing Mary as an integral participant in the work of the missionary Church, we can see how the instinct of the present Holy Father linking Mary to both evangelization and proselytism offers interesting possibilities. First, it causes Catholics to remember the rightful place Our Lady should occupy in all things Catholic. Second, it is not unreasonable to imagine that even proselytizers who are using Marian imagery for less than honest or noble purposes may indeed find themselves (or at least members of their communities) devoted to the Mother of the Lord. In this way, she will in truth be precisely what John Paul II says she is, the genuine source of Christian unity:

> If the mystery of the Word made flesh enables us to glimpse the mystery of the divine motherhood and if, in turn, contemplation of the Mother of God brings us to a more profound understanding of the mystery of the Incarnation, then the same must be said for the mystery of the Church and Mary's role in the work of salvation. By a more profound study of both Mary and the Church, clarifying each by the light of the other, Christians who are eager to do what Jesus tells them — as their Mother recommends (cf. Jn. 2:5) — will be able to go forward together on this "pilgrimage of faith." Mary, who is still the model of this pilgrimage, is to lead them to the unity which is willed by their one Lord and so much desired by those who are attentively listening to what "the Spirit is saying to the Churches" today (Rev. 2:7, 11, 17).[23]

In a very tender, informative, and insightful article in *Our Lady's Dowry*, the newsletter of the first Anglican parish in the United States to enter into full communion with the Catholic Church, the editor explains both the historical and present significance of the expression "Our Lady's Dowry." James Orr writes that "it means that England, and all English-speaking people, were assigned to Mary as a permanent gift which no one could take away. Hence, England belongs to Mary, and although in many respects her dowry has been robbed from her, she still lawfully possesses it." Therefore, he goes on, "every portion, however small, which returns to Mary increases her dowry."

Orr recalls that within the context of his Bull *Apostolicae Curae* of 1896, Pope Leo XIII prayed, "O Blessed Mother of God and our own most gentle Queen and Mother, look down in mercy upon England thy dowry and upon all who gently hope and trust in thee. . . ."

Of course, this is the very point of that verse in Father Faber's popular hymn:

> Faith of our Fathers, Mary's prayer,
> Shall win all nations unto thee;
> And through the truth that comes from God,
> Mankind shall then indeed be free.

The editor concludes his reflections on a note that would also serve us well in the present circumstances: "We cannot know, we cannot tell, what precious portions will one day return to the special care of Mary and enrich her dowry. But we can rest in the assurance that those brave souls will find rest for their convictions and peace at the feet of the Queen of Unity."[24] Surely, this applies to the whole family of faith and is not limited to England or English-speaking peoples.

The Fundamentalist proselytizers' use of Mary that has occupied our attention in this study, then, may indeed be their unwitting participation in a divine plan to bring together into one family again dispersed brothers and sisters through the agency of a loving Mother.

Endnotes

1. As the Reverend Avery Dulles, S.J., observes: ". . . there is increasing recognition that Catholics and conservative Evangelicals share many things in common, including a reverence for the canonical Scriptures and adherence to the central doctrines of the Trinity, the Incarnation, the atoning death and bodily resurrection of Jesus. In the realm of moral teaching, conservative Evangelicals, like Catholics, tend to be opposed to abortion and to defend traditional family values" ("John Paul II and the New Evangelization," *America* [February 1, 1992]: 54).

2. See NCCB, "National Pastoral Plan for Hispanic Ministry," *Origins (*December 10, 1987), nn. 83-84.
   At their Fourth General Conference, the Latin American bishops called for a catechesis that explains the mystery of the Church as sacrament of salvation and communion, the mediation of the Virgin Mary and the saints, and the mission of the Church hierar-

chy. (See *Nueva Evangelización, Promoción Humana, Cultura Cristiana* [Bogotá: Ediciones Paulinas, 1992], n. 142.)

3. Once again Dulles offers some insight: "American Catholics are wary of evangelization for a variety of reasons. They see it as the chosen trademark of revivalist and fundamentalistic sects, some of them virulently anti-Catholic. They distrust the biblicism, the individualism, and the emotionalism, and the aggressive proselytism of Protestant evangelistic preachers" (Dulles, 52).

4. Eleace King, *Proselytism and Evangelization: An Exploratory Study* (Washington, D.C.: Center for Applied Research in the Apostolate, 1991), 7.

5. See Puebla IV, n. 15.

6. Ibid., n. 143.

7. Pope John Paul II, "Opening Address to the Fourth General Conference of the Latin American Episcopate," *Origins* (October 22, 1992): 326.

In that same address, the Pope expanded on that theme thus: "Because of its eminently Catholic roots, the deep-seated popular religiosity of your faithful, with its extraordinary values of faith and piety, of sacrifice and solidarity, when properly evangelized and joyfully celebrated, and directed toward the mysteries of Christ and the Virgin Mary, may serve as antidote to the sects and help safeguard fidelity to the message of salvation" (ibid.).

8. Pope John Paul II, "Mary Was Star of the First Evangelization of America," *L'Osservatore Romano*, October 7, 1992, 4.

The Holy Father's reliance on Puebla suggests the value of a careful reading of that document, in which the bishops devote significant attention to the question of "Mary in the Life of the People of God in Latin America." (See John Eagleson and Philip Scharper, eds., *Puebla and Beyond: Documentation and Commentary* [Maryknoll, New York: Orbis Books, 1979], nn. 282-303.)

9. Ibid.

The Guatemalan hierarchy apply this to their own situation: "The mystery of the intercession of Mary, assumed now into Heaven, and of the pouring out of the Holy Spirit is prolonged throughout the history of evangelization in the Church. In our great Marian sanctuaries, from Guadalupe to Altagracia, the Luján apparition and so many others in each country . . . Mary accompanies us and will accompany us in the great task of the New Evangelization which we undertake. She will obtain for us the continued outpouring of the Spirit" (179).

10. Ibid.

The Bishops of Texas have picked up this theme from the Pope: "We place such evangelization teams under the special protection of Our Lady of Guadalupe, the Mother of the Evangelization of the Americas. Jesus Himself had given His Mother to us as He hung dying on the cross: '. . . and from that hour the disciple took her into his own home' (John 19:27). If we are ever to promote house-churches, small ecclesial communities, parish families and diocesan unity, there is no better way to begin than by taking Mary into our homes" (Catholic Bishops of Texas, *Mission: Texas* [Lubbock, Texas, 1989]: 14).

In even greater depth and detail, CELAM made the following observations:

◆ The Virgin Mary has been presented as the Gospel's highest realization. She is "the great sign" who invites us to enter into communion with the Father and the Son.

◆ Guadalupe and other Marian shrines on the continent are signs of the encounter of the Church's Faith with Latin American history.

◆ Paul VI affirmed that devotion to Mary has a special place in the genuine piety of the Church and in Christian worship. John Paul II observed that Marian devotion pertains intimately to the very identity of the Latin American people.

◆ The people know that Mary is encountered in the Catholic Church. Marian piety has been the resistant bond that has maintained fidelity to the Church.

◆ Mary will be the Mother teacher of the Faith, the preeminent teacher of the Gospel in Latin America.

◆ Mary gives a feminine dimension to religion that contributes to love and respect for life. She is the "sacrament," as it were, of God's maternal characteristics (89-91).

11. Stefano DeFiores and Salvatore Meo, eds., *Nuovo Dizionario di Mariologia* [*New Dictionary of Mariology*] (Cinisello Balsamo [Milan]: Edizioni Paoline, 1986), s.v. "Evangelizzazione" by T. F. Ossanna (p. 548).

12. Bertetto Domenico, "Maria e l'Attività Missionaria di Cristo e della Chiesa" ["Mary and the Missionary Activity of Christ and of the Church"], in *Portare Cristo all'Uomo. Congresso del Ventennio dal Concilio Vaticano II* [*Bearer of Christ to Men. Congress of the Twentieth Anniversary of Vatican Council II*] (Rome: Pontificia Università Urbaniana, 1985), 457.

13. Ibid., 467.

14. See *La Presenza di Maria nella Missione Evangelizzatrice del Popolo di Dio* [*The Presence of Mary in the Evangelizing Mission of the People of God*] (Rome: Collegamento Mariano Nazionale, 1973), 16-28.

15. Ibid., 41.

16. Ibid., 43.

17. See the contributions of Mazzoleni, Cupia, Pagani, and Weber in the same volume.

18. Francesco Franzi, "Principi e Linee Pastorali Derivanti dalla Presenza Operante di Maria nella Evangelizzazione" ["Principles and Pastoral Services from the Active Presence of Mary in Evangelization"], ibid., 106-110.

19. Ibid., 117.

20. Ibid., 125.

21. Antonio Gaspari, "Rediscovering Mary," *Inside the Vatican* (May 1995): 48-51.

22. Stefano DeFiores, *Maria: Presenza Viva nel Popolo di Dio* [*Mary: Living Presence in the People of God*] (Rome: Edizioni Monfortane, 1980), 407.

23. Pope John Paul II, *Redemptoris Mater* (Boston: Daughters of St. Paul, 1987), n. 30.

24. James Orr, "Every Portion Counts," *Our Lady's Dowry* 13, no. 2: 1-4.

Appendix 1

The 1878 Niagara Creed*

So many in the latter times have departed from the faith, giving heed to seducing spirits, and doctrines of devils; so many have turned away their ears from the truth, and turned unto fables; so many are busily engaged in scattering broadcast the seeds of fatal error, directly affecting the honor of our Lord and the destiny of the soul, we are constrained by fidelity to Him to make the following declaration of our doctrinal belief, and to present it as the bond of union with those who wish to be connected with the Niagara Bible Conference.

I

We believe "that all Scripture is given by inspiration of God," by which we understand the whole book called the Bible; nor do we take the statement in the sense in which it is sometimes foolishly said that works of human genius are inspired, but in the sense that the Holy Ghost gave the very words of the sacred writings to holy men of old; and that His Divine inspiration is not different in degrees, but extends equally and fully to all parts of these writings, historical, poetical, doctrinal, and prophetical, and to the smallest word, and inflection of a word, provided such word is found in the original manuscripts: 2 Tm 3:16, 17; 2 Pt 1:21; 1 Cor 2:13; Mk 12:26, 36; 13:11; Acts 1:16; 2:4.

II

We believe that the Godhead eternally exists in three Persons, the Father, the Son, and the Holy Spirit; and that these three are one God, having precisely the same nature, attributes, and perfections, and worthy of precisely the same homage, confidence, and obedi-

---

*As found in Ernest R. Sandeen, *The Roots of Fundamentalism: British and American Millenarianism, 1800-1930* (Chicago: University of Chicago Press, 1970), 273-277.

223

ence: Mk 12:29; Jn 1:1-4; Mt 28:19, 20; Acts 5:3, 4; 2 Cor 13:14; Heb 1:1-3; Rv 1:4-6.

III

We believe that man, originally created in the image and after the likeness of God, fell from his high and holy estate by eating the forbidden fruit, and as the consequence of his disobedience the threatened penalty of death was then and there inflicted, so that his moral nature was not only grievously injured by the fall, but he totally lost all spiritual life, becoming dead in trespasses and sins, and subject to the power of the devil: Gn 1:26; 2:17; Jn 5:40; 6:53; Eph 2:1-3; 1 Tm 5:6; 1 Jn 3:8.

IV

We believe that this spiritual death, or total corruption of human nature, has been transmitted to the entire race of man, the man Christ Jesus alone excepted; and hence that every child of Adam is born into the world with a nature which not only possesses no spark of Divine life, but is essentially and unchangeably bad, being in enmity against God, and incapable by any educational process whatever of subjection to His law: Gn 6:5; Ps 14:1-3; 51:5; Jer 17:9; Jn 3:6; Rom 5:12-19; 8:6, 7.

V

We believe that, owing to this universal depravity and death in sin, no one can enter the kingdom of God unless born again; and that no degree of reformation however great, no attainment in morality however high, no culture however attractive, no humanitarian and philanthropic schemes and societies however useful, no baptism or other ordinance however administered, can help the sinner to take even one step toward heaven; but a new nature imparted from above, a new life implanted by the Holy Ghost through the Word, is absolutely essential to salvation: Is 64:6; Jn 3:5, 18; Gal 6:15; Phil 3:4-9; Ti 3:5; Jas 1:18; 1 Pt 1:23.

VI

We believe that our redemption has been accomplished solely by the blood of our Lord Jesus Christ, who was made to be sin, and made a curse, for us, dying in our room and stead; and that no repentance, no feeling, no faith, no good resolutions, no sincere efforts, no submission to the rules and regulations of any church, or of all the churches that have existed since the days of the Apostles, can add in the very least to the value of that precious blood, or to the merit of that finished work, wrought for us by Him who united in His Person true and proper divinity with perfect and sinless humanity: Lv 17:11; Mt 26:28; Rom 5:6-9; 2 Cor 5:21; Gal 3:13; Eph 1:7; 1 Pt 1:18, 19.

VII

We believe that Christ, in the fulness of the blessings He has secured by His obedience unto death, is received by faith alone, and that the moment we trust in Him as our Saviour we pass out of death into everlasting life, being justified from all things, accepted before the Father according to the measure of His acceptance, loved as He is loved, and having His place and portion, as linked to Him, and one with Him forever: Jn 5:24; 17:23; Acts 13:39; Rom 5:1; Eph 2:4-6, 13; 1 Jn 4:17; 5:11, 12.

VIII

We believe that it is the privilege, not only of some, but of all who are born again by the Spirit through faith in Christ as revealed in the Scriptures, to be assured of their salvation from the very day they take Him to be their Saviour; and that this assurance is not founded upon any fancied discovery of their own worthiness, but wholly upon the testimony of God in His written Word, exciting within His children filial love, gratitude, and obedience: Lk 10:20; 12:32; Jn 6:47; Rom 8:33-39; 2 Cor 5:1, 6-8; 2 Tm 1:12; 1 Jn 5:13.

IX

We believe that all the Scriptures from first to last center about our Lord Jesus Christ, in His Person and work, in His first and second coming; and hence that no chapter even of the Old Testament is properly read or understood until it leads to Him; and moreover that all the Scriptures from first to last, including every chapter even of the Old Testament, were designed for our practical instruction: Lk 24:27,

44; Jn 5:39; Acts 17:2, 3; 18:28; 26:22, 23; 28:23; Rom 15:4; 1 Cor 10:11.

X

We believe that the Church is composed of all who are united by the Holy Spirit to the risen and ascended Son of God, that by the same Spirit we are all baptized into one body, whether we be Jews or Gentiles, and thus being members one of another, we are responsible to keep the unity of the Spirit in the bond of peace, rising above all sectarian prejudices and denominational bigotry, and loving one another with a pure heart fervently: Mt 16:16-18; Acts 2:32-47; Rom 12:5; 1 Cor 12:12-27; Eph 1:20-23; 4:3-10; Col 3:14, 15.

XI

We believe that the Holy Spirit, not as an influence, but as a Divine Person, the source and power of all acceptable worship and service, is our abiding Comforter and Helper, that He never takes His departure from the Church, nor from the feeblest of the saints, but is ever present to testify of Christ, seeking to occupy us with Him, and not with ourselves nor with our experiences: Jn 7:38, 39; 14:16, 17; 15:26; 16:13, 14; Acts 1:8; Rom 8:9; Phil 3:3.

XII

We believe that we are called with a holy calling to walk, not after the flesh, but after the Spirit, and so to live in the Spirit that we should not fulfill the lusts of the flesh; but the flesh being still in us to the end of our earthly pilgrimage needs to be kept constantly in subjection to Christ, or it will surely manifest its presence to the dishonor of His name: Rom 8:12, 13; 13:14; Gal 5:16-25; Eph 4:22-24; Col 3:1-10; 1 Pt 1:14-16; 1 Jn 3:5-9.

XIII

We believe that the souls of those who have trusted in the Lord Jesus Christ for salvation do at death immediately pass into His presence, and there remain in conscious bliss until the resurrection of the body at His coming, when soul and body reunited shall be associated with Him forever in the glory; but the souls of unbelievers remain after death in conscious misery until the final judgment of the great white throne at the close of the millennium, when soul and body reunited shall be cast into the lake of fire, not to be annihilated, but to be punished with everlasting destruction from the presence of the Lord, and from the glory of His power: Lk 16:19-26; 23:43; 2 Cor 5:8; Phil 1:23; 2 Thes 1:7-9; Jude 6:7; Rv 20:11-15.

XIV

We believe that the world will not be converted during the present dispensation, but is fast ripening for judgment, while there will be a fearful apostasy in the professing Christian body; and hence that the Lord Jesus will come in person to introduce the millennial age, when Israel shall be restored to their own land, and the earth shall be full of the knowledge of the Lord; and that this personal and premillennial advent is the blessed hope set before us in the Gospel for which we should be constantly looking: Lk 12:35-40; 17:26-30; 18:8; Acts 15:14-17; 2 Thes 2:3-8; 2 Tm 3:1-5; Ti 2:11-15.

Appendix 2

Questionnaire Regarding Proselytism

Are you aware of any churches or groups proselytizing in your diocese? If so, specify which ones.

All of the (arch)dioceses surveyed were aware of proselytism to some extent. Most commonly named were: Jehovah's Witnesses, Mormons, various Fundamentalist/Evangelical churches (especially active in college campus ministry in some states), proponents of maintaining cultural identity (in the case of Native Americans), and the Moslems (in the African-American community).

In your diocese, which ethnic minorities seem to be the most vulnerable to proselytizing?

In order, indicating the most targeted groups: Hispanics, African-Americans, Native Americans and Vietnamese.

What would you say are the principal means used by non-Catholics to proselytize in your diocese?

Door-to-door visitations; promises of employment, food, and other material assistance; invitation/transportation to church and church-sponsored activities.

Is Marian imagery used?
Yes: 21%
No: 38%
Not sure: 41%

What would you say is the most successful means used by others to proselytize in your diocese?

All of the principal means are effective, to varying degrees, because they convey a personal interest in the individual, which is often lacking in the Catholic community.

Proselytizing by non-Catholic groups is a serious problem in my diocese.

Agree: 69%

Disagree: 31%

The Catholic Church in my diocese is doing an effective job of evangelizing ethnic minorities.

Agree: 48%

Disagree: 52%

The Church's neglect in promoting popular devotions (processions, Marian devotions, novenas, etc.) has hampered the Church's outreach to ethnic minorities.

Agree: 86%

Disagree: 14%

Bibliography

I. General Works on Fundamentalism and Evangelical Theology

ADRIS Newsletter. Review of *Fundamentalisms Observed*, ed. by Martin E. Marty and R. Scott Appleby. January/March 1992, 5.

Alabama and Mississippi, Bishops of. "A Pastoral Letter on Fundamentalism." *The Catholic Answer*, March/April 1990, 48-56.

Ammerman, Nancy T. "North American Protestant Fundamentalism." In *Fundamentalisms Observed*, eds. Martin E. Marty and R. Scott Appleby, 1-65. Chicago: University of Chicago Press, 1991.

Anderson, H. George, et al. *The One Mediator, the Saints, and Mary*. Minneapolis: Augsburg Fortress Press, 1992.

Anti-Defamation League. *The Religious Right: The Assault on Tolerance and Pluralism in America*. New York: Anti-Defamation League/B'nai B'rith, 1994.

Appleby, R. Scott. "Unflinching Faith: What Fires Up the World's Fundamentalists?" *U.S. Catholic*, December 1989, 6-13.

Arinze, Francis Cardinal. "The Challenge of New Religious Movements." *Origins*, April 25, 1991, 748-753.

Arthur, Chris. "Intolerance Explained." *Times Higher Education Supplement*, June 12, 1992, 12.

Atwood, Thomas. "Through a Glass Darkly: Is the Christian Right Overconfident It Knows God's Will?" *Policy Review*, Fall 1990, 46ff.

Baer, John E. *A Catholic Analysis of the Idea of 'Revelation' in the Protestant 'Fundamentalist' Movement in the United States*. Rome: Catholic Book Agency, 1963.

Ball, William Bentley, ed. *In Search of a National Morality: A Manifesto for Evangelicals and Catholics*. San Francisco: Ignatius Press, 1992.

Balmer, Randall. *Mine Eyes Have Seen the Glory*. New York: Oxford University Press, 1989.

Barr, James. *Beyond Fundamentalism*. Philadelphia: Westminster Press, 1984.
_____. *Fundamentalism*. Philadelphia: Westminster Press, 1978.

Barth, Karl. *Church Dogmatics*, Volume I, Part 2. Edinburgh: T. & T. Clark, 1963.

Bell, Charles. "City of Faith: What We Believe." *Daily News*, March 31, 1986, C-8.

Bergant, Dianne. "Fundamentalists and the Bible." *New Theology Review*, May 1988, 36-50.

Berkhof, Louis. *Systematic Theology*. Grand Rapids, Michigan: Eerdmans Publishing Co., 1939.

Berkouwer, G. C. *The Conflict with Rome*. Philadelphia: Presbyterian & Reformed Publishing Co., 1958.

_____. *The Second Vatican Council and the New Catholicism*. Grand Rapids, Michigan: Eerdmans Publishing Co., 1965.

Boadt, Lawrence. "Fundamentalism." *New Catholic World*, January/February 1985, 2.

Boone, Kathleen C. *The Bible Tells Them So: The Discourse of Protestant Fundamentalism*. Albany, New York: State University of New York Press, 1989.

Bouwsma, William J. *John Calvin: A Sixteenth-Century Portrait*. New York: Oxford University Press, 1988.

Brown, Raymond E. *Biblical Exegesis and Church Doctrine*. New York: Paulist Press, 1985.

_____. *Responses to 101 Questions on the Bible*. New York: Paulist Press, 1990.

Brown, Raymond E., et al., eds. *The Jerome Biblical Commentary*. Englewood Cliffs, New Jersey: Prentice-Hall, 1968. S. v. "The Gospel according to Matthew," by John L. McKenzie.

_____. *The New Jerome Biblical Commentary*. Englewood Cliffs, New Jersey: Prentice-Hall, 1990. S. v. "The Gospel according to Matthew," by Benedict Viviano.

Bryan, William Jennings. *In His Image*. Freeport, New York: Books for Libraries Press, 1971.

Burke, John. "When Catholics Share the Bible with Other Christians." *New Catholic World*, January/February 1985, 23-25.

Burtt, Edwin A. *Types of Religious Philosophy*. New York: Harper and Brothers, 1951.

Butler, Jon. "Making the Old-Time Religion New." *Wilson Quarterly*, Autumn 1992, 79-82.

Byrd, Joann. "Coverage of Christians," *Washington Post*, July 14, 1993, C-6.

Carey, George. *A Tale of Two Churches*. Downers Grove, Illinois: InterVarsity Press, 1984.

Carroll, Jackson, et al. *Religion in America: 1950 to the Present*. New York: Harper & Row, 1979.

Catechism of the Catholic Church. San Francisco: Ignatius Press-Librairie Editrice Vaticane, 1994.

Catholics Answer Jimmy Swaggart. Florissant, Missouri: Pax Tapes, n.d.

Christian Research Institute. *Should Christians Practice the Celebration of Easter?* San Juan Capistrano, California: Christian Research Institute, 1993.

Cohen, Norman J., ed. *The Fundamentalist Phenomenon: A View from Within, A Response from Without.* Grand Rapids, Michigan: Eerdmans Publishing Co., 1990.

Colacci, Mario. *The Doctrinal Conflict between Roman Catholic and Protestant Christianity.* Minneapolis: T. S. Denison and Co., 1962.

Cole, Stewart G. *The History of Fundamentalism.* New York: R. R. Smith, Inc., 1931.

Coleman, John. "Who are the Catholic Fundamentalists?" *Commonweal,* January 27, 1989, 42-47.

Coskren, Thomas M. "Fundamentalists on Campus." *New Catholic World,* January/February 1985, 38-41.

Countryman, William. *Biblical Authority or Biblical Tyranny? Scripture and the Christian Pilgrimage.* Philadelphia: Fortress Press, 1981.

Cox, Harvey. *Fire from Heaven: The Rise of Pentecostal Spirituality and the Reshaping of Religion in the Twenty-first Century.* Reading, Massachusetts: Addison-Wesley Publishing Co., 1994.

Cozens, M. L. *A Handbook of Heresies.* London: Sheed and Ward, 1974.

Cromartie, Michael, ed. *No Longer Exiles: The Religious New Right in American Politics.* Washington, D.C.: Ethics and Public Policy Center, 1992.

Curley, Brian E. "Fundamentalism and Its Challenge to Catholic Religious Education." *New Catholic World,* January/February 1985, 34-37.

Dakin, Arthur. *Calvinism.* London: Duckworth, 1940.

D'Angelo, Louise. *The Catholic Answer to the Jehovah's Witnesses: A Challenge Accepted.* Meriden, Connecticut: Maryheart Catholic Information Center, 1981.

de la Potterie, Ignace. "Exegesis: Awed and Not Perplexed." *30 Days,* No. 11 (1992), 52-53.

DeMarco, Donald. "The Dispute between Galileo and the Catholic Church." *Homiletic and Pastoral Review,* May 1986, 53ff., and June 1986, 23ff.

Diamond, Sara. "Watch on the Right: Change in Strategy," *The Humanist,* January/February 1994, 34-36.

_____. *Spiritual Warfare: The Politics of the Christian Right.* Chapel Hill: University of North Carolina Press, 1993.

Dinges, William D., and James Hitchcock. "Roman Catholic Traditionalism and Activist Conservatism in the United States." In *Fundamentalisms Observed*, eds. Martin E. Marty and R. Scott Appleby, 66-141. Chicago: University of Chicago Press, 1991.

Dobson, Edward. "Fundamentalism — Its Roots." *New Catholic World*, January/February 1985, 4-9.

Dolan, Jay P. *Catholic Revivalism*. Notre Dame, Indiana: University of Notre Dame Press, 1978.

Dulles, Avery. *Models of Revelation*. Garden City, New York: Doubleday & Co., 1983.

_____. "Paths to Doctrinal Agreement: Ten Theses." *Theological Studies*, March 1986, 32-47.

_____. *Revelation and the Quest for Unity*. Washington, D.C.: Corpus Books, 1968.

Fackre, Gabriel. "Positive Values and Honorable Intentions: A Critique of Fundamentalism." *New Theology Review*, May 1988, 58-73.

Falwell, Jerry, et al., eds. *The Fundamentalist Phenomenon: The Resurgence of Conservative Christianity*. Garden City, New York: Doubleday & Co., 1981.

Feinberg, Charles, ed. *The Fundamentals for Today*. Grand Rapids, Michigan: Kregel Publishers, 1958.

Finke, Roger, and Rodney Stark. *The Churching of America, 1776-1990*. New Brunswick, New Jersey: Rutgers University Press, 1992.

_____. "How the Upstart Sects Won America." *Journal for the Scientific Study of Religion*, 1989, 27-44.

Flannery, Austin. *Vatican Council II: Conciliar and Post-Conciliar Documents*. Northport, New York: Costello Publishing Co., 1980.

Foster, J. M. "Rome, the Antagonist of the Nation." In *The Fundamentals for Today* (Volume II), ed. Charles Feinberg, 495-503. Grand Rapids, Michigan: Kregel Publications, 1958.

Fox, Robert J. *Protestant Fundamentalism and the Born Again Catholic*. Alexandria, South Dakota: Fatima Family Apostolate, 1991.

Frankl, Razelle. *Televangelism: The Marketing of Popular Religion*. Carbondale, Illinois: Southern Illinois University Press, 1987.

Freeman, Matthew. *The San Diego Model: A Community Battles the Religious Right*. Washington, D.C.: People for the American Way, 1993.

Furniss, Norman F. *The Fundamentalist Controversy: 1918-1931*. New Haven: Yale University Press, 1954.

Gerrish, B. A. *Reformers in Profile*. Philadelphia: Fortress Press, 1967.

Gnuse, Robert. *The Authority of the Bible: Theories of Inspiration, Revelation and the Canon of Scripture.* New York: Paulist Press, 1985.

Goode, Stephen. "Exploring the Passion of Faiths." *Insight*, June 1, 1992, 12ff.

Grant, Robert M., and David Tracy. *A Short History of the Interpretation of the Bible.* Philadelphia: Fortress Press, 1984.

Gritsch, Eric W. *Born Againism: Perspectives on a Movement.* Philadelphia: Fortress Press, 1982.

Hadden, Jeffrey K., and Anson Shupe, eds. *Secularization and Fundamentalism Reconsidered.* New York: Paragon House, 1989.

Hanegraaff, Hendrik. "Is Roman Catholicism a Cult?" *Christian Research Institute Perspective*, n.d.

_____. "What Separates Evangelicals from Catholics?" *Christian Research Institute Perspective*, n.d.

Hase, Karl Von. *Handbook to the Controversy with Rome.* London: The Religious Tract Society, 1906.

Hatch, Nathan O., and Mark A. Noll. *The Bible in America: Essays in Cultural History.* New York: Oxford University Press, 1982.

Hayes, Zachary. "Fundamentalist Eschatology: Piety and Politics." *New Theology Review*, May 1988, 21-35.

Henry, Carl F. H. *Basic Christian Doctrines: Contemporary Evangelical Thought.* New York: Holt, Rinehart and Winston, 1962.

_____. "Thoughts on the Conflict over Justification." *Christian Research Journal*, Spring 1995, 50-51.

Hertzke, A. D. *Representing God in Washington.* Knoxville, Tennessee: University of Tennessee Press, 1988.

Higgins, James J. "A Catholic Looks at Fundamentalism." *Liguorian*, October 1981, 48-53.

_____. "Fundamentalism and the Church." *Liguorian*, October 1986, 40ff.

Hislop, Alexander. *The Two Babylons or the Papal Worship.* Neptune, New Jersey: Loizeaux Brothers, 1959.

Hodge, Charles. *Systematic Theology.* Grand Rapids, Michigan: Eerdmans Publishing Co., 1973 (reprint).

Hoekema, Anthony A. *The Four Major Cults.* Grand Rapids, Michigan: Eerdmans Publishing Co., 1986.

Hofstadter, Richard. *Anti-Intellectualism in American Life.* New York: Alfred A. Knopf, 1963.

Hoppe, Leslie J. "The Bible Tells Me So." *The Bible Today*, September 1991, 279-283.

Howell, Kenneth. Telephone interview by author, April 14, 1992.

Hutchinson, William R. *The Modernist Impulse in American Protestantism.* Cambridge, Massachusetts: Harvard University Press, 1976.

Irenée de Lyon. *Contre les Hérésies.* Paris: Editions Cerf, 1969.

Jamieson, George. *Discussions on the Atonement: Is It Vicarious?* Edinburgh: William Blackwood and Sons, 1887.

Jelen, Ted G. and Clyde Wilcox. "The Christian Right in the 1990's," *The Public Perspective,* March/April 1993, 10ff.

John Paul II, Pope. "Bible Experts Must be Guided by Spirit." *L'Osservatore Romano,* April 28, 1993, 3ff.

_____. *Catechesi Tradendae.* Boston: St. Paul Editions, 1979.

Jurgens, William A. *The Faith of the Early Fathers.* Collegeville, Minnesota: Liturgical Press, 1970.

Kaplan, George R. "Shotgun Wedding: Notes on Public Education's Encounter with the New Christian Right," *Phi Delta Kappan,* May 1994, K1-12.

Kaplan, Lawrence, ed. *Fundamentalism in Comparative Perspective.* Amherst: University of Massachusetts Press, 1992.

Keating, Karl. *Catholicism and Fundamentalism: The Attack on 'Romanism' by 'Bible Christians.'* San Francisco: Ignatius Press, 1988.

_____. "Fundamentalism." *Extension,* January 1990, 18-19.

Kelley, Dean. *Why Conservative Churches Are Growing.* New York: Harper & Row, 1972.

Kepp, Michael. "Fast Track to Paradise." *Catholic World Report,* February 1992, 22-27.

Kimball, William R. *The Bible and Roman Catholicism.* South Lake Tahoe, California: Christian Equippers International, 1985.

Kreeft, Peter. "The Fundamentalists: Whose Bible Is It, Anyway?" *National Catholic Register,* August 30, 1992, 5.

LaVerdiere, Eugene. "Must A Christian Be Born Again?" *New Catholic World,* January/February 1985, 20-22.

_____. "There's No Such Thing as a Catholic Fundamentalist." *U.S. Catholic,* September 1989, 36-38.

Lehmann, Helmut T., ed. *Luther's Works.* Philadelphia: Fortress Press, 1970.

Lehmann-Haupt, Christopher. "God, Self and Evil from a Fundamentalist View." *New York Times,* April 4, 1994.

Leith, John H., ed. *Creeds of the Churches.* Louisville: John Knox Press, 1982.

Leon, Luis D. G. "*Somos Un Cuerpo en Cristo:* Notes on Power and the

Body in an East Los Angeles Chicano/Mexicano Pentecostal Community." *Latino Studies Journal*, September 1994, 60-86.

Lepin, M. *Les Théories de M. Loisy: Exposé et Critique*. Paris: Beauchesne et Cie., 1910.

Lienesch, Michael. *Redeeming America: Piety and Politics in the New Christian Right*. Chapel Hill: University of North Carolina Press, 1993.

Loisy, Alfred. *The Gospel and the Church*. Philadelphia: Fortress Press, 1976.
_____. *My Duel with the Vatican: The Autobiography of a Catholic Modernist*. New York: Greenwood Press, 1968.

Loome, Thomas Michael. *Liberal Catholicism, Reform Catholicism, Modernism*. Mainz, Germany: Matthias-Grunewald-Verlag, 1979.

Lull, Timothy F., ed. *Martin Luther's Basic Theological Writings*. Minneapolis: Fortress Press, 1989.

Mahan, Walter L. *The Unveiling of End-Time Events*. Nashville, Tennessee: Winston-Derek, 1993.

Mailer, Norman, "By Heaven Inspired," *New Republic*, October 12, 1992, 24ff.

Marrow, Stanley B. *The Words of Jesus in our Gospels: A Catholic Response to Fundamentalism*. New York: Paulist Press, 1979.

Marsden, George M. "Defining American Fundamentalism." In *The Fundamentalist Phenomenon: A View from Within, A Response from Without*, ed. Norman J. Cohen, 22-37. Grand Rapids, Michigan: Eerdmans Publishing Co., 1990.
_____. *Fundamentalism and American Culture: The Shaping of Twentieth Century Evangelicalism, 1870-1925*. New York: Oxford University Press, 1980.
_____. "Fundamentalism as an American Phenomenon: A Comparison with English Evangelicalism." *Church History*, June 1977, 215-232.
_____. *Reforming Fundamentalism: Fuller Seminary and the New Evangelicalism*. Grand Rapids, Michigan: Eerdmans Publishing Co., 1987.
_____. *Understanding Fundamentalism and Evangelicalism*. Grand Rapids, Michigan: Eerdmans Publishing Co., 1991.

Martin, David. *Tongues of Fire: The Explosion of Protestantism in Latin America*. Oxford: Basil Blackwell, 1990.

Martin, Walter. *Essential Christianity: A Handbook of Basic Christian Doctrines*. Ventura, California: Regal Books, 1980.

Marty, Martin E. "Modern Fundamentalists." *America*, September 27, 1986, 133-135.

Marty, Martin E., and R. Scott Appleby, eds. *Fundamentalisms Observed*. Chicago: University of Chicago Press, 1991.

McBride, Alfred, O. Praem. *The Second Coming of Jesus*. Huntington, Indiana: Our Sunday Visitor, Inc., 1993.

McNeill, John T. *The History and Character of Calvinism*. New York: Oxford University Press, 1954.

McNeill, John T., ed. *Calvin: Institutes of the Christian Religion*. Philadelphia: Westminster Press, 1960.

Meacham, Jon. "What the Religious Right Can Teach the New Democrats," *Washington Monthly*, March/April 1993, 45ff.

Medhurst, T. W. "Is Romanism Christianity?" In *The Fundamentals for Today* (Volume II), ed. Charles Feinberg, 485-494. Grand Rapids, Michigan: Kregel Publications, 1958.

Methodist League for Faith and Life. *The Case of Methodism Against Modernism*. Philadelphia: 1929.

Miley, John. *Systematic Theology* (two volumes). New York: Eaton and Mains, 1892 and 1894.

Monti, Dominic V. "World Out of Time: The Origins of the Fundamentalist Movement." *New Theology Review*, May 1988, 5-20.

Mozley, J. K. *The Doctrine of the Atonement*. London: Gerald Duckworth & Co., 1962.

Nash, Ronald. "Was the New Testament Influenced by Pagan Religions?" *Christian Research Journal*, Winter 1994, 8-15.

National Conference of Catholic Bishops (Ad Hoc Committee on Biblical Fundamentalism). "Pastoral Statement for Catholics on Biblical Fundamentalism." *Origins*, November 5, 1987, 376-377.

Navarre Bible. *St. Matthew*. Dublin: Four Courts Press, 1988.

Neuhaus, Richard J., and Michael Cromartie. *Piety and Politics: Evangelicals and Fundamentalists Confront the World*. Washington, D.C.: Ethics and Public Policy Center, 1987.

Neuner, J., and J. Dupuis, eds. *The Christian Faith in the Doctrinal Documents of the Catholic Church*. New York: Alba House, 1982.

Nevins, Albert J. *Answering a Fundamentalist*. Huntington, Indiana: Our Sunday Visitor, Inc., 1990.

Nunn, H.P.V. *What Is Modernism?* New York: Macmillan Co., 1932.

O'Meara, Thomas F. *Fundamentalism: A Catholic Perspective*. New York: Paulist Press, 1990.

_____. "Fundamentalism and the Christian Believer." *The Priest*, March 1988, 39-42.

Packer, J. I. *'Fundamentalism' and the Word of God: Some Evangelical Principles*. Grand Rapids, Michigan: Eerdmans Publishing Co., 1982.

Parker, T.H.L. *Calvin's Preaching*. Louisville: Westminster/ Knox, 1992.

Pelikan, Jaroslav. *Luther the Expositor*. St. Louis: Concordia Publishers, 1959.

Pepper, Howard. *Current Catholicism*. San Juan Capistrano, California: Christian Research Institute, 1979.

Petre, M. D. *Alfred Loisy: His Religious Significance*. Cambridge: Cambridge University Press, 1944.

Pierson, A. T. "Antagonism to the Bible." *Our Hope*, January 1909, 475ff.
_____. *Knowing the Scriptures*. New York: Gospel Publishing House, 1910.

Pontifical Biblical Commission. "Instructio de Historica Evangeliorum Veritate." *Catholic Biblical Quarterly*, July 1964, 299-312.

Poulat, Emile. *Histoire, Dogme et Critique dans la Crise Moderniste*. Paris: Casterman, 1962.

Pryke, W. Maurice. *Modernism as a Working Faith*. Cambridge: W. Heffer and Sons, 1926.

Pucelik, T. M. Review of *Fundamentalisms Observed*, ed. by Martin E. Marty and R. Scott Appleby. In *Choice* (July/August 1992): 10.

Quick, Oliver Chase. *Liberalism, Modernism and Tradition*. New York: Longmans, Green and Co., 1922.

Ramm, Bernard. *After Fundamentalism*. San Francisco: Harper & Row, 1983.

Rauch, Jonathan. *Kindly Inquisitors*. Chicago: University of Chicago Press, 1993.

Reid, J.K.S. *Calvin: Theological Treatises*. Philadelphia: Westminster Press, 1954.

Rivenburg, Roy. "Odysseys of Faith," *Sunday Star-Ledger*, October 4, 1992, 39.

Roberts, Kenneth. *Father Roberts Answers Jimmy Swaggart*. West Covina, California: St. Joseph's Catholic Tapes and Books, 1986.

Rome and the Study of Scripture. St. Meinrad, Indiana: Grail Publications, 1962.

Ruether, Rosemary Radford. Review of *Fundamentalisms Observed*, ed. by Martin E. Marty and R. Scott Appleby. In *The New York Times Book Review* (January 26, 1992): 32.

Rumble, Leslie. "The 'Bible Only' Theory." *This Rock*, December 1992, 18-22; January 1993, 20-26.

Rutler, George W. *Christ and Reason: An Introduction to Ideas from Kant to Tyrrell*. Front Royal, Virginia: Christendom Press, 1990.

Salmaan, Abu al-Hasan. Review of *Fundamentalisms Observed*, ed. by Martin

E. Marty and R. Scott Appleby. In *Muslim World Book Review* 12 (1992): 5.

Samples, Kenneth, and Dan Kistler. *Catholicism Bibliography.* San Juan Capistrano, California: Christian Research Institute, 1989.

Sandeen, Ernest R. *The Origins of Fundamentalism: Toward a Historical Interpretation.* Philadelphia: Fortress Press, 1968.

————. *The Roots of Fundamentalism: British and American Millenarianism, 1800-1930.* Chicago: University of Chicago Press, 1970.

Schreck, Alan. *Catholic and Christian: An Explanation of Commonly Misunderstood Catholic Beliefs.* Ann Arbor, Michigan: Servant Publications, 1984.

Schrotenboer, Paul G. *Roman Catholicism: A Contemporary Evangelical Perspective.* Grand Rapids, Michigan: Baker Book House, 1988.

Shriver, Peggy L. "Guardians of Fundamentalism's Fortress." *New Catholic World*, January/February 1985, 15-19.

Smyth, Newman. *Passing Protestantism and Coming Catholicism.* New York: Charles Scribner & Sons, 1908.

Sonn, Tamara. Review of *Fundamentalisms Observed*, ed. by Martin E. Marty and R. Scott Appleby. In *Journal of Asian Studies* (November 1992): 12.

Sproul, R. C. *Essential Truths of the Christian Faith.* Wheaton, Illinois: Tyndale House Publishers, 1992.

Stackhouse, John G. "Are Fundamentalists All Alike?" *Christianity Today*, November 23, 1992, 37.

Steinfels, Peter. "Beliefs." *New York Times*, February 20, 1993, 8.

————. "Fundamentalism: Last Spasm of the 20th Century?" *New York Times*, April 4, 1993, A21.

Stephens, W. P. *Zwingli: An Introduction to His Thought.* New York: Oxford/Clarendon, 1992.

Stransky, Thomas F. "A Catholic Looks at American Fundamentalists." *New Catholic World*, January/February 1985, 10-13.

Stravinskas, Peter M. J. *The Catholic Response.* Huntington, Indiana: Our Sunday Visitor, Inc., 1985.

————. *Constitutional Rights and Religious Prejudice: Catholic Education as the Battleground.* Milwaukee: Catholic League for Religious and Civil Rights, 1983.

Strozier, Charles B. *Apocalypse: On the Psychology of Fundamentalism in America.* Boston: Beacon Press, 1994.

Sungenis, Robert, et al. *Shock Wave 2000! Harold Camping's 1994 Debacle.* Green Forest, Arizona: Green Leaf Press, 1994.

Swaggart, Jimmy. *Catholicism and Christianity.* Baton Rouge, Louisiana: Jimmy Swaggart Ministries, 1986.

Tappert, Theodore G., ed. *The Book of Concord.* Philadelphia: Fortress Press, 1981.

Thompson, K. C. *Once for All.* London: The Faith Press, 1962.

Thorkelson, Willmar. "Scholar: Interpret Bible in Community," *The Lutheran,* October 1992, 36.

Tillich, Paul. *Systematic Theology.* Chicago: University of Chicago Press, 1951.

Toon, Peter. *Protestants and Catholics: A Guide to Understanding the Differences among Christians.* Ann Arbor, Michigan: Servant Publications, 1984.

Turvasi, Francesco. *The Condemnation of Alfred Loisy and the Historical Method.* Rome: Edizioni di Storia e Letteratura, 1979.

Von Balthasar, Hans Urs. *The Office of Peter and the Structure of the Church.* San Francisco: Ignatius Press, 1986.

Walker, Williston. *John Calvin: The Organiser of Reformed Protestantism.* New York: Schocken Books, 1969.

Warfield, Benjamin. "The Deity of Christ." In *The Fundamentals for Today,* ed. Charles Feinberg, 235-240. Grand Rapids, Michigan: Kregel Publications, 1958.

Weber, Timothy P. *Living in the Shadow of the Second Coming.* Chicago: University of Chicago Press, 1987.

Wendell, François. *Calvinism: The Origins and Development of His Religious Thought.* New York: Harper & Row, 1950.

Whalen, William. *Separated Brethren.* Huntington, Indiana: Our Sunday Visitor, Inc., 1979.

Whealon, Archbishop John F. "Challenging Fundamentalism." *America,* September 27, 1986, 136-138.

White, James. *Answers to Catholic Claims: A Discussion of Biblical Authority.* Southbridge, Massachusetts: Crowne Publications, 1990.

Wiley, H. Orton. *Introduction to Christian Theology.* Kansas City, Missouri: Beacon Hill Press, 1949.

Williams, George Huntson. *Anselm: Communion and Atonement.* St. Louis: Concordia Publishing House, 1960.

Williams, Paul L., ed. *Faith and the Sources of Faith.* Scranton: Northeast Books, 1985.

Williams, Peter W. *Popular Religion in America.* Chicago: University of Illinois Press, 1989.

Williamson, Peter, and Kevin Perrotta, eds. *Christianity Confronts Modernity*. Ann Arbor, Michigan: Servant Books, 1981.

Wilson, George W. *Methodist Theology vs. Methodist Theologians*. Cincinnati: Jennings and Pye, 1904.

Wood, A. Skevington. *The Principles of Biblical Interpretation: As Enunciated by Irenaeus, Origen, Augustine, Luther, and Calvin*. Grand Rapids, Michigan: Eerdmans Publishing Co., 1967.

Wuthnow, Robert. "Fundamentalism in the World." *The Christian Century*, April 29, 1992, 456ff.

_____. "The World of Fundamentalism." *The Christian Century*, April 22, 1992, 426ff.

II. Works Related to Proselytism and Evangelization

Abalos, David. Letter to author, December 5, 1994.

Abbott, Diane. "Leaving the Faith for Fundamentalism." *The Catholic Answer*, November/December 1989, 8-10.

Aboody, Charles. Telephone interview by author, December 6, 1994.

Ackerman, Todd. "The Rustlers." *National Catholic Register*, September 18, 1988, 1ff.

Alfaro, Juan. Telephone interview by author, March 12, 1992, and April 28, 1994.

Amato, Angelo. "Mariologia in Contesto." *Marianum: Ephemerides Mariologiae*, 1980.

Angela, Sister. Telephone interview by author, March 12, 1992, and April 27, 1994.

Arinze, Francis Cardinal. *The Essence of Evangelization*. Dublin: Veritas Publications, 1990.

"¿Aumentan Grupos Evangélicos y Pentecostales entre Indigenas?" *Today's Catholic*, September 3, 1993, 34.

Babcock, James. Telephone interview by author, December 6, 1994.

Barkley, Roy. "The Fundamentalist Threat." *Homiletic and Pastoral Review*, February 1988, 45-53.

Bedford, Michael. "Fundamentalists Storm Philippines for Christ." *National Catholic Reporter*, December 14, 1990, 25.

Berger, Joseph. "Koreans Breathe New Life into Queens Church." *New York Times*, July 30, 1986, B-1.

Bernardin, Joseph Cardinal. "Cardinal Urges Polish Ministry Follow-Up." *The Chicago Catholic*, May 25, 1984, 18.

Bertram, Robert W. "A Constructive Lutheran Theology of the Saints." *Dialog*, October 1992, 265-271.

Bevilacqua, Anthony Cardinal. Letter to author, May 6, 1993.

Bifet, Juan Esquerda. *Mary, Our Lady in the Mission of the Church*. Rome: Centro Internazionale di Animazione Missionaria, 1985.

Blackall, John C. "The Hispanic Presence." *Homiletic and Pastoral Review*, December 1984, 31ff.

Boettner, Loraine. *Roman Catholicism*. Philadelphia: Presbyterian & Reformed Publishing Co., 1974.

Boucher, John, J. "Reaching Out to Fundamentalists." *The Catholic Answer*, March/April 1989, 40-44.

Brennan, Walter T. "Theological Reflection: From *Marialis Cultus* to Mission — A New Challenge in Liturgy, Devotions and Popular Religion." *Marian Studies*, 1992, 132-159.

Brewer, Bartholomew. *Pilgrimage from Rome*. Greenville, South Carolina: Bob Jones University Press, 1982.

Briggs, Kenneth. "Among Hispanic Catholics, Another Pattern of Practice." *New York Times*, January 9, 1983, E-14.

Brooke, James. "Pragmatic Protestants Win Catholic Converts in Brazil." *New York Times*, July 4, 1993, A-1.

Burke, John. "When Catholics Share the Bible with Other Christians." *New Catholic World*, January/February 1985, 23-25.

Caldecott, Stratford. "Lay Movements and the Challenge of Faith." *National Catholic Register*, February 1, 1987, 1ff.

Caponetto, Antonio. *The Black Legends and Catholic Hispanic Culture*. St. Louis: Central Bureau of the Catholic Verein of America, 1991.

Carson, Thomas. Telephone Interview at the Episcopal Church Center, New York City, August 27, 1983.

Catéchisme de L'Église Catholique. Paris: Mame-Librairie Editrice Vaticane, 1992.

Catholic News Service. "Catholic Immigrants Welcomed — by Others." *The Catholic Advocate*, March 25, 1992, 18.

Catholics Answer Jimmy Swaggart. Florissant, Missouri: Pax Tapes, n.d.

Catoir, John. "Fundamentalists on the Move." *America*, September 27, 1986, 142-144.

Cheevers, Jack. "Mormon Recruiting Stirs Up Refugees." *The Tribune*, July 27, 1986, A-17.

Chick, Jack T. *Are Roman Catholics Christians?* Chino, California: Chick Publications, n.d.

Chilson, Richard. "A Call to Catholic Action." *America*, September 27, 1986, 148ff.

_____. "Two Visions." *New Catholic World*, January/February 1985, 42-44.

Chiniquy, Charles. *The Secrets of the Confessional*. Chino, California: Chick Publications, 1983.

Christensen, Mark. "Coming to Grips with Losses: The Migration of Catholics into Conservative Protestantism." *America*, January 26, 1991, 58-59.

"Christian Witness and Proselytism: A Study Document." *The Ecumenical Review*, January 1971, 9-19.

Clark, Eugene V., ed. *Teaching the Catholic Faith: Central Questions for the '90s*. New York: St. John's University Press, 1991.

Coffey, Tony. *Once a Catholic: What You Need to Know about Roman Catholicism*. Eugene, Oregon: Harvest House Publishers, 1993.

Coleman, John. Review of *The Social Sources of Sectarianism: Sects and New Religious Movements in Contemporary Society*, by Bryan R. Wilson. In *Theological Studies*, March 1992: 171-172.

Collegamento Mariano Nazionale. *La Presenza di Maria nella Missione Evangelizzatrice del Popolo di Dio*. Rome: Santuario della Madonna del Divino Amore, 1973.

Conferencia Episcopal de Guatemala (Departamento de Laicos). *Elementos para una Reflexión Pastoral en Preparación de la IV Conferencia General del Episcopado Latinoamericano*. Bogotá: 1990.

Conferencia General del Episcopado Latinoamericano. *Nueva Evangelización, Promoción Humana, Cultura Cristiana*. Bogotá: Ediciones Paulinas, 1992.

Consejo Episcopal Latinoamericano. *La Evangelización en el Presente y en el Futuro de América Latina*. Caracas: Puebla, 1979.

_____. "Latin America: Rise and Walk!" *Origins*, May 25, 1995, 22-23.

Conway, Pierre. "Keep Your Bible Closed." *Homiletic and Pastoral Review*, June 1986, 28ff.

Cowell, Alan. "In Baltics, Pope's Message Is for the Eastern Orthodox." *New York Times*, September 7, 1993, A-4.

Cunningham, W. Patrick. "Facing the Fundamentalists." *Homiletic and Pastoral Review*, May 1988, 56-59.

Dakin, Arthur. *Calvinism*. London: Duckworth, 1940.

Dart, John. "Immigrants Called 'Ripe Harvest Field' for Churches." *Los Angeles Times*, Part II, April 20, 1985, 6.

Dashbach, Edwin. "Fundamentalism in Appalachia: One Priest's Experience." *The Priest*, February 1985, 3-4.

Deck, Allan Figueroa. *The Challenge of Evangelical/Pentecostal Christianity to Hispanic Catholicism in the United States*. Notre Dame, Indiana: Cushwa Center for the Study of American Catholicism, 1992.

_____. "Fundamentalism and the Hispanic Catholic." *America*, January 26, 1985, 64-66.

_____. "Proselytism and Hispanic Catholics: How Long Can We Cry Wolf?" *America*, December 10, 1988, 485-490.

_____. *The Second Wave: Hispanic Ministry and the Evangelization of Cultures*. New York: Paulist Press, 1989.

_____. Review of *The Liberating Spirit: Toward an Hispanic American Pentecostal Social Ethic*, by Eldin Villafañe. In *Theological Studies* (September 1994): 594-595.

Deck, Allan Figueroa, and Joseph A. Nuñez. "Religious Enthusiasm and Hispanic Youths." *America*, October 23, 1982, 233ff.

DeFiores, Stefano. *Maria: Presenza Viva nel Popolo di Dio*. Rome: Edizioni Monfortane, 1980.

_____, and Salvatore Meo. *Nuovo Dizionario di Mariologia*. Milan: Edizioni Paoline, 1986.

DePaolis, Velasio. *The Pastoral Care of Migrants in the Teaching and in the Directives of the Church*. New York: Center for Migration Studies, 1983.

Dinges, William D. "The Vatican Report on Sects, Cults and New Religious Movements." *America*, September 27, 1986, 145-147.

Dodds, Bill. "Sects and the Hispanic Family." *Our Sunday Visitor*, June 18, 1995, 12.

_____. "Strangers Need Not Apply." *Our Sunday Visitor*, August 2, 1992, 10-11.

_____. "Target: The Hispanic Catholics." *Our Sunday Visitor*, August 19, 1990, 10-11.

Dolan, Jay P. *The American Catholic Experience*. Garden City, New York: Doubleday & Co., 1985.

Domenico, Bertetto. "Maria e l'Attività Missionaria di Cristo e della Chiesa." In *Portare Cristo all'Uomo* (Proceedings of the Congresso del Ventennio dal Concilio Vaticano II), 455-472. Rome: Pontificia Università Urbaniana, 1985.

Duinn, J. "Hispanic Catholics." *New Covenant*, January 1990, 9-11.

Dulles, Avery. "John Paul II and the New Evangelization." *America*, February 1, 1992, 52ff.

Eagleson, John, and Philip Scharper, eds. *Puebla and Beyond: Documentation and Commentary*. Maryknoll, New York: Orbis Books, 1979.

Elya, Bishop John. Telephone interview by author, December 6, 1994.

Espaillat, Benny. Telephone interview by author, April 27, 1994.

"Evangelist Is Given Six-Year Prison Term." *New York Times*, September 18, 1994, 43.

Falasca, Stefania. "Interview with Cardinal Sodano: Defending the Essential." *30 Days*, No. 11 (1992), 24-27.

_____. "Santo Domingo: Fall of the Walls of Old." *30 Days*, No. 11 (1992), 16-21.

Feuerherd, Peter. "Catholic Immigrants Leave Fold." *National Catholic Register*, June 28, 1992, 1ff.

"Fewer Latinos Now Are Identifying Themselves as Catholic." *Long Island Catholic*, March 23, 1994, 12.

Fitzpatrick, Joseph P. "The Hispanic Poor in the American Catholic Middle-Class Church." *Thought*, Spring 1988, 189-200.

_____. Review of *Is Latin America Turning Protestant? The Politics of Evangelical Growth*, by David Stoll. In *Theological Studies* (March 1992): 172-174.

Flannery, Austin. *Vatican Council II: Conciliar and Post-Conciliar Documents*. Northport, New York: Costello Publishing Co., 1980.

Fox, Robert J. *Protestant Fundamentalism and the Born Again Catholic*. Alexandria, South Dakota: Fatima Family Apostolate, 1991.

Galilea, S. *Catholics and the Sects*. Quezon City, Philippines: Claretian Publications, n.d.

_____. *The Challenge of Popular Religiosity*. Quezon City, Philippines: Claretian Publications, 1988.

Gallup, George. Letter to author, October 31, 1994.

Gallup, George, and Jim Castelli. *The American Catholic People*. Garden City, New York: Doubleday & Co., 1987.

Gallup, George, and Sarah Jones. *100 Questions and Answers: Religion in America*. Princeton, New Jersey: Princeton Religion Research Center, 1989.

Gallup Organization. *Unchurched American*. Washington, D.C.: Paulist National Catholic Evangelization Association, 1988.

Gapi, François-Marie. "Les Religions Traditionelles et le Dialogue Interreligieux." *Bulletin: Pontificium Consilium pro Dialogo inter Religiones*, No. 82 (1993), 70-76.

Gaspari, Antonio. "Rediscovering Mary." *Inside the Vatican*, May 1995, 48-51.

Gesy, Lawrence J. *Today's Destructive Cults and Movements*. Huntington, Indiana: Our Sunday Visitor, Inc., 1993.

Gilles, Anthony E. *Fundamentalism: What Every Catholic Needs to Know.* Cincinnati, Ohio: St. Anthony Messenger Press, 1984.

Goldman, Ari. "Religion Notes: Hispanic Americans Move Up in U.S. Catholic Church; They Also Move Out to Evangelical Groups." *New York Times*, March 26, 1994, 26.

Gonzalez, Roberto O. "The New Evangelization and Hispanics in the United States." *America*, October 19, 1991, 268ff.

Gonzalez, Roberto O., and Michael LaVelle. *The Hispanic Catholic in the United States: A Socio-Cultural and Religious Profile.* New York: Northeast Catholic Pastoral Center for Hispanics, 1985.

Gracida, Bishop René. "Whatever Happened to the Diocese of Masuccaba?" *The Catholic Answer*, September/October 1991, 54-57.

Graves, Jim. "Evangelical Movement Offers Challenges to Catholics." *Diocese of Orange Bulletin*, August 1992, 7ff.

Greeley, Andrew M. *The Catholic Myth: The Behavior and Beliefs of American Catholics.* New York: Scribner, 1990.

_____. "Defection among Hispanics." *America*, July 23 and July 30, 1988, 61-62.

Hansen, Laurie. "Plainly Speaking: Pope Uses Strong Words to Denounce Latin American Sects." *Catholic New York*, October 22, 1992, 7.

Henry, Carl F. H. *Basic Christian Doctrines: Contemporary Evangelical Thought.* New York: Holt, Reinhart and Winston, 1962.

Hill, Clifford. "Immigrant Sect Development in Britain: A Case of Status Deprivation." *Social Compass*, 1971, 236ff.

Hislop, Alexander. *The Two Babylons or the Papal Worship.* Neptune, New Jersey: Loizeaux Brothers, 1959.

Hispanic Bishops of California. "Responding to Proselytism." *Origins*, June 23, 1988, 82-85.

Hodge, Charles. *Systematic Theology.* Grand Rapids, Michigan: Eerdmans Publishing Co., 1973 (reprint).

Hoge, Dean. *Converts, Dropouts, Returnees: A Study of Religious Change among Catholics.* Washington, D.C.: United States Catholic Conference, 1981.

_____. "Why the Decline in New Adult Catholics?" *Catholic Evangelization*, September/October 1988, 5-7.

Holland, Clifton L. *The Religious Dimension in Hispanic Los Angeles.* South Pasadena, California: William Carey Library, 1974.

Holler, Stephen C. "Mary and the Poor in Latin America Since Vatican II: Responses of the Church to Marian Popular Religion." Ph.D. dissertation, St. Louis University, 1992.

Holton, Robert. "Spanish Spirits on the Airwaves." *Our Sunday Visitor*, June 4, 1995, 5.

_____. "Where is the Church's Visibility?" *Our Sunday Visitor*, May 2, 1993, 14.

Hoornaert, Eduardo. "La Evangelización según la Tradición Guadalupana," In *Maria en la Pastoral Popular*, 89-110. Bogotá: Ediciones Paulinas, 1976.

Icaza, Rosa. Telephone interview by author, April 28, 1994.

Jarbo, Raymond. Interview by author, April 24, 1994, Ontario, Oregon.

John Paul II, Pope. "Address of February 12, 1988, to Italian Bishops on Liturgical Course." *L'Osservatore Romano*, March 14, 1988, 5.

_____. "Catholic Laity and Migration." *L'Osservatore Romano*, September 7, 1987, 3ff.

_____. "Christ Is Hope of Latin America." *L'Osservatore Romano*, October 27, 1993, 5.

_____. *Christifideles Laici*. Vatican City: Libreria Editrice Vaticana, 1988.

_____. "The Church on Her Way." *L'Osservatore Romano*, August 25, 1980, 7.

_____. "Continue the Evangelization Efforts." *Newsletter of the Confraternity of Catholic Clergy*, May 1992, 3.

_____. "I Entrust to Mary the Difficult Personal Situation of Migrants." *L'Osservatore Romano*, November 7, 1988, 2ff.

_____. "Mary Was Star of the First Evangelization of America." *L'Osservatore Romano*, October 7, 1992, 4.

_____. "Opening Address to the Fourth General Conference of the Latin American Episcopate." *Origins*, October 22, 1992, 321-332.

_____. "The Problems of Migration." *The Pope Speaks*, Volume 31, No. 4, 1986, 354-360.

_____. "Proselytizing of Migrants by Sects Is a Challenge the Church Must Meet." *L'Osservatore Romano*, August 6, 1990, 1ff.

_____. *Redemptor Hominis*. Boston: St. Paul Editions, 1979.

_____. *Redemptoris Missio*. Vatican City: Libreria Editrice Vaticana, 1990.

_____. "Structures of Participation Must Reflect the Church's True Nature." *L'Osservatore Romano*, October 13, 1993, 3ff.

_____. "The Task of the Latin American Bishops." *Origins*, March 24, 1983, 659-662.

_____. "You Are Constructing a Human Multiracial Community in the Light of Christianity." *L'Osservatore Romano*, August 4, 1980, 8ff.

Johnson, Benton, et al. "Mainline Churches: The Real Reason for Decline." *First Things*, March 1993, 13-18.

Jurgens, William A. *The Faith of the Early Fathers.* Collegeville, Minnesota: Liturgical Press, 1970.

"Jury Convicts An Evangelist in Tax Evasion," *New York Times*, June 12, 1994, 30.

Kayal, Philip. Letter to author, December 5, 1994.

Keating, Karl. "Answering the Fundamentalist Challenge." *Homiletic and Pastoral Review*, July 1985, 32ff.

_____. *Catholicism and Fundamentalism: The Attack on 'Romanism' by 'Bible Christians.'* San Francisco: Ignatius Press, 1988.

Kepp, Michael. "In Brazil, Renewal Is Thriving." *National Catholic Register*, March 7, 1993, 1ff.

King, Eleace. *Proselytism and Evangelization: An Exploratory Study.* Washington, D.C.: Center for Applied Research in the Apostolate, 1991.

_____. Telephone interview by author, January 31, 1994, and April 27, 1994.

King, Eleace, and Francis Gillespie. *Final Report on the Survey of Attitudes towards Proselytism of Ethnic Minorities.* Washington, D.C.: Center for Applied Research in the Apostolate, 1988.

Kroeger, James H. "Cruciform Dialogue in Mission." *Bulletin: Pontificium Consilium pro Dialogo inter Religiones*, No. 83 (1993), 147-152.

Laghi, Archbishop Pio. "Stemming the Outflow of Hispanic Catholics." *Origins*, November 24, 1988, 386-388.

LaVerdiere, Eugene. "Fundamentalism: A Pastoral Concern." *The Bible Today*, January 1983, 5-11.

LeBar, James J. *Cults, Sects, and the New Age.* Huntington, Indiana: Our Sunday Visitor, Inc., 1989.

_____. "The Fundamentalist Challenge." *The Catholic Answer*, November/December 1992, 46-51.

Lehmann, Helmut T., ed. *Luther's Works.* Philadelphia: Fortress Press, 1970.

Lehmann, Karl. "The Meaning of a New Evangelization of Europe." *Communio*, Winter 1992, 541-548.

Levada, Archbishop William. "Hispanic Ministry's Changing Face." *Origins*, June 1, 1995, 46-48.

Lewis, Vincent P. "How to Proclaim — and Defend — the Faith." *The Catholic Answer*, January/February 1992, 34-37.

Loesch, Juli. "We're Losing the Hispanics." *National Catholic Register*, August 18, 1985, 1ff.

Lopez y Guzman, Antonio. "Mexican-Americans: A Vibrant Spirituality." *Catholic Twin Circle*, August 9, 1992, 4-5.

Lull, Timothy F., ed. *Martin Luther's Basic Theological Writings*. Minneapolis: Fortress Press, 1989.

Lynch, Edward A. "The Retreat of Liberation Theology." *Homiletic and Pastoral Review*, February 1994, 12-21.

Madrid, Patrick. Telephone interview by author, April 26, 1994.

Maldonado, David. "Hispanic Protestantism: Historical Reflections," *Apuntes*, Spring 1991, 3-16.

Marchetto, Ezio. *The Catholic Church and the Phenomenon of Migration: An Overview*. New York: Center for Migration Studies, 1989.

Marty, Martin E., and Frederick E. Greenspahn, eds. *Pushing the Faith: Proselytism and Civility in a Pluralistic World*. New York: Crossroad, 1988.

McClory, Robert J. "Why Did the Catholic Cross the Road?" *U.S. Catholic*, January 1991, 6-12.

McDonald, Kevin. "Dialogue and Proclamation: A Comment from an Ecumenical Perspective." *Bulletin: Pontificium Consilium pro Dialogo inter Religiones*, No. 83 (1993), 127-134.

McGuinness, Matthew. Telephone interview by author, April 27, 1994.

McNeill, John T., ed. *Calvin: Institutes of the Christian Religion*. Philadelphia: Westminster Press, 1960.

Meo, Salvatore. "Maria Stella Dell'Evangelizzazione," In *l'Annuncio del Vangelo Oggi*, 763-780. Rome: Pontificia Università Urbaniana, 1977.

Moingt, Joseph. "Séductions Fondamentalistes." *Etudes*, December 1988, 667-679.

Mol, Hans. "Theory and Data on the Religious Behavior of Migrants." *Social Compass*, 1979, 36ff.

National Conference of Catholic Bishops. "The Hispanic Presence: Challenge and Commitment." *Origins*, January 19, 1984, 529-540.

_____. "National Pastoral Plan for Hispanic Ministry." *Origins*, December 10, 1987, 449-463.

_____ [Bishops' Committee on Migration, Office of Pastoral Care of Migrants and Refugees]. "Pastoral Care of Vietnamese Catholics in the United States: A Preliminary Report." Unpublished, Washington, D.C.: National Conference of Catholic Bishops, 1985.

_____ [Bishops' Committee on Migration]. *Today's Immigrants and Refugees*. Washington, D.C.: United States Catholic Conference, 1988.

_____ [Administrative Committee]. *Together, A New People: Pastoral*

Statement on Migrants and Refugees. Washington, D.C.: United States Catholic Conference, 1980.

_____ [Bishops' Committees on Ecumenical and Hispanic Affairs] and CELAM. "Fostering Ecumenism in the U.S. Hispanic Community." *Origins*, March 23, 1995, 658-660.

Nevins, Albert J. *Answering a Fundamentalist*. Huntington, Indiana: Our Sunday Visitor, Inc., 1990.

O'Connor, Charles. Telephone interview by author, May 2, 1994.

O'Connor, Liz. "Research Shows Where Catholics Go." *Long Island Catholic*, March 4, 1992, 1ff.

Olson, James S. *Catholic Immigrants in America*. Chicago: Nelson Hall, 1987.

O'Mahoney, Thomas. "Suicide of the Missions." *Religious Life*, February 1992, 1ff.

Orsi, Robert Anthony. *The Madonna of 115th Street: Faith and Community in Italian Harlem, 1880-1950*. New Haven: Yale University Press, 1985.

Ossanna, T. F. "Evangelizzazione." *Nuovo Dizionario di Mariologia*, ed. by Stefano DeFiores and Salvatore Meo. Milan: Edizioni Paoline, 1986.

Padilla, Gilbert. "Proselytism, Conservatism, and the Hispanics." *Pastoral Life*, November 1989, 13-21.

Patton, Cindy. "Public Enemy: Fundamentalists in Your Face." *Voice Literary Supplement*, February 1993, 1ff.

Paul VI, Pope. *Evangelii Nuntiandi*. Washington, D.C.: United States Catholic Conference, 1976.

Pelikan, Jaroslav. *Luther the Expositor*. St. Louis: Concordia Publishers, 1959.

Peña, Bishop Raymond. "Incorporating Hispanics into the U.S. Church." *Origins*, January 22, 1987, 574-579.

_____. Interview by author, November 11, 1992, Washington, D.C.

_____. Telephone interview by author, April 28, 1994.

"Philippine Bishops' Statement on Biblical Fundamentalism." *Origins*, February 23, 1989, 627-628.

Poblete, Renato. *Movimiento Pentecostal y Iglesia Católica*. Santiago, Chile: Centro Bellarmino, 1984.

Pontifical Commission for the Spiritual Care of Migrants and Itinerants. *Solidarity in Favour of New Migrations*. Vatican City: PCSCMI, 1991.

Pontificio Consiglio della Pastorale per I Migranti e gli Itineranti. *Migrazione e Diritto Ecclesiale*. Padua, Italy: Edizioni Messaggero, 1992.

"Pope Reflects on Needs of Ecclesial Integration." *L'Osservatore Romano*, September 2, 1985, 2.

Princeton Religion Research Center. *The Unchurched American — 10 Years Later*. Princeton, New Jersey: Princeton Religion Research Center, 1988.

"Proselytism." *Extension*, June 1991, 19-22.

"Protestant Growth." *One World*, March 1993, 21-22.

"Protestant Growth." *One World*, March 1994, 20.

Pulido, Alberto L. "Searching for the Sacred: Conflict and Struggle for Mexican Catholics in the Roman Catholic Diocese of San Diego, 1936-1941." *Latino Studies Journal*, September 1994, 37-59.

Quigley, Thomas. "Overview: Myths about the Latin American Church." *Origins*, October 28, 1993, 362-368.

Ramírez, Bishop Ricardo. "Bringing Ecumenism to Hispanic Christians." *Origins*, May 28, 1992, 40-44.

_____. "Hispanics Leaving the Catholic Church." *National Catholic Register*, July 28, 1985, 2.

_____. Interview with National Catholic News Service, April 29, 1986.

Ratzinger, Joseph Cardinal. *Instruction on Christian Freedom and Liberation*. Boston: St. Paul Editions, 1986.

Reed, Ralph. "Christianity vs. Fanaticism." *The Wall Street Journal*, March 16, 1993, 6.

Rehkemper, Robert. Telephone interview by author, March 11, 1992.

Reid, J.K.S. *Calvin: Theological Treatises*. Philadelphia: Westminster Press, 1954.

Reynolds, John Mark. "Are Fundamentalists Really So Bad?" *New Oxford Review*, October 1992, 5-8.

Rodriguez, Benjamin. Telephone interview by author, October 5, 1992.

Rodríguez, Bishop Plácido. Interview by author, November 17, 1992, Washington, D.C.

_____. "Hispanic Catholics: How Culture Shock Can Charge Up a Parish." An interview by *U.S. Catholic*, December 1986, 33-39.

Rodriguez, Richard. *Hunger of Memory: The Education of Richard Rodriguez*. New York: Bantam Press, 1988.

Román, Bishop Agustín. Interview by author, November 16, 1992, Washington, D.C.

Rome, Michael. "Reaping the Whirlwind." *Catholic World Report*, February 1992, 18-19.

Saliba, John A. "Vatican Response to the New Religious Movements." *Theological Studies*, March 1992, 3-39.

Sanchez, Archbishop Robert. "Responding Pastorally to Sect Activity among Immigrants." *Origins*, January 11, 1990, 526-529.

Sandidge, Jerry L. "The Pentecostal Movement and Ecumenism: An Update." *Ecumenical Trends*, July/August 1989, 102-106.

Schindler, David L. "Towards a Eucharistic Evangelization." *Communio*, Winter 1992, 549-575.

Schreck, Alan. *Catholic and Christian: An Explanation of Commonly Misunderstood Catholic Beliefs*. Ann Arbor, Michigan: Servant Publications, 1984.

Schreiter, Robert J. "The Challenge of Fundamentalism." *New Theology Review*, May 1988, 3-4.

Scott, Michael. Interview by author, April 28, 1994, Bayonne, New Jersey.

Shaughnessy, Gerald. *Has the Immigrant Kept the Faith?* New York: Macmillan Co., 1925.

Sheehan, Bishop Michael. "Seizing the Catholic Moment." *The Catholic Answer*, July/August 1989, 26-32.

Sheehan, Pete. "Why Catholics Leave." *Long Island Catholic*, March 4, 1992, 1ff.

Sirico, Robert A. "The Catholic Crack-Up." *National Review*, August 23, 1993, 47-50.

Sly, Julie. "The Church Fights Back to Stop Defections." *Our Sunday Visitor*, February 10, 1985, 8-9.

_____. "The Fundamentalists and Catholic Hispanics." *Our Sunday Visitor*, January 27, 1985, 4-5ff.

_____. "The Fundamentalist Crusade for Hispanic Catholics." *Our Sunday Visitor*, February 3, 1985, 8.

Soseman, Richard. Telephone interview by author, October 7, 1992.

Sox, David. "The Fundamentalist Tide." *The Tablet*, May 10, 1986, 481-483.

"Spanish-Language Resources." *Christian Research Institute Newsletter*, November/December 1993, 11.

Spear, Lois. "The Church Fights Back to Stop Defections." *Our Sunday Visitor*, February 10, 1985, 8-9.

_____. "Fundamentalism 'Interferes' in Church Life, Priest Says." National Catholic News Service, May 7, 1986.

Stahel, Thomas H. "The Sects in Paraguay." *America*, September 27, 1986, 139-141.

Steinfels, Peter. "Shepherds or Wolves? Whatever, Flocks Grow." *New York Times*, October 27, 1992, A4.

Stoll, David. *Is Latin America Turning Protestant? The Politics of Evangelical Growth*. Berkeley: University of California Press, 1990.

Stravinskas, Peter M. J. *The Catholic Response*. Huntington, Indiana: Our Sunday Visitor, Inc., 1985.

_____. *Proselytism among Today's Immigrants: A Preliminary Report*. Washington, D.C.: United States Catholic Conference, 1987.

"Study Says Church Failing to Reach Immigrants." *Long Island Catholic*, June 10, 1992, 7.

Suquia, Angel Cardinal. "The New Evangelization: Some Tasks and Risks of the Present." *Communio*, Winter 1992, 515-540.

Suren, Victor. "Integration of Catholic Immigrants." *Social Justice Review*, October 1960, 196ff.

Suro, Robert. "Hispanic Shift of Allegiance Changes Face of U.S. Religion." *New York Times*, May 14, 1989, 1.

Tessarolo, Giulivo, ed. *'Exsul Familia': The Church's Magna Charta for Migrants*. New York: St. Charles Seminary, 1962.

Texas, Catholic Bishops of. *Mission: Texas*. Lubbock, Texas: 1989.

Tomasi, Silvano M. Letter to author, May 6, 1993.

_____. Interview by author, May 29, 1993, Rome, Italy.

_____. *A Lesson from History: The Integration of Immigrants in the Pastoral Practice of the Church in the United States*. New York: Center for Migration Studies, 1987.

_____. "Pastoral Action and the New Immigrants." *Origins*, February 13, 1992, 580-584.

_____. *The Pastoral Challenges of the New Immigration*. New York: Center for Migration Studies, 1990.

_____. *The Response of the Catholic Church in the United States to Immigrants and Refugees*. New York: Center for Migration Studies, 1984.

Tomko, Jozef Cardinal. "On Relativizing Christ: Sects and the Church." *Origins*, April 25, 1991, 753f.

Toon, Peter. *Protestants and Catholics: A Guide to Understanding the Differences among Christians*. Ann Arbor, Michigan: Servant Publications, 1984.

Tornielli, Andrea. "Interview with Cardinal Ratzinger: Testimonies in the Pagan Age." *30 Days*, No. 11 (1992), 28-32.

Trabold, Robert. "Building an Immigrant Community" (master's thesis, Long Island University, 1982).

"A United States of Latin America?" *Catholic World Report*, November 1992, 7.

Valderrey, José. "Sects in Central America." *Pro Mundi Vita*, Bulletin 100, 1985, 7ff.

Vatican Press Office. "Communiqué: College of Cardinals Meeting." *Origins*, April 25, 1991, 745ff.

"Vatican Report on Sects, Cults and New Religious Movements." *Origins*, May 22, 1986, 1-10.

Vidal, Jaime R. "Proselytism of Hispanic Migrants: A Challenge to the American Church." *Migration World*, No. 2 (1991), 13ff.

Vilar, Juan Diaz. Interview by author, October 27, 1992, Jersey City, New Jersey.

_____. *Religious Sects*. New York: Catholic Book Publishing Co., 1992.

_____. *Las Sectas: Un Defasio a la Pastoral*. New York: Northeast Catholic Pastoral Center for Hispanics, 1985.

_____. "The Success of the Sects among Hispanics in the United States." *America*, February 25, 1989, 174-181.

Wagner, C. Peter. "A Vision for Evangelizing the Real America." *International Bulletin of Missionary Outreach*, Volume 10, No. 2, 62ff.

Walker, Williston. *John Calvin: The Organiser of Reformed Protestantism*. New York: Schocken Books, 1969.

Weinandy, Thomas. "Why Catholics Find It So Hard to Evangelize." *New Covenant*, October 1993, 18-19.

West, John. Telephone interview by author, December 13, 1993.

Whalen, William. *Strange Gods: Contemporary Religious Cults in America*. Huntington, Indiana: Our Sunday Visitor, Inc., 1981.

_____. "Strange Gods: Cults Are Still with Us and Remain a Cause for Concern." *Our Sunday Visitor*, October 28, 1984, 3ff.

Whealon, Archbishop John F. "Fighting Fundamentalism." *America*, October 12, 1985, 211-212.

Whelan, Marsha. Telephone interview by author, April 27, 1994.

Wiley, H. Orton. *Introduction to Christian Theology*. Kansas City, Missouri: Beacon Hill Press, 1949.

Wilkins, Sally. "Fundamentalists Make a Home of Their Church." *Our Sunday Visitor*, July 29, 1990, 4-5.

_____. "Understanding the Appeal of God's Word." *Our Sunday Visitor*, July 22, 1990, 4-5.

Wilson, Bryan R. *The Social Sources of Sectarianism: Sects and New Religious Movements*. New York: Oxford/Clarendon, 1990.

Working Paper for 1994 Special Synod for Africa. "Evangelizing Mission of the Church in Africa." *Origins*, March 11, 1993, 653ff.

Yao, Richard. *There Is a Way Out.* New York: Luce Publications, 1983.

_____. Interview with *National Catholic Reporter*, June 21, 1985, 3.

Young, James Lee. "Hispanic Southern Baptists." *The Historical Commission News of the Southern Baptist Convention*, April 27, 1983.

Zanghi, Giuseppe Maria. "Eglise, Icône de la Trinité, pour le Dialogue et l'Annonce." *Bulletin: Pontificium Consilium pro Dialogo inter Religiones*, No. 83 (1993), 135-146.

III. Mary in Catholicism, Classical Protestantism, and Fundamentalism

Anderson, H. George, et al. *The One Mediator, the Saints, and Mary.* Minneapolis: Augsburg Fortress Press, 1992.

Barth, Karl. *Church Dogmatics*, Volume I, Part 2. Edinburgh: T. & T. Clark, 1963.

Blackbourn, David. *Marpingen: Apparitions of the Virgin Mary in Nineteenth-Century Germany.* New York: Alfred A. Knopf, 1994.

Bouwsma, William J. *John Calvin: A Sixteenth-Century Portrait.* New York: Oxford University Press, 1988.

Brown, Raymond E. *The Birth of the Messiah.* Garden City, New York: Doubleday & Co., 1977

Brown, Raymond E., et al. *Mary in the New Testament.* New York: Paulist Press, 1978.

Cantalamessa, Raniero. *Mary, Mirror of the Church.* Collegeville, Minnesota: Liturgical Press, 1992.

Carroll, Eamon R. "Theology on the Virgin Mary: 1966-1975." *Theological Studies*, June 1976, 253-289.

Carter, David. *Mary and Ecumenical Sensitivity.* Surrey, England: Ecumenical Society of the Blessed Virgin Mary, 1994.

Catéchisme de L'Église Catholique. Paris: Mame-Librairie Editrice Vaticane, 1992.

Catholics Answer Jimmy Swaggart. Florissant, Missouri: Pax Tapes, n.d.

Chapman, Mark E. "Sancta Maria, Sancta Ecclesia: A Lutheran Possibility for a Marian Ecclesiology." Lecture in Washington, D.C.: October 2, 1993.

Cole, William J. "Was Luther a Devotee of Mary?" *Marian Studies*, 1970, 94-202.

Congar, Yves. *Christ, Our Lady and the Church.* Westminster, Maryland: Newman Press, 1957.

Cranfield, C.E.B. "Some Reflections on the Subject of the Virgin Birth." *Scottish Journal of Theology* 41 (1988), 177-189.

Dakin, Arthur. *Calvinism*. London: Duckworth, 1940.

Daly, Cahal. "Luther Loved Mary." *The Word*, May 1969, 24-26.

Dawe, Donald G. *Mary, Pilgrimages and Protestants: Do They Belong Together?* Surrey, England: Ecumenical Society of the Blessed Virgin Mary, 1993.

Deiss, Lucien. *Mary, Daughter of Sion*. Collegeville, Minnesota: Liturgical Press, 1972.

DeLubac, Henri. *The Splendor of the Church*. San Francisco: Ignatius Press, 1986.

Farrelly, Joseph P. *The Origins of Marian Ecumenism and the Ecumenical Society of the Blessed Virgin Mary*. Surrey, England: Ecumenical Society of the Blessed Virgin Mary, 1994.

Ferguson, Ron. *Chasing the Wild Goose: The Iona Community*. Glasgow: Collins, 1988.

Finley, Mitch. "A Protestant Celebrates Mary." *Our Sunday Visitor*, May 9, 1993, 5.

Flannery, Austin. *Vatican Council II: Conciliar and Post-Conciliar Documents*. Northport, New York: Costello Publishing Co., 1980.

Frazier, T. L. "Assumptions Made about Mary." *This Rock*, May/June 1992, 12-18.

Graef, Hilda. *Mary: A History of Doctrine and Devotion*. Westminster, Maryland: Christian Classics, 1990 (reprint).

Greenacre, Roger. *I Sing of a Maiden*. Wallington, England: Ecumenical Society of the Blessed Virgin Mary, 1992.

Henry, Carl F. H. *Basic Christian Doctrines: Contemporary Evangelical Thought*. New York: Holt, Reinhart and Winston, 1962.

Hislop, Alexander. *The Two Babylons or the Papal Worship*. Neptune, New Jersey: Loizeaux Brothers, 1959.

Hodge, Charles. *Systematic Theology*. Grand Rapids, Michigan: Eerdmans Publishing Co., 1973 (reprint).

Hodges, Marcus. *Why Did St. Thomas Aquinas Reject the Doctrine of the Immaculate Conception?* Wallington, England: Ecumenical Society of the Blessed Virgin Mary, 1992.

Holton, Robert. "The Children of Guadalupe." *Our Sunday Visitor*, December 11, 1994, 12-13.

Jelly, Frederick. "Mary in Theology and Piety Since Vatican II." *Dialog*, October 1992, 245-250.

Jensen, Robert W. "An Attempt to Think about Mary." *Dialog*, October 1992, 259-264.

Jepsen, Dee. *Jesus Called Her Mother*. Minneapolis: Bethany House Publishers, 1993.

John Paul II, Pope. *Behold Your Mother: Mary in the Life of the Priest*. Boston: St. Paul Books and Media, 1988.

_____. "Hail the Blessed Mother of God!" *L'Osservatore Romano*, June 30, 1993, 3.

_____. *Redemptoris Mater*. Boston: St. Paul Books and Media, 1987.

Johnson, Elizabeth A. "Mary the Female Face of God." *Theological Studies*, September 1989, 500-526.

Jurgens, William A. *The Faith of the Early Fathers*. Collegeville, Minnesota: Liturgical Press, 1970.

Keating, Karl. *Catholicism and Fundamentalism: The Attack on 'Romanism' by 'Bible Christians.'* San Francisco: Ignatius Press, 1988.

Kreeft, Peter. "Answering the Fundamentalists: Mary and the Saints." *National Catholic Register*, September 27, 1992, 5.

Küng, Hans, and Jurgen Moltmann, eds. *Mary in the Churches*. New York: Seabury Press, 1983.

Laurentin, René. *Mary in the Communion of Saints*. Surrey, England: Ecumenical Society of the Blessed Virgin Mary, 1973.

_____. *Structure et Théologie de Luc I-II*. Paris: Gabalda, 1964.

Lees, Charles. "Archbishop Gawlina, Martin Luther, and the Magnificat." *Mary Today*, March/April 1965, 26-28.

Lehmann, Helmut T., ed. *Luther's Works*. Philadelphia: Fortress Press, 1970.

Lull, Timothy F., ed. *Martin Luther's Basic Theological Writings*. Minneapolis: Fortress Press, 1989.

Macquarrie, John. *Mary for All Christians*. Grand Rapids, Michigan: Eerdmans Publishing Co., 1990.

Madrid, Patrick. "Any Friend of God's Is a Friend of Mine." *This Rock*, September 1992, 1ff.

Martin, Walter. "The Christmas Message and Old Testament Prophecy." *Christian Research Newsletter*, November/December 1992, 4.

Mascall, E. L., ed. *The Mother of God*. London: Dacre Press, 1949.

Mateo, Father. *Refuting the Attack on Mary*. San Diego: Catholic Answers, 1993.

McCurry, James. "Our Lady of Guadalupe: Evangelizer of the Americas." *Marian Studies*, 1992, 9-16.

McDonald, Kevin. "Mary in Recent Ecumenical Documents." *One in Christ*, 1986 (No. 4), 35-38.

McHugh, John. *The Mother of Jesus in the New Testament*. Garden City, New York: Doubleday & Co., 1975.

_____. Review of *Chosen by God: Mary in Evangelical Perspective*, ed. by David F. Wright. In the *Newsletter of the Ecumenical Society of the Blessed Virgin Mary* (January 1991): 5.

McNeill, John T., ed. *Calvin: Institutes of the Christian Religion*. Philadelphia: Westminster Press, 1960.

Miller, Charles. *Mary and the Eucharist: A Seventeenth-Century Anglican View*. Surrey, England: Ecumenical Society of the Blessed Virgin Mary, 1992.

Miller, Elliot. "The Mary of Roman Catholicism" (Part I). *Christian Research Journal*, Summer 1990, 9-15.

_____. "The Mary of Roman Catholicism" (Part II). *Christian Research Journal*, Fall 1990, 27-33.

Miller, Elliot, and Kenneth R. Samples. *The Cult of the Virgin: Catholic Mariology and the Apparitions of Mary*. Grand Rapids, Michigan: Baker Book House, 1992.

Nevins, Albert J. *Answering a Fundamentalist*. Huntington, Indiana: Our Sunday Visitor, Inc., 1990.

Newman, John Henry. *Mary, the Second Eve*. Rockford, Illinois: TAN Books and Publishers, 1982.

Oberman, Heiko A. *The Virgin Mary in Evangelical Perspective*. Philadelphia: Fortress Press, 1971.

O'Carroll, Michael. *Theotokos: A Theological Encyclopedia of the Blessed Virgin Mary*. Wilmington, Delaware: Michael Glazier, 1982.

O'Meara, Thomas F. *Mary in Protestant and Catholic Theology*. New York: Sheed and Ward, 1965.

Orr, James. "The Virgin Birth of Christ." In *The Fundamentals for Today*, ed. Charles Feinberg, 241-250. Grand Rapids, Michigan: Kregel Publications, 1958.

Orr, James. "Every Portion Counts." *Our Lady's Dowry*, Volume 12, No. 2, 1-4.

Orsi, Robert Anthony. *The Madonna of 115th Street: Faith and Community in Italian Harlem, 1880-1950*. New Haven: Yale University Press, 1985.

Paul VI, Pope. *Marialis Cultus*. Washington, D.C.: United States Catholic Conference, 1974.

Pelikan, Jaroslav. *Luther the Expositor*. St. Louis: Concordia Publishers, 1959.

Ramsey, Boniface. "Matrimony: The Early Church." *The Catholic Answer*, September/October 1993, 41-46.

Ratzinger, Joseph Cardinal. "Without Mary, God's Entrance into History Would Not Reach Its Conclusion." *Inside the Vatican*, May 1995, 52-53.

Reid, J.K.S. *Calvin: Theological Treatises*. Philadelphia: Westminster Press, 1954.

Romero, C. Gilbert. *Hispanic Devotional Piety: Tracing the Biblical Roots*. Maryknoll, New York: Orbis Books, 1991.

Saward, John. *Redeemer in the Womb: Jesus Living in Mary*. San Francisco: Ignatius Press, 1993.

Schlink, Basilea. *Mary, the Mother of Jesus*. London: Marshall Pickering, 1986.

Schreck, Alan. *Catholic and Christian: An Explanation of Commonly Misunderstood Catholic Beliefs*. Ann Arbor, Michigan: Servant Publications, 1984.

Senn, Frank C. "Mary in Ecumenical Dialogue and Liturgical Convergence." *Dialog*, October 1992, 251-258.

Sicari, Antonio. "Mary, Peter and John: Figures of the Church." *Communio*, Summer 1992, 190-207.

Stacpoole, Alberic, ed. *Mary's Place in Christian Dialogue*. Slough, England: St. Paul Publications, 1982.

Stravinskas, Peter M. J. *The Catholic Response*. Huntington, Indiana: Our Sunday Visitor, Inc., 1985.

Thurian, Max. *Mary, Mother of All Christians*. New York: Herder & Herder, 1964.

Toon, Peter. *Protestants and Catholics: A Guide to Understanding the Differences among Christians*. Ann Arbor, Michigan: Servant Publications, 1984.

Turnbull, Stephen. *Devotion to Mary among the Hidden Christians of Japan*. Surrey, England: Ecumenical Society of the Blessed Virgin Mary, 1992.

Walker, Williston. *John Calvin: The Organiser of Reformed Protestantism*. New York: Schocken Books, 1969.

Wallwork, Norman. *The Cult of Our Lady in the Presbyterian and Catholic Ministries of W. E. Orchard*. Surrey, England: Ecumenical Society of the Blessed Virgin Mary, 1990.

Wiley, H. Orton. *Introduction to Christian Theology*. Kansas City, Missouri: Beacon Hill Press, 1949.

Wright, David F., ed. *Chosen by God: Mary in Evangelical Perspective*. London: Marshall Pickering, 1989.

Zacchello, Joseph. *Secrets of Romanism*. Neptune, New Jersey: Loizeaux Brothers, n.d.

IV. Mary Among the Proselytizers

Abalos, David. Letter to author, December 5, 1994.

Alfaro, Juan, of the Hispanic Ministry Department of the Archdiocese of San Antonio. Telephone interviews by author, March 12, 1992, and April 28, 1994.

Angela, Sister, of the Dallas Diocesan Office for Evangelization. Telephone interviews by author, March 12, 1992, and April 27, 1994.

Bail, Paul. "Latinos Remain Loyal to the Virgin." *National Catholic Register*, August 18, 1985, 7.

Barth, Karl. *Church Dogmatics*, Volume I, Part 2. Edinburgh: T. & T. Clark, 1963.

Bentley, Amy. *The Conversion of a Catholic Nun*. San Diego: Mission to Catholics International, n.d.

Berry, Charles A. *The Conversion of a Catholic Priest*. San Diego: Mission to Catholics International, n.d.

Bevilacqua, Anthony Cardinal. Letter to author, May 6, 1993.

Boettner, Loraine. *Roman Catholicism*. Philadelphia: Presbyterian & Reformed Publishing Co., 1974.

Brewer, Bartholomew F. *The Conversion of a Catholic Priest*. San Diego: Mission to Catholics International, n.d.

————. *Pilgrimage from Rome*. Greenville, South Carolina: Bob Jones University Press, 1982.

Catholics Answer Jimmy Swaggart. Florissant, Missouri: Pax Tapes, n.d.

Chick, Jack T. *Are Roman Catholics Christians?* Chino, California: Chick Publications, n.d.

————. *Why Is Mary Crying?* Chino, California: Chick Publications, n.d.

Chiniquy, Charles. *The Gift*. Philadelphia: Continental Press, n.d.

————. *The Secrets of the Confessional*. Chino, California: Chick Publications, 1983.

Coffey, Tony. *Once a Catholic: What You Need to Know about Roman Catholicism*. Eugene, Oregon: Harvest House Publishers, 1983.

Dodds, Bill. "Strangers Need Not Apply." *Our Sunday Visitor*, August 2, 1992, 10-11.

Doran, Eileen. *The Conversion of a Catholic Nun*. San Diego: Mission to Catholics International, n.d.

Espaillat, Benny, of the Boston Archdiocese. Telephone interview by author, April 27, 1994.

Facio, Manuel. Telephone interview by author, April 27, 1994.

Gallup, George. Letter to author, October 31, 1994.

Gallup, George, and Jim Castelli. *The American Catholic People.* Garden City, New York: Doubleday & Co., 1987.

Gonzalez, Roberto O., and Michael LaVelle. *The Hispanic Catholic in the United States: A Socio-Cultural and Religious Profile.* New York: Northeast Catholic Pastoral Center for Hispanics, 1985.

Hislop, Alexander. *The Two Babylons or the Papal Worship.* Neptune, New Jersey: Loizeaux Brothers, 1959.

Hispanic Bishops of California. "Responding to Proselytism." *Origins,* June 23, 1988, 82-85.

Icaza, Rosa, of the Mexican-American Cultural Center in San Antonio. Telephone interview by author, April 28, 1994.

Jarbo, Raymond. Interview by author, April 24, 1994, Ontario, Oregon.

John Paul II, Pope. "The Church on Her Way." *L'Osservatore Romano,* August 25, 1980, 7.

Kimball, William R. *The Bible and Roman Catholicism.* South Lake Tahoe, California: Christian Equippers International, 1985.

King, Eleace. *Proselytism and Evangelization: An Exploratory Study.* Washington, D.C.: Center for Applied Research in the Apostolate, 1991.

_____. Telephone interviews by author, January 31, 1994, and April 27, 1994.

King, Eleace, and Francis Gillespie. *Final Report on the Survey of Attitudes towards Proselytism of Ethnic Minorities.* Washington, D.C.: Center for Applied Research in the Apostolate, 1988.

Kreeft, Peter. "Answering the Fundamentalists: Mary and the Saints." *National Catholic Register,* September 27, 1992, 5.

Lopez y Guzman, Antonio. "Mexican-Americans: A Vibrant Spirituality." *Catholic Twin Circle,* August 9, 1992, 4-5.

Madrid, Patrick. "Any Friend of God's Is a Friend of Mine." *This Rock,* September 1992, 1ff.

_____. Telephone interview by author, April 26, 1994.

Mateo, Father. *Refuting the Attack on Mary.* San Diego: Catholic Answers, 1993.

McClory, Robert J. "Why Did the Catholic Cross the Road?" *U.S. Catholic,* January 1991, 6-12.

McGuinness, Matthew, of the Diocese of Wichita. Telephone interview by author, April 27, 1994.

National Conference of Catholic Bishops. "National Pastoral Plan for Hispanic Ministry." *Origins*, December 10, 1987, 449-463.

O'Connor, Charles, former director of the Hispanic Apostolate for the Diocese of Metuchen. Telephone interview by author, May 2, 1994.

Orsi, Robert Anthony. *The Madonna of 115th Street*. New Haven, Connecticut: Yale University Press, 1985.

O'Steen, Robert. "Some 'Catholic' Churches Really Aren't Catholic." *The Florida Catholic*, May 13, 1994, B3.

Padilla, Gilbert. "Proselytism, Conservatism, and the Hispanics." *Pastoral Life*, November 1989, 13-21.

Peña, Bishop Raymond. Interview by author, November 11, 1992, Washington, D.C.

_____. Telephone interview by author, April 28, 1994.

Pezzotta, Anthony. *I Found Everything When I Found Christ*. San Diego: Mission to Catholics International, n.d.

"Philippine Bishops' Statement on Biblical Fundamentalism." *Origins*, February 23, 1989, 627-628.

Rehkemper, Robert, vicar general of the Diocese of Dallas. Telephone interview by author, March 11, 1992.

Rodriguez, Benjamin. Telephone interview by author, October 5, 1992.

Rodríguez, Bishop Plácido. Interview by author, November 16, 1992, Washington, D.C.

Román, Bishop Agustín. Interview by author, November 16, 1992, Washington, D.C.

Samples, Kenneth, and Dan Kistler. *Catholicism Bibliography*. San Juan Capistrano, California: Christian Research Institute, 1989.

Sanchez, Archbishop Robert. "Responding Pastorally to Sect Activity among Immigrants." *Origins*, January 11, 1990, 526-529.

Scott, Michael, of Perth Amboy, New Jersey. Interview by author, April 28, 1994, Bayonne, New Jersey.

Shaughnessy, Gerald. *Has the Immigrant Kept the Faith?* New York: Macmillan Co., 1925.

Stoll, David. *Is Latin America Turning Protestant? The Politics of Evangelical Growth*. Berkeley: University of California Press, 1990.

Stravinskas, Peter M. J. *Proselytism among Today's Immigrants: A Preliminary Report*. Washington, D.C.: United States Catholic Conference, 1987.

Tomasi, Silvano M. Letter to author, May 6, 1993.

_____. Interview by author, May 29, 1993, and January 14, 1994, Rome, Italy.

Turnbull, Stephen. *Devotion to Mary among the Hidden Christians of Japan*. Surrey, England: Ecumenical Society of the Blessed Virgin Mary, 1992.

Vilar, Juan Diaz. "The Success of the Sects among Hispanics in the United States." *America*, February 25, 1989, 174-181.

_____. Interview by author, October 27, 1992, Jersey City, New Jersey.

West, John. Telephone interview by author, December 13, 1993.

Whelan, Marsha, of the Archdiocese of Miami. Telephone interview by author, April 27, 1994.

Woodrow, Ralph. *Babylon Mystery Religion*. Riverside, California: Ralph Woodrow Evangelistic Association, Inc., 1981.

Index

The reader is advised that, for a number of reasons, this index is not arranged in the conventional manner. For example, some proper names appear as they normally would, that is, last names first, followed by one's given name, while the remainder appear with last names following the first names (particularly where saints' names are concerned). Another difference involves the use of capitalization; because quoted material is used verbatim as a rule, there may be seeming inconsistences in the text (for instance, capitalizing versus lowercasing words such as Resurrection and Immaculate Conception). Most entries having both a singular and plural form (for instance, Baptist, Baptists) as well as various forms of the same words (Ecuador, Ecuadorans; Presbyterian Church, Presbyterianism, Presbyterians) are shown in only one form. Other modifications (including the arbitrary use of cross-references) are obvious.

Gordon, Adoniram Judson 19
Grace Theological Seminary 33
Greenacre, Roger 78, 90
Guatemala 8, 125, 132, 134, 135, 151,
    153, 154, 156, 157, 158, 160,
    161, 220

H
Haiti 129, 148, 150, 187
Hatch, Nathan 51
Hauerwas, Stanley 55
Hayes, Zachary 25, 46
Henry, Carl 80
Heritage USA 30
Hispanic 6, 128, 136, 148, 149, 155,
    156, 160, 162, 163, 166, 168,
    174, 175, 176, 177, 178, 184,
    187, 190, 192, 193, 202, 204,
    206, 210, 211, 212, 228
Hodge, Archibald Alexander 19
Hodge, Charles 37, 79
Holiness Pentecostalism 32
Holy Office 44
Holy Scripture — **see** Scripture
Holy See 125, 136, 143, 150, 168,
    177
Holy Spirit; **also** Holy Ghost 15, 18,
    19, 36, 38, 39, 49, 77, 216, 220,
    223, 224, 226
Holy Trinity — **see** Trinity
homosexual 62, 209
Hondurans 132
Humani Generis 39, 58
hyperdulia 98

I
Icaza, Rosa 189
iconoclast 73, 77
Immaculate Conception 73, 77, 78,
    80, 81, 84, 95, 100, 104, 105,
    110, 172, 174, 209
Incarnation 14, 71, 81, 84, 88, 89, 90,
    104, 116, 119, 122, 143, 218,
    219
Indochinese 148
intercession of saints 76

intercessory role of Mary 174, 198
Irenaeus, St. 85, 88
Israel 30, 37, 46, 47, 227

J
Jamieson, George 42
Jarbo, Raymond 189
Jehovah's Witnesses 14, 55, 125, 145,
    179, 185, 187, 228
Jews; **also** Judaism 21, 30, 83, 89, 226
John, St. 96, 102
John Paul II, Pope 82, 91, 94, 97, 126,
    128, 130, 134, 138, 140, 142,
    143, 145, 149, 151, 152, 154,
    190, 192, 211, 214, 218, 219,
    221
John the Baptist, St. 96
John XXIII, Pope 97, 141
Johnson, Benton 31, 35
Jonah 38
Judaeo-Christian 21
Judaism — **see under** Jews
justification 41, 42, 96

K
Kant, Immanuel 20
Kayal, Philip 191, 207
Kelley, Dean 137
Kimball, William R. 171
King, Eleace 7, 12, 151, 157, 160
Koran 170
Koreans 148

L
Lamentabili 44
Lane, Tony 84, 85, 96
Latimer, Hugh 78
Latin America 10, 12, 14, 15, 126,
    127, 128, 131, 133, 134, 135,
    136, 144, 145, 153, 156, 157,
    160, 167, 178, 186, 192, 219,
    221
Latino Protestant converts 186
latria 98
LaValle, Michael 132
Laws, Curtis Lee 26

Our Sunday Visitor...
Your Source for Discovering the Riches of the Catholic Faith

Our Sunday Visitor has an extensive line of materials for young children, teens, and adults. Our books, Bibles, booklets, CD-ROMs, audios, and videos are available in bookstores worldwide.

To receive a FREE full-line catalog or for more information, call **Our Sunday Visitor** at **1-800-348-2440**. Or write, **Our Sunday Visitor** / 200 Noll Plaza / Huntington, IN 46750.

Please send me: __ A catalog
Please send me materials on:
    __ Apologetics and catechetics   __ Reference works
    __ Prayer books   __ Heritage and the saints
    __ The family   __ The parish

Name_____

Address_____Apt._____

City_____State___Zip_____

Telephone (   )_____

A73BBABP

Please send a friend: __ A catalog
Please send a friend materials on:
    __ Apologetics and catechetics   __ Reference works
    __ Prayer books   __ Heritage and the saints
    __ The family   __ The parish

Name_____

Address_____Apt._____

City_____State___Zip_____

Telephone (   )_____

A73BBABP

Our Sunday Visitor
200 Noll Plaza
Huntington, IN 46750
1-800-348-2440
OSVSALES@AOL.COM

Your Source for Discovering the Riches of the Catholic Faith